Healing Healthcare

Also by Roger K. Howe:

Where Have We Failed?
A Systemic Analysis of U.S. Health Care

Healing Healthcare

How to Fix Our Broken Healthcare System

Roger K. Howe, MD, MMM

Durban House

Printed in the United States of America.

For information address:
Durban House Press, Inc.
5001 LBJ Freeway, Suite 700
Dallas, Texas 75244

Library of Congress Cataloging-in-Publication Data

Howe, Roger K.

Healing Healthcare / Roger K. Howe

Library of Congress Control Number: 2007943813

p. cm.

ISBN: 978-0-9800067-3-5
0-9800067-3-2

First Edition

10 9 8 7 6 5 4 3 2 1

Visit our Web site at
http://www.durbanhouse.com

Table of Contents

Acknowledgements

Writing a book is only one small piece of a much larger process. A book flows from a question or set of questions which must be posed by someone—frequently, not independently by the author. Then the ideas require development, testing, contemplation, argumentation, and refinement. Finally, the writing must be done, revised, edited, formatted, laid out, and printed into a book. Through all of this, the author must be patient, persistent, and faithful; it certainly helps to have someone else who believes in the project and the ability of the author to get it done.

This last role has been filled for me by Nancy Howe, my wife, companion, and soulmate, who, despite all of my day-to-day shortcomings as a person and partner, continues to believe in me and in my ability to do this work. She has read every word I have written, has asked questions and made suggestions, and has otherwise helped at every step of the way. But more important than all of that, she has encouraged me to continue by her unflagging belief that this was something I could and should do. I could not have done it without her.

There have, of course, been others. Some provided the question—the "so, what do you think we should do now?" question. The first to do so were a bright and attentive group of master's degree students in Shreveport, Louisiana. Then there were the early morning risers in the Forum at the Universalist-Unitarian Church of Little Rock, Arkansas, who were persistent about asking the same question.

Others helped to challenge and hone ideas. The most memorable of these was my uncle, Al Trumpler, who asked the challenging questions that caused me to rethink a whole section of the book.

I especially appreciate the time and energy of Wes Curry. Wes edited my first book and has continued to advise me in spite of being "retired." He spent considerable time editing this book for content and flow. His comments were greatly appreciated.

The path to publication for this book has not been easy. H. K. Stewart has been invaluable in completing the editing task, suggesting changes in presentation and editing my writing for clarity and flow.

It takes a community to raise a child; it takes a community to write and publish a book. There have been too many who have contributed—including many whose only contribution was moral support in times when that was what was needed—to name each one. Thank you all.

Part One

How to Design a
Better Healthcare System

Chapter 1

Introduction

"All progress is precarious, and the solution of one problem brings us face to face with another problem."
—Martin Luther King, Jr.

Healing healthcare—fixing the healthcare system in the United States—is a daunting undertaking. It has been the subject of books, journal articles, and political movements. Some have gone so far as to decry the complete lack of a healthcare system in the United States.[1]

So why is our healthcare system so difficult to fix?

Healthcare—A Complex System

To begin with, healthcare is a complex system. Systems theory tells us about the operation of complex systems. Complex systems do not come into being because someone organizes them, for example. They come into being when many individual pieces are operating in relationship to one another according to a set of underlying rules. Such complex systems are self-generating and self-repairing. They are incredibly resistant to change. External forces applied to them produce results not only in the local area of the applied force, but also in entirely unanticipated ways far from that original force.

A School of Fish

One example of a complex system is a school of fish. A school of fish forms because there are a number of fish of a certain species in the same volume of water. Some fish do not form schools; others do. The ones that do act as though they are programmed to obey certain internal rules, and it is the presence of those rules that creates the school. There is no drill sergeant among the fish issuing instructions; there is no organizing mind; in fact, there does not appear to be any communication at all between the individual fish in the school. But the school continues to swim together anyway.

One could create a set of rules that seems likely to create schooling behavior. Let me propose three rules for the individual fish in a school. I think you will agree that these would probably work just fine:

- Stay as close as possible to the center of the group of fish.
- Stay at least one inch away from the nearest object in the water (whether it is a fish in the school or a rock or a predator).
- Swim at five miles per hour.

What we will find is that there will be a certain amount of churning activity within the school as fish try to obtain or are displaced from central positions in the school. "Stay as close as possible to the center of the school" is a survival rule—the closer an individual fish is to the center of the school, the less likely that fish is to be eaten by a predator. The school will generally swim around in the volume of water available, but the internal churning will also manifest as a random variation in the direction the school is swimming. As the location of the center changes, the direction each fish must swim to get closer to it will change, and this will change the direction of the school as a whole. And if a rock intervenes, or a predator attacks and eats a few fish, the location of the center changes as the fish swim to avoid the rock or predator. As a result, the school's direction and even its overall shape will change.

This makes a good basic illustration of the functioning of a system. But what about the "unanticipated effects" thing? This is where the relationship between systems theory and chaos theory comes into play.

Chaos Theory

One of the classic illustrations of chaos theory is that a butterfly flaps its wings in China and causes a hurricane in the Caribbean. While this is an exaggeration, it is certainly illustrative of unanticipated consequences. The butterfly did not intend to cause the hurricane. No one who watched the butterfly would anticipate the possibility of a hurricane. But the hurricane happens at the remote end of a chain of events started by the flapping of the wings.

In reality, unforeseen consequences of significant magnitude do happen. If, for example, our school of fish is swimming deep in an enclosure of rocks that rise nearly to the surface, they may continue to go around and around, never breaking out of the enclosure because there is nothing to cause them to go near the surface and beyond the top of the rocks. On the other hand, if a moray eel pops out of a hole in one of the rocks one day and eats one of the fish, the school's direction and balance will change, even if only a little. Because of the way the eel attacked, the school's direction shifts slightly upward, and the next day, the fish swim over the rocks and out of the enclosure, never to return. This was certainly not the intent of the eel, but it took only a slight stimulus to create the change that ended with a dramatic result.

Healthcare as a Complex System

Healthcare fulfills the criteria for a complex system. Certainly no one deliberately created the mess we find ourselves in. Certainly no one seems to be in charge. Change is constant, but directed change is difficult. (The system is self-organizing and self-repairing.) Like a school of fish, the healthcare system is made up of many small units (doctors, hospitals, labs, physical therapy offices, etc.).

The relationships among the small units can be described,[2] and it might even be possible to speculate about the underlying rules. People are more complicated than fish, however, so the rules are likely to be more complicated as well.

Because healthcare is a system, we can predict that efforts to "fix" the system will be met by internal adjustments that can result in unforeseen consequences. We can also predict that one of the surest ways not to fix the system is to pick some small aspect of it and work to fix that one aspect. Regardless of the result on that part, there will be effects on other parts—effects no one would have anticipated.

Sometimes these unanticipated consequences may be helpful. More often, they are destructive to the overall aims one intended in trying to fix the system in the first place. Sometimes the unanticipated side effects are instructive to those who plan the next steps. Frequently, they merely frustrate reformist efforts and lead to a sense of futility.

Interestingly, these adjustments are just as frustrating to those within the system as they are to those outside of it.[3] They are no easier for the insiders to foresee than they are for outsiders to predict, and they are not under the control of any individual or small group of individuals. This is the nature of complex systems.

How can we avoid the morass and gain the high road to system redesign? The landscape of the last hundred years of healthcare is littered with the battered and burned-out remains of many reformist efforts. Some of these efforts have come from within the medical and hospital professions; others have come from the outside, including political solutions. Each has looked at some small piece of the puzzle, each has attempted a solution for a defined problem—and each has suffered from the twin problems of being too focused and too fixed.

Solutions That Are Too Focused

Being too focused means the problem is defined as some aspect of the system, which leads to attempts to fix only that one problem. Regardless of the effect on that focal problem, though, other effects in the system mitigate any advantage one may have gained in solving it. Examples are many—and "managed care" is one of the more recent and prominent of them.

Managed care was invented as a way to engage the efforts of physicians in controlling the cost of medical care. It turned out that there were so many ways to save costs that a whole industry sprang up to answer the call—and to make money off the solutions. While the original concept may have been laudable, the result was a feeding frenzy in which physicians and hospitals suffered—and some patients ended up with less care than they needed. The effort to contain cost was highly successful. The side effect was a backlash that has essentially emasculated the managed care movement. Even if there is some beneficial after-effect, current managed care organizations will have a hard time capitalizing on it. The industry has effectively been hobbled by regulations. In the meantime, costs are spiraling up at a multiple of the growth rate of the nation's Gross Domestic Product.

Solutions That Are Too Fixed

Being too fixed has to do with choosing solutions that are absolute and inflexible. Here are two examples:

- In California, as in many other states, the legislature noted that instilling a solution of silver nitrate into the eyes of newborn babies would prevent ophthalmia neonatorum, a complication of gonorrhea in the mother which causes blindness in the baby. The state's lawmakers passed a law requiring that this treatment be applied to every baby born in the state. Silver nitrate is very irritating and causes its own newborn eye disease. It is not very effective for trachoma, another less-common eye infection that can cause blindness. Eventually, the use of erythromycin eye drops was advocated as a treatment that would prevent both ophthalmia neonatorum and trachoma, and would be much less irritating. The law continued to require silver nitrate. Physi-

7

cians were faced with the choice of doing what was right and doing what was legal. It took years to get the law changed.

• When the Medicare law was passed in the mid-1960s, it was a parallel to then-existing catastrophic medical insurance available commercially. Its purpose was to pay for the overwhelming cost of hospitalization. It did not intend to cover ambulatory care or the relatively minor cost of prescription medications. Basically, it was there to cover the elderly for the catastrophic care to which the elderly are so liable. Between the mid-1960s and now, medical care has shifted. The cost of prescription medications has increased at several times the rate of inflation every year for two or three decades. Coverage has fallen behind the need. Now, because of changes in care patterns and cost patterns, Medicare may be spending more money for hospital care because its recipients cannot afford the medication they need to keep them out of the hospital.

What Might Work?

I think we now have some idea of what won't work. What is the alternative? The answer is not simple and involves a leap of faith. If solving bits and pieces of the problem won't work, and fixed, rigid solutions won't work, then we must set about creating a global solution that will be all-encompassing and flexible enough to meet the changing needs and aspects of the system.

The purpose of this book is to explore how we might go about doing that.

Chapter 2

Getting Started

"Opportunities are usually disguised as hard work, so most people don't recognize them."

—*Ann Landers*

As I mentioned in the previous chapter, the healthcare system is a complex system. There is certainly a lot wrong in it.[1-11] If we are going to design a global solution, it will help to start with some idea of the result we seek. What kind of healthcare system do we want to have? What results should it produce? How should it work?

Problems in developing and implementing a solution are based in part on problems in our schizophrenic approach to health care[12] as a society:

- We complain bitterly about the cost of prescription medications, but spend freely on herbal medications of uncertain effectiveness.

- We understand and are outraged at the fact that people are mistreated by the healthcare system, but we continue to patronize dispensers of medical care without regard to quality.

- We use *Consumer Reports* to guide our purchases of refrigerators and automobiles, but there is no *Consumer Reports* to help select physicians and hospitals.

- We eat too much at fast food restaurants and watch TV rather than exercise, and then expect the healthcare system to patch us up when our bodies cannot take it any longer.

- We have set up a quality control system that indicates we would rather be sick and damaged and have a chance to be rich via a lawsuit than take care of ourselves or select healthcare providers as carefully as we select washing machines.

Just what is it that we want? This inconsistent, self-contradictory approach reflects a lack of societal consensus about what we want the healthcare system to be and to do for us.

I think the basic question is not about defining what kind of system we need, nor about how care should be paid for. It is about what we want the healthcare system to do. Once we know what outcomes we want, we can talk about what components we must assemble to get a system to produce those outcomes. From a list of currently available parts, we can determine how we need to modify the parts to allow them to fit into the mechanism we need to build to get the outcomes we want.

The purpose of this book is to answer the question "Where do we go from here?" To answer that question, I will walk through the process of establishing a set of goals, building a system to accomplish those goals, and analyzing the process necessary to change the current system into the designed one.

When we start by defining what we think a health care system should do, we start by setting positive expectations. By defining the functional goals, we create the context to consider the structure we will need to fulfill those defined goals—including the relationships among the parts. The clarity we gain by having our overall functional and structural goals defined will provide us a goal against which to measure progress. If we make changes that move the whole system in the right direction, we will know. If some reforms are progressing faster than others, we will know where to apply more effort.

Understanding the functional goals and the structural needs in advance enables us to look at the current system and develop a gap analysis—a comparison of where we are to where we want to be. A gap analysis will allow us to understand how we must move the current system to get to our goals. The gap analysis will help us understand what we need to do to create the changes that will close the gaps.

Will this work? It is an orderly way of approaching system change that has worked in industrial system realignments. I think it has a much better chance of working than anything we have tried so far.[13] The system we have is so woefully inadequate that a new approach seems warranted.

I will propose a set of functional goals, define them, and justify them.[14] Before I do, let me be clear that I do not believe my list is the definitive list. I think the people of the United States deserve an opportunity to have a say in defining functional goals for the healthcare system. Ideally, there should be a long series of town meetings, then a set of composite goals should be proposed and voted on in some way to assure that everyone has the opportunity to have input. That said, I would not be surprised if the list came out looking something like this one (in no particular order of importance):

- It should provide universal access to a defined standard of health care.

- It should be affordable for the individual and for society.

- It should provide care that is safe and effective. (This is a quality statement.)

- It should be available. (Financial access is not enough.)

- It should be comprehensive. (And the financing/regulatory systems accompanying it should be flexible enough to accommodate changes in science and practice.)

- It should be personal. (The relationship between physician and patient is among the most intimate relationships most of us ever have, and it needs preservation and protection.)

- It should be professional. (Ethical standards should be enforced by the profession, and the profession should be in a position to banish unethical members.)

In the next several chapters, I will discuss each of these aspects and explain why I think each is worth enumerating. In subsequent sections of the book, I will consider the structures necessary to accomplish these goals, measure the distance to be traveled, and suggest some things we need to be doing to close the gap.

Chapter 3

Access to Coverage

"This country will not be a good place for any of us to live in unless we make it a good place for all of us to live in."
—*Theodore Roosevelt*

The issue of access to coverage is one of the indictments against the current American system. More than 40 million people in the United States do not have any form of financial coverage for health care needs. In fact, as many as 45 million people were uninsured at some time during 2005. There are several reasons to contend all Americans should have financial coverage for health care. Any of the following should be adequate argument for universal coverage:

America, the Greatest Country on Earth

If we really are to contend that we are the "greatest country on earth," that contention loses credibility if we do not do a good job of caring for our own population. Universal health care coverage is a characteristic of virtually every other industrialized nation. If we truly are a great nation, why aren't we doing as well for our population as these other countries are doing for theirs?[1,2]

Who Has the Greatest Life Expectancy?

Despite the huge amounts we spend on health care in our country, we lag behind most of the industrialized countries in life expectancy.[3] There are many conclusions that can be drawn—some of them fantastic, some reasonable, and some disheartening—but the most dramatic difference between the United States and other countries with longer life expectancies is the presence of universal coverage in those other countries.

Medical Indigence

Without some "third-party payer" on one's side, virtually all Americans are medically indigent. In an era when the initial hospital care for a premature newborn can cost more than $250,000 and the care for a severe burn can run well over $1 million, no one can reasonably afford the cost of care. Many of us have insurance, so we are okay. The problem has its twists even beyond that, however. What care we tend to get echoes what care we have coverage for. When all we have is hospital coverage, hospital utilization tends to go up. If we have no pharmaceutical coverage, we tend not to take prescription drugs (especially the expensive ones), and instead we utilize something we do have coverage for.

The medications prescribed most commonly for seniors cost more than $100 per month per prescription. When your income from Social Security is $1,500 per month, you have a pension for another $800, your rent costs $1,100 a month and utilities another $400, do you spend the remaining $800 per month on medications your doctor has prescribed or on food?

For many people, even the premiums for health insurance are too expensive. Some of the uninsured are uninsured because they cannot afford coverage—either because they are too poor to afford any coverage, or because they have illnesses that make the premiums too high for any reasonable person to afford. Some of the uninsured are uninsured because their employers either no longer offer health insurance or expect large premium contributions from them that they cannot afford.[4,5] Some of the uninsured are uninsured because they "choose" to be so, either because they have made the same choice as the senior citizen in the last paragraph, or because they think, "I am healthy and I do not need insurance."

People who do not have insurance tend to delay needed care and to seek care in the most expensive and least effective arena— the emergency room. But they cannot pay for it. The emergency room cannot absorb the cost of that care. It can only redistribute it to other clients. In essence, that redistribution assures that we all pay for the cost of caring for the uninsured. From an entirely practical standpoint, wouldn't it be preferable for everyone to have access to the preventive and early-care services that could prevent more emergency room and catastrophic care visits?

Moral Imperative

Some would contend that it is simply immoral for the richest country on earth to do so poorly in providing health care services to its least fortunate citizens. The ethical principle of distributive justice applies: in an environment of plenty, the most vulnerable should not be denied the resources to meet their needs merely because they are politically disenfranchised.[6,7,8]

Economic Imperative

Closely tied to the moral imperative is the economic imperative, which is also bound up in the principle of distributive justice. If the economic cost of leaving people uninsured is more than the economic cost of insuring them, then they should be insured. Some serious analyses suggest this is the case.[9]

Historical Imperative

The United States has always been home to groups who support community action and a sense of community responsibility. From the Pilgrims to the Amish, including Native Americans shore to shore, we are a people who invests greatly in community welfare and support of our communities. Only recently, as the scales have tipped so dramatically toward urbanization, has our national sense of community waned. It still exists in communities small enough to allow it. To have a sense of community among more than a few thousand is hard, though, and it is impossible to identify oneself as a member of a community of a million. But the sense of community our grandparents knew still draws us. The thought of the community gathering for a barn raising or an Independence Day picnic or a community dance is still enticing.

In this tradition of community, we have always taken care of the weak, the infirm, and the disabled among us. Universal health insurance doesn't just make sense; it is a necessity within such a tradition.

Financial Imperative

From a financial standpoint, it makes great sense to grant everyone access to personal, preventive, and early-treatment care. Not only does optimizing the health of our population optimize one of our greatest natural resources, it is also a way to decrease the overall cost of care.

"The Wheels Are Coming Off"

The current system is spiraling out of control—and if we don't fix it, we face a disaster in the making. Universal coverage looks like one way of averting the disaster. Where does such a doomsday assessment come from? A story may light the way:

I was recently at a meeting of lay people, employers, and health professionals gathered to work on the healthcare system in Arkansas. One woman shared a story about a friend of hers, then followed it with an important question.

Her friend, who is uninsured, was feeling ill. (The uninsured woman's husband works at a place that offers health insurance, but they cannot afford the employee part of the premium.) She called her family physician, but he refused to see her because she owed him several hundred dollars, which she could not pay because she had no money. He suggested she go to the emergency room of the local hospital, so she did. They evaluated her and found, among other things, that her blood sugar was 650 (normal is up to 115). She received extensive treatment over two days at the hospital and was discharged feeling much better. Her bill is $5,000, which she will be unable to pay.

The woman telling the story then asked, who pays for this care?

The first answer is that the hospital does. It absorbs the loss, and if enough such losses occur, it goes out of business. But many hospitals would recognize this "uncompensated care" as being a cost of doing business, and they would build this into their cost structure when they negotiate with insurance companies. These hospitals would ask for higher reimbursement from other payers to make up for the losses on the self-pay business.

What happens to the insurance companies if the hospitals are constantly asking for more money to make up for uncompensated care? Insurance company costs rise. Insurance companies tolerate losses even less than hospitals do, so they raise their premiums. When they raise their premiums, that cost either must be borne by the employer or passed on to the employees as an increase in their contribution to premiums. The higher the employee contribution becomes, the fewer employees who can afford (or choose to pay) the premium at all. So more of them drop health insurance, which leads to more uninsured people showing up at the hospital ill or requiring medical care they cannot pay for. And hospital costs rise even more.

This is a positive feedback loop. It will build and build until something happens to stop it. That something could be a literal meltdown of the entire system.[10,11,12] Or it could be that we see the danger and take action to avert it.

What Does Universal Access Mean?

Does universal access to coverage mean a single-payer system? No, I don't think it means that at all. President Clinton's proposal was not a single-payer system, but it would have gone almost all the way to universal coverage. Given that we are Americans and as such we love pluralistic solutions to almost everything, I think it likely we would be most happy with a pluralistic solution—if we can develop one that will fulfill all of our success criteria.

Does universal access to coverage mean that everyone must be covered? I think so. I think we must start with the level playing field of "everyone is in," so that underwriting standards can be applied across the board. We should not allow some people to "opt out"—to choose not to be covered in trade for not paying into the system. As we have seen, the problem with allowing opt-outs is that it undermines the financial basis of the system. Those at least risk will opt out because their contribution is likely to be higher than the cost of their care. For them, not being covered looks cheaper than the premium or tax imposed to provide the coverage. But it is precisely because some people must pay "too much" that those who are ill will be able to receive coverage at a reasonable price. The point of lock-in is that it requires the enrollment of the entire population, which levels out the underwriting issue.

A federal, single-payer system could fill the role. All premiums would be taxes; all people would be covered—much as the Medicare program currently works for seniors. There are drawbacks to such a system that would need to be confronted, which I will discuss later in this book.

Would we permit people who are covered under the program to seek care outside of the system? Perhaps. It would depend on how a "black market" in healthcare would affect the viability of our solution. If the presence of a secondary cash market threatened the existence of the primary solution, then we would have to find a way to keep it from happening. If it did not, then I think Americans would want to have a secondary resource available to them.[13]

What about foreigners who need care while they are in the United States? This is a secondary issue that must be discussed and resolved. I believe we can and should pay for the healthcare needs of everyone who needs care while they are on United States soil, regardless of where they came from or how they got here (provided they did not come to the United States to seek healthcare). Mostly, this is for the financial reasons mentioned above: if they become catastrophically ill, we are going to pay anyway because they will not be able to do so. It makes more sense to make care available at the front end. This does not mean that people from all over the world could come to the United States for medical care and expect our system to pay for it. One of the issues to be resolved will be how to tell the difference.

Conclusion

To fulfill our self-image as the "greatest country," as well as to fulfill our moral obligations, to reduce the cost to society of health care, and to prevent the catastrophic collapse of our current "system," we must advocate for and develop an acceptable system to accomplish universal coverage for health care. It need not be a single-payer system. It may or may not be an exclusive system, but it must lock every American into participation in coverage, even if not in care. The goal: everyone in America should have financial access to healthcare.

Chapter 4

Affordable Cost

"Blessed are the young, for they shall inherit the national debt."
—*Herbert Hoover*

A major concern about health care is its affordability. We are in the early years of another cost spiral. The annual expenditure on medications has been increasing between 10% and 20% for several years, and the cost of hospital care also continues to rise. Health insurance premiums have gone up by double digits each year for several years, driving employers to look for ways to avoid the increased overhead.

Affordability is an interesting concern in that it means different things to different people. From the employer's point of view, it means the cost of health insurance should not drive his product to a price higher than comparable goods produced in other countries. This is clearly a concern for many of our industries and for the people who work within them whose jobs are at stake.

Affordability is a concern for the body politic because of the increasing taxes that must be levied to pay for government programs. Taxes are higher in some countries than in the United States because of the need to support a health care process paid for by the government.

Affordability is a concern for the individual not only because of the impact of premium costs on taxes and wages, but also because of direct costs such as co-payments, deductibles, and co-insurance. These direct costs are in place to act as barriers to the casual abuse of the health care system. They not only reduce the premium cost to the payer, but they are also designed to reduce the rate of access to the system by forcing potential patients to think about the personal cost of accessing the system. If the cost is too high compared to the potential benefit, the person will find another way to cope with the immediate health problem, and money will have been saved.

There are a number of ways of dealing with the affordability issue. Three ways that have already been used come to mind, and a successful plan will probably need to define a role for each of these to achieve a truly affordable national system over the long haul.

In Oregon, citizens attended a long string of "town hall" meetings and defined the priorities for the state health plan. The plan was designed to encompass as many people as possible while still acknowledging budget constraints. All health care was reduced to a single list of priorities. The needs of the identified population were projected actuarially, and a line was drawn through the list at the point where the money ran out. Everything above the line was covered. Everything below the line was not. In recent years, there has been an increasing demand to change the benefit structure to pay for more and more medical interventions. Now the list of coverage for the Oregon Medicaid program looks like that of many other states—and the availability of coverage to those not eligible for Medicaid has tightened considerably.

If we are to establish a national, inclusive plan that is heterogeneous—administered by various methods for different segments of the population—we must set some "minimum necessary" coverage to create a standard. I would propose that the standard be set by a method similar to that used in Oregon. If some people want to buy additional insurance to cover medical expenses not covered by the basic plan, they should be free to do so. If some people are wealthy enough to be able to pay for additional care, so be it. The wealthy will always be able to buy things the rest of us cannot, but at least we can determine a level of service available to all Americans under a universal access plan.

Another cost-control method is to set limits on prices for medical services or on the reimbursement available for those services. There was a period under President Nixon when medical fees were frozen, but I know of no other time when this technique was used. In general, limits have been set not on prices but on reimbursements from the particular plan. Patients who do not have some powerful entity negotiating on their behalf generally pay much higher prices than are paid on behalf of those who are represented by insurance companies or the government.

While limiting fees may seem draconian, limiting fees and limiting reimbursements amount to the same thing if there is but one payer—with the psychological difference that when fees are limited, the payer may choose to pay the full fee, and when reimbursement is limited, the provider may charge any fee he/she desires. The higher the fee goes, the lower the fixed reimbursement becomes as a percent of the fee, and the "worse" the system seems to be. In a heterogeneous system, this can result in "gaming" of the system by the avaricious—seeing patients who pay relatively well and avoiding those who do not (or whose insurance does not). This has deprived many government-sponsored patients of care when the medical community has uniformly determined that rendering care to those patients results in too little reward for too much work.

For reimbursement controls to work, they must be uniform: all sources of payment must have access to the same payment schedule. The down side to such a system is the risk that over-control of reimbursement could drive providers from the market. Recent events in the payment for Medicare services offer an interesting lesson in price controls. The federal government does not negotiate reimbursements with providers—whether they are physicians, hospitals, durable medical equipment (DME) companies, or home health agencies. The government dictates the prices and allows the providers to decide whether to participate. The arcane formulas for compensating physicians in recent years have resulted in a series of decreases in reimbursement—so much so that over three years, reimbursements have dropped by more than 10%. In an industry where profits are normally in the low single digits, such a reduction can be disastrous. Uniform pricing may be desirable as a cost-control mechanism, but it needs to be an intense and careful mechanism to make the appropriate adjustments in payments over time.

The third cost-control method is patient participation in the cost of care. This comes in several forms:

- The patient can participate in the cost of the premium by making payments to a fiscal intermediary for the health coverage.

- The patient can have a deductible to meet—an amount of money that must be paid before the coverage begins.

- The patient may have co-payments to pay—a fixed amount per encounter.

- The patient may have coinsurance—a percentage of the allowed bill that must be paid by the patient.

Often, more than one cost-sharing technique may apply.

Government programs sometimes apply another cost-sharing technique: means testing—an assessment of the ability of the supplicant to pay his/her own way. In most government programs, means testing is an "all or nothing" test. Either the applicant qualifies as being sufficiently destitute (or sufficiently old) and is therefore eligible for a particular program, or he/she does not qualify. In many private systems where means tests are applied, they result in a sliding scale payment due from the applicant, the size of the payment being proportional to the ability of the applicant to pay. If we are discussing means testing in regard to a universal program, only this latter interpretation makes sense. Means testing for Medicare was proposed a number of years ago and was first adopted, then rescinded, by Congress after strenuous objections from the AARP.

A progressive tax structure, in which higher income individuals are taxed at higher rates than lower income individuals, is itself a kind of means test, even though it is applied not to those who are recipients of largess but to those who pay for it whether or not they ever receive its benefits.

The funding and cost sharing of a national program will probably need to include all of these techniques in some manner or another. Means testing is an interesting way to set the premium contribution for each participant, as well as co-payments, deductibles, and co-insurance. I indicated earlier that we are all, except the very richest of Americans, medically indigent if we are without insurance. However, we are not all equally medically indigent. There are some who have no money—they may be the homeless, the disabled, or the unemployed. Such people may be unable to afford a co-payment of a single dollar to access care—and such a co-payment becomes not just a disincentive but an absolute barrier to care. There are others of us with thousands of dollars of financial reserves. We can easily afford a $15 or $25 co-payment and should, perhaps, also be subject to some requirement to fund part of the cost of the program with an annually recalculated contribution to the premium cost. This is what means testing is all about.

Regardless of what we choose to do for cost control, I think it is imperative that all three methodologies discussed above (limits on coverage, reimbursement controls, and means-tested participation) be part of the system. The goal is to have a system that is affordable to society and to individuals, but still offers sufficient incentives for people to continue seeking jobs in the health care sector and allows them to make a decent living.

Chapter 5

Health Insurance? Entitlement Program? Health Coverage? Medical Coverage?... What Is It Really?

"A superstition is a premature explanation that overstays its time."

—*George Iles*

Finding terminology that is not "loaded" for one or more of the participants in the conversation is one of the difficulties of talking about how health care is financed. Each term in the title of this chapter is correct in some ways and incorrect in others, and it is helpful to explore what is right and wrong with each of them.

The Insurance Paradigm

Third-party payment for health care began as insurance in the classical sense of the word—and policies that look a lot like insurance are still available. To understand what this means, though, we need to tease out what "insurance" is, and what characteristics would make a payment mechanism for health care look like an insurance policy.

At its core, buying an insurance policy is a lot like placing a bet. When you buy, for instance, a term life insurance policy, you are making a bet that you will die within the next year; the insurance company is making a bet that you will not die within the next year. You pay the premium, and if you do not die (i.e., the company wins the bet), the company keeps the money. If you die (i.e., you win the bet), your beneficiary collects the face value of the insurance policy. The "odds" on the bet are represented in the disproportion between the premium and the face value of the policy.

Similarly, when you buy fire insurance on your home, in essence you are betting that you will have a fire that will destroy your home. You pay the premium. If your home is not destroyed by fire, the insurance company wins the bet and it keeps the premium. If your house does burn down, then you win the bet, and the company pays you the amount indicated in the policy. The same analogy can be applied to auto insurance and all kinds of liability insurance.

There are several problems in applying this concept to medical coverage. First, the events on which you are betting in your life insurance policy and your fire insurance policy are events beyond your control. In fact, if you kill yourself, the insurance company may void your policy and refuse to pay any benefits. If you light your own house on fire, not only may the insurance company not pay you, but you may also go to jail. Your use of health care services, however, is under your control to a large degree. No one would bet that you will not use any health care services this year, since all you have to do is stand in line at any doctor's office to do so.

Second, the events for which you buy insurance are generally catastrophes. They are events that you hope will not happen, but you buy the insurance policy (you bet against your own hopes and desires) to cover the contingency. Even though your primary hope is the same as the insurance company's, you buy insurance because you want to make sure you won't be wiped out if the worst happens. The premium is small compared to the personal cost if the event happens, so you see the payment of the premium as being a low-cost way of "hedging your bets."

So, at age 22, you are just starting a career and your wife of six months has just had a positive pregnancy test. You are betting on (putting the majority of your energy and effort into) having a long life and a successful career, anticipating grandchildren in 25 years or so and retirement in 40 years. You buy life insurance to hedge your bet. If something should happen to you, your wife and child will have assets to allow them to live in spite of the loss of the income you would have brought them had you lived. You will not be around to expound on what a catastrophe your death was, but your widow and children will be, and that is exactly how they will feel about it. This is a significant contrast to developing a cold and going to see a doctor about it.

Third, the payout from an insurance policy is defined and limited. Your life insurance policy pays an exact amount, and it specifies the conditions under which that amount is paid. (For example, it will not pay anything if you kill yourself within three years, but it will pay double the policy amount if your death is from an accident, and triple if you are on a public conveyance such as a bus, tram, train, or airplane.) Your fire policy on your home is equally specific. (For example, it does not pay for the first $500, but will pay the remaining amount up to the $250,000 estimated value of your home to restore it to its previous condition, or it will pay you cash in that amount if the home is declared to be a total loss.) Personal liability policies are equally specific. They may or may not cover guests in your home or people working around your home. In contrast, the amount of the potential payout from a health insurance policy is undefined and may only be limited by a "lifetime maximum" of some large amount like $1 million.

If you take apart the business of an insurance company and analyze the business model, what you find is a well-protected bet. If you follow individuals covered by life insurance, it is likely they will pay premiums for many years before they die, and the insurance company is able not only to accumulate the premiums over time, but also to invest them and gain the benefit of the return on those investments.

The young man with the pregnant wife may decide to buy a $10,000 life insurance policy that costs $160 per year in premiums. In ten years, he will have paid in $1,600 for which he will have received nothing but the assurance of added financial stability in case of his death. In the meantime, the insurance company has been earning 7.5% annually on his premiums, or about $2,250. In twenty years, the total premiums paid will be $3,200, but the insurance company will have accumulated $6,928.75. After twenty-five years, the insurance company will have accumulated more than the $10,000 face value of the insurance policy. By the time the insured is 60, he will have paid in $6,400, and he will still be paying $160 per year, but the insurance company will have amassed $36,361.04. The nature of the business model is that there is a sufficient lag between selling an insurance policy and paying the benefit that the insurance company has plenty of time to make money off the investment to more than cover the cost of the benefit.

A number of years ago, I was surprised to look at the annual reports of a major insurance company in which I had purchased stock. (I didn't make money on the stock, but the education was worth the lack of profit.) This company would calculate a loss ratio (the ratio of total payments—losses—to the premiums collected) and a "combined loss and expense ratio" (add the losses to the expense of running the business and compare that to the premiums collected). Often, the loss ratio was over 98% and the combined loss and expense ratio was over 100%—yet the company was profitable! The difference was in the investment income.

In contrast to this, when a health insurance company sells policies, it generally expects to spend 80-90% of the premium received on medical services rendered to the beneficiary. The cost of doing business will take up about 10-15% of the premium, and whatever is left over is profit (or can be invested to produce another income stream). This is a very different business model.

When are health policies like insurance? They are like insurance policies when they perform in the same way as insurance does:

- They are a way you hedge your bet about your health.

- They have a limited and defined payout.

- That payout is not expected to happen and is not under your direct control.

What would such a policy look like? One form it takes is a hospital indemnity policy—one that pays a flat amount per day of confinement in the hospital. Another form it takes is specific disease insurance. If your kidney fails, the policy will pay $20,000 per year for dialysis or $100,000 toward a kidney transplant. Or perhaps it will just pay you $100,000 for having kidney failure, and you get to figure out how to use the money. A third form it could take is a high-deductible plan, where the deductible is high enough that any reasonably foreseeable health care needs will cost less than the deductible. This might be a deductible of $10,000 a year. The plan might pay 100% of costs over the initial deductible up to a specified total annual payment. (The size of the deductible needs to be set so that the probability of reaching it is small—$10,000 may well not be high enough.)

These three examples generally conform to the requirements for insurance. They are a hedge—a bet you make against your anticipation to cover a contingency. You do not anticipate that you will use them, and the insurance company is happy to pick up that side of the bet because you are unlikely to experience the triggering event. And the payout is defined and limited.

These characteristics are not what medical coverage generally is like. The biggest contrast is with HMO coverage, which has no threshold event, no effective limitation on coverage, and in which it is everyone's expectation that you will use services. (The expectation is that the HMO will arrange for you to have whatever services you need to detect potential health problems as early as possible so that treatment will be less expensive and complications less likely.) Here, instead of betting you will not use services, the HMO is expected to help you use at least some services (or so the theory says).

In life insurance, the vast majority of the people covered by a particular company do not die in any one year. In medical coverage, the vast majority of the people covered do use at least some medical services each year.

In contrast to the carefully worded statements about what the company will and will not pay for in your home or auto insurance, health insurance companies do not have any effective limitation on how much they may pay. They do not even have any effective voice in the choices of which services you receive, from whom, or at what price. My collision insurance is quite clear that my car will be repaired by the lowest of three bids from repair shops approved by my insurer, and that those bids will include all necessary items for the repair. My medical coverage (which thinks it is an HMO!) does not restrain which contracted specialists I might see, what tests they can order, or how often I can be seen. There is no requirement that I get several bids, or that the company will pay the lowest. There is no requirement that the company be able to review the plan of care to assure it is complete and not excessive. The company is obligated to pay for whatever health services I ask for and can arrange. This is not so much like an insurance program as it is like an entitlement program, which brings us to the next comparison.

An Entitlement Program

An entitlement program should include some process to determine whether a particular person is eligible for the program. Once entitlement is determined, the person is entitled to a defined benefit from the program without further question. There is a limit on what the eligible person is entitled to receive, inherent to the entitlement.

For example, Supplemental Security Income (SSI) is an entitlement program. If an individual is deemed to be eligible for SSI, then he or she is entitled to certain benefits, usually a set amount of income per month based on various factors. But the entitlement is not unlimited.

How does all this relate to health care? First, for most medical programs, there is a determination of entitlement—one must qualify for Medicare or Medicaid, for example, or purchase qualification by paying premiums for commercial insurance. However, on the defined-benefit side, problems arise. First, in a practical sense, the extent of the benefit is not defined. Second, in an equally practical sense, the benefactor does not control the extent of the benefit. When people consider health care benefits to be an entitlement, they tend to overuse services, driving the cost up. (See the discussion on "moral hazard" in Chapter 14.) This is part of what is causing health care expenditures to rise at their current rate, and it is part of what will cause health care to become unaffordable in the near future. If we approach our medical coverage as cost-conscious shoppers looking for an insurance policy with the best premium price, but treat our health care as an unconstrained entitlement, we will overspend the premium, break every budget, and run the system into bankruptcy.

If you are running an entitlement program, you figure out what population you are serving, what proportion will be eligible, and how much each person will be entitled to receive. With this information, you can calculate the upper limit of what your entitlement funding should be. After adding an amount for overhead, you will know how much it will cost to do business. As people come in and are found to be eligible, you hand them their entitlement—a check for $20 per week or whatever it may be. You can go wrong by miscalculating the number of eligibles, or you can go wrong if the amount of the entitlement changes. Otherwise, it is predictable. Health care, however, is not so predictable. No one pre-calculates the cost of care for an automobile accident or schedules the discovery of their cancer for the third of May.

An Interesting Hybrid

On the other hand, some of the cost ought to be predictable —an annual physical examination, a pap smear and a mammogram, a colonoscopy, tests for cholesterol. It is possible to define a scientifically valid set of cost-effective screening tools for detecting certain diseases early enough to make a difference in overall health status, outcome, or cost of care. The list is surprisingly shorter than most people realize. Nonetheless, there is such a list.[1] If we know these things, we can construct a defined benefit program (with definable costs) that covers this care as a benefit program and covers anything else that happens as insurance—with a significant deductible so the insurance "kicks in" only when there is a significant, unanticipated, health-related mishap. For this protection, we use "insurance" techniques—for example, where many pay for the benefit of the few, but the benefit, when paid, is of a potentially mind-boggling magnitude.

Why don't we do this? Currently, the efforts in this direction are in the form of the "high-deductible health plan." This kind of plan, authorized by the Medicare Modernization Act in 2003, offers a defined wellness benefit paid in full from the first dollar, and the rest of health care is relegated to a high-deductible plan. We do not yet know how this will work. However, it is possible to point to some potential obstacles in the path of a universal application of this kind of plan. The major difficulty is the deductible. No matter what level of participation one demands from enrollees, some would be unable to pay the high deductible and would be barred from receiving care. This means universal application of this kind of plan would require there to be at least two plans available—a means-tested one that would cover all care without enrollee expense, and one for the rest of us that would impose enrollee participation in the cost.

The other problem with separating health care into two categories is that it requires drawing absolute boundaries where there are none in practice. Even where there are apparently some boundaries, reality is not so clear. For example, since there are different codes for screening mammography and diagnostic mammography, it should be easy to separate the preventive test (screening mammography) from the illness-related test (diagnostic mammography). However, for some women, a screening mammogram does not give enough information for an adequate screening examination—perhaps because of unusually dense breasts or because of what is called "fibrocystic disease." For these women, the annual examination is not a screening mammogram but a diagnostic one, even though it is being done for screening purposes. Is it reasonable that Ms. Smith should have her annual mammogram paid in full by her insurance while Ms. Johnson must pay the full cost for hers under the same plan?

Some tests are preventive at some times and not at others. Cholesterol screening is recommended as a preventive test starting at age 35 for men and 45 for women, but only every five to ten years. This implies that if the test is done more frequently, it is no longer a screening test. Instead, it is probably being done to monitor an abnormality. And what if it is done on a 25-year-old?

In addition, there are many more "screening" and "wellness" tests and interventions than evidence to support them. For instance, exercise stress testing for heart disease—to assess the risk of heart attacks—is advanced as a screening test. When someone has chest pain that suggests coronary artery disease, this test is very helpful in letting us know who does not need further evaluation and treatment. On the other hand, the test is of little value for people who have no symptoms and can exercise normally.

There is also a large, hazy area between wellness care and catastrophic care. Many people with minor illnesses receive expensive diagnostic testing to reassure them or their physicians that the minor illness does not represent anything more serious than it seems on the surface. Are these tests screening tests or not? Do they belong in the basic benefit or in the high-deductible insurance plan? If we put them in the insurance plan, then a lot of people are going to be paying a lot of money "out of pocket" for a lot of health care services.

Or maybe not. Maybe we will learn to forego some of these tests. Instead of having an MRI today, we wait a couple weeks to see how the illness responds to treatment. If it responds, we don't need the MRI at all. If it doesn't, then maybe it is worth the $1,000 cost. We just don't know how this behavior pattern will play out because no one has been doing high-deductible health plans (as currently defined) long enough and with enough people to have a sense of how they work.

Health Coverage

The very term "health coverage" is a misnomer. We really don't have "health" coverage; we have "sickness" coverage. The things healthy people can do to keep themselves healthy are not generally things they need to go to a doctor—or any other kind of "healer"—for, such as the following:

- Eating a balanced diet
- Getting some sun exposure but not an excessive amount
- Being physically active
- Maintaining a balance between calories consumed and calories expended in exercise
- Not smoking
- Drinking alcohol in moderation or not at all
- Not taking illicit drugs
- Following safe sexual practices
- Using a seat belt when driving

- Driving at or below the speed limit

- Learning to avoid or cope with stress

- Avoiding excessively risky activities

- Following safety rules at work, home, and play

- Using caution with firearms

- Washing one's hands during flu season

There are also health-maintaining benefits in immunizations. Taking low-dose aspirin helps maintain health for people in whom blood clotting is more dangerous than bleeding—such as those susceptible to strokes, heart attacks, or blood clots in the legs. Taking vitamins may help those with unbalanced diets, but in general, vitamin consumption is not particularly helpful.

What about annual physical examinations, or pap smears, mammograms, blood fat determinations, blood pressure checks, PSA tests, sonograms for aneurysms, and other screening tests? These are not to keep people healthy. They are to detect disease at an early stage so it can be treated sooner with the hope the treatment will lead to less risk and better outcomes. They are mostly blunt instruments, though—none blunter than the annual physical examination, whose value is miniscule—and none of them prevent any disease.

Medical Coverage

"Medical coverage," then, is the term we may be left with to describe the process of arranging payment for medical care or health care. However, this term implies that it refers only to coverage for medical care, as opposed to health care (see the next section below). This would clearly be incorrect in many instances, since preventive services and non-standard providers are often covered under "medical coverage." As a term, "medical coverage" is superior to medical insurance, since it keeps us out of the insurance paradigm. It also does not get too specific about how the coverage is provided, which is probably good. We should use a term that is flexible enough to allow us as much latitude as possible in resolving the problem of how to do it.

"Medical coverage" would, for instance, cover services exclusively offered within a single medical provider system. It would cover a plan in which having a particular diagnosis would result in the payment to the victim of a certain amount of money to be spent by that individual in whatever way he or she saw fit. It would also cover the kinds of arrangements we more frequently see in which health care services are divided into those that are covered and those that are not, with the ones covered resulting in some sharing of financial responsibility between the patient and the third-party payer.

As I use the term in this book, I intend "medical coverage" to encompass any and all possible ways of providing the financial resources to pay for covered health care services. I do not intend to limit it to sickness care, though that is most of what it encompasses. I also do not wish to imply any particular funding mechanism. The text will do that, not the label.

"Health Care" Versus "Medical Care"

What then of the term "health care?" In this book, I have and will continue to use the term "health care" to indicate a broader range of services than I encompass under the term "medical care." By "medical care," I mean standard sickness care—care provided to sick people to alleviate illness, provided by physicians and their adjuncts (hospitals, surgicenters, imaging centers, and the professionals who populate them). By "health care," I refer to both "medical care" and a broader range of services provided by other licensed and unlicensed healers to maintain or enhance wellness. In "health care," I would include cosmetic surgery and massage therapy, but I would not include the purchase of food, shelter, clothing, heaters, coolers, vaporizers, dehumidifiers, or other environmental modifiers unless they are specifically prescribed by a physician as part of the treatment for an identified and diagnosed illness.

Conclusion

It seems that what we have is neither a system of health insurance (or medical insurance) nor an entitlement program, though it has aspects of both insurance and entitlement. In some ways for the participants, it has the best aspects of a Marxian system of requiring contributions from each according to ability to pay and providing benefits to each according to need.

There is an experiment in progress to see what will result from an obvious, if not explicit, combining of the two in the form of the high-deductible health plan. In the meantime, what we have is a relatively unstructured, mostly unlimited, benefit program.

For the purposes of this book, I have defined the terms "health care" and "medical care" and will continue to use the term "medical coverage" to refer to ways of providing financial access to health care services.

In this chapter, we have examined one aspect of the structure of medical coverage from a high altitude. In the midst of that process is some party—neither the caregiver nor the patient—who must manage the transfer of cash from whoever is ultimately paying (e.g., employer, government) to the provider on behalf of the patient. In the next chapter, I will discuss that third-party payer's role.

Chapter 6

The Third-Party Payer

"Judge a tree from its fruit, not from the leaves."

—Euripides

The company managing funds to pay for medical care is a
"third-party payer." The third-party payer is in essence a conduit by
which money paid in by one entity (usually an employer or the government) is used to fund the health care required by an identified
population. The third-party payer may merely administer this flow
(a relationship called "administrative services only" or ASO), or the
third-party payer may be at risk for the cost of care—collecting a
fixed monthly amount (the premium) from the sponsor and committing to keep health care costs within that boundary (or lose money
on the arrangement). In the latter, the third-party payer obviously
has an interest in how its money is being spent.

The role of the third-party payer looks like a "black box" process to most people. It is hard to understand what is going on at
"the insurance company" or "the HMO" unless you take time and
effort to see it. When you are feeling well, you have no motivation
to read the long certificate that is the contract indicating what your
medical coverage will and will not pay for. When you are ill, you have
neither the time nor the patience for checking on the rules. Most of
us remain blissfully ignorant about our medical coverage until we

disagree with the third-party payer about a payment decision. But if we are to plan a new health care system, we had better understand the roles of all of the players. Unless we decide to outlaw third-party payers (which would make most of us instantly medically indigent), we will need at least one third-party payer for any system we choose to institute. Let us walk in the shoes of the third-party payer for the space of a chapter.

Open for Business

You have just opened Utopia Medical Plan. Operations commence on the first of January. You are in charge of the business. You receive what seems like a lot of money—$150 million—to be paid to your company at the rate of $12.5 million per month. In return, you are responsible for paying for the health care needs of a population of 50,000 people for the entire year. That means you have an average of $3,000 ($250 per month) per man, woman, and child in your population. Offhand, that seems as though it ought to be plenty. You will need office space, furnishings, equipment, a computer system for claims payment, and supplies. And you will need employees to operate the computers, answer the phones, and keep the company running. You will face challenges along the way, some of which may force you to change your business plan during the year.

For the sake of this exercise, I have compressed events and magnified them somewhat—but none of the crises that confront Utopia Medical Plan are invented. I have personally seen each of them in the real life of real third-party payers.

Budget

A good businessman starts with a budget. You start by assuming that your medical expense ratio (the cost of care) will consume about 88% of the available funds. This leaves you with 12% for operating expenses and margin. Your computer system will cost $4.5 million to lease for a year. The office space and furnishings will run $2 million per year. Computers and other specialized equipment (scanners, fax machines, telephones) will cost another $1.2 million. You estimate salaries at $1.5 million per year. With other items added in, your budget looks something like Figure 1.

Figure 1: Budget for Utopia Medical Plan

	Monthly	Annual	
Income	$12,500,000	$150,000,000	
Expenses			
Cost of care	$11,000,000	$132,000,000	88%
Salaries	$125,000	$1,500,000	
Benefits	$43,750	$525,000	
Computer system	$375,000	$4,500,000	
Rent	$166,667	$2,000,000	
Equipment	$100,000	$1,200,000	
Postage	$15,000	$180,000	
Supplies	$10,000	$120,000	
Phone & utilities	$54,167	$650,000	
Other	$5,000	$60,000	7%
TOTAL	$11,894,583	$142,735,000	95%
Net	$605,417	$7,265,000	5%

January: Initial Operations

Your contract with the sponsor of the plan says that the enrollees will pay $15 toward the cost of a physician office visit, 20% of any outpatient service not rendered in a physician's office, and $500 toward any hospitalization. Because you are a new company, you have no contracts with providers. You believe local provider fees are reasonable, so this is not a major concern to you. However, you also realize there is a financial benefit to the provider in receiving payment from you within 20 days as compared to having to bill the patient repeatedly for payment, so you expect to obtain contracts for some reduction in their standard fees.

In January you start paying claims. Because you are a new plan, you are not covering any claims from the previous year. Claims are slow coming in, so rapid processing is not a challenge. You believe this is an advantage for you, because you are rapidly getting a reputation for being a prompt payer. You have hired a contract manager to craft and negotiate contracts with the providers who recognize the value of your prompt payments. You give your contract manager until the end of February to get contracts signed with providers, dating back to the first of January.

By the end of January, you have paid out about $4 million in medical care expenses. Your contract manager is very successful in getting physicians and hospitals to agree to a contract that specifies that payment will be at 75% of normal billed charges. You are very pleased with this progress. More than half of the providers who have sent you bills are now under contract, and your contract manager informs you the rest are soon to follow. You believe your payments should decrease by 25%.

You have 21 employees (counting yourself): a claims supervisor and 10 claims processors, a contract manager, a medical director, an accountant (whom you have named CFO) with one helper, an IT manager, and four people answering telephones in customer service. So far, things are going well. The cash flow for the month looks like Figure 2 on page 45.

February: Price Creep

You are receiving weekly reports from your claims supervisor on number of claims processed and dollars paid. By mid-February, you note that the cost per claim has not gone down since January. On the contrary, it has gone up. On investigation, you find that a number of providers (especially the hospital most commonly used by your members) have raised their fees since signing your contract.

The norm seems to be a 50% increase. Instead of paying 75% of what you paid in January, you are paying about 112.5% of what you paid in January when you compare service by service.

You realize you will not achieve predictable costs without a predictable fee schedule. Since a reduction from billed charges did not achieve good predictability, you decide to send your contract manager back out to re-contract—this time with a fixed-fee schedule representing 75% of the January fee levels. There is much more resistance to these contracts, and many providers refuse to sign them, so you threaten to send your patients elsewhere. Your providers grumble about your lousy payment rates, but gradually they come into line.

January Cash Summary	
Income	$12,500,000
Medical Cost	$4,000,000
Feb	$0
Mar	$0
Apr	$0
May	$0
Jun	$0
Jul	$0
Aug	$0
Sep	$0
Oct	$0
Nov	$0
Dec	$0
Total	$4,000,000

Figure 2: January Cash Flow

Med Exp Ratio	32.0%
Operating Costs	
Salary	$112,083
Benefits	$39,229
Other	$725,833
Total	$877,146
Cash Flow	$7,622,854
Bank Balance	
opening	0
closing	$7,622,854

The plan sponsor (the organization sending you the $12.5 million each month) calls to say they have been receiving complaints from doctors claiming you are trying to starve them to death by paying only half of what they are billing. You check some claims and notice that they have not rolled back their fees, so their complaint that you are only paying them half of what they bill is correct. You explain the change in fee schedules to the plan sponsor, offering to share the data. The plan sponsor chuckles and says, "No need. They did that to me when I ran the plan myself. I'm just glad you have to handle them now."

You realize you will be reprocessing a number of claims, so you hire two more claims processors and two more customer service agents (anticipat-

February Cash Summary	
Income	$12,500,000
Medical Cost	
Jan	$4,000,000
Feb	$5,500,000
Total	$9,500,000
Net of Medical	$3,000,000
Med Exp Ratio	**76.0%**
Operating Costs	
Salary	$131,667
Benefits	$46,083
Other	$727,333
Total	$905,083
Cash Flow	$2,094,917
Bank Balance	
opening	$7,622,854
closing	$9,717,771

ing that, if your sponsor is getting calls, you will be also). In addition, you hire one person to work with the contract manager to provide information and support services to the providers, and another accountant, because the bookkeeping is becoming complicated.

In February, you pay another $4 million of January claims and $5.5 million of February claims. Many February claims will need to be ad-

Figure 3: February Cash Flow

justed. You hope that the dollar figure goes down as adjustments are made during March. Your medical expenses were $9.5 million compared to a budget of $11 million, so you are concerned because you are just beginning, and you will continue to receive claims for January and February services for several more months. (See Figure 3.)

March: High Impact Case

In mid-March, your medical director comes to you with the news that you have a high-cost hospitalization on your hands. He anticipates that your payment on this case will end up at more than a million dollars. You and he discuss how you can more effectively monitor hospital utilization, since that can clearly create huge costs. As a result of your conversation, the medical director audits two dozen recent hospital stays and discovers delays in service and lays in discharge plus five unnecessary admissions, all of which have cost the plan more than $100,000. Between the two of you, you decide the potential for this level of savings justifies hiring some nurses and implementing a concurrent review process for hospital stays, similar to that employed by other local payers. You hire an experienced nurse supervisor with managed care experience, three nurses, and two clerical people for a new Care Management department. You realize this new process will cause more phone calls and concerns, so you add two more customer service agents and another provider relations agent.

During March, you are pleased to note that the January claim volume is decreasing—down to $1.5 million. (See Figure 4.)

Figure 4: March Cash Flow

April: Consolidation and Unnecessary Services

As April proceeds, your weekly reports from your claims supervisor indicate a reduction in claims for January and February dates of service. April is moving a bit more slowly than March did, but not much. You wonder if people were saving up to have medical things done in the second quarter of the year.

Your medical director reports that the

March Cash Summary	
Income	$12,500,000
Medical Cost	
Jan	$1,500,000
Feb	$3,740,000
Mar	$5,400,000
Total	$10,640,000
Net of Medical	**$1,860,000**
Med Exp Ratio	**85.1%**
Operating Costs	
Salary	$166,667
Benefits	$58,333
Other	$728,983
Total	$953,983
Cash Flow	$906,017
Bank Balance	
opening	$9,717,771
closing	$10,623,788

nurses are very busy. Cost savings from avoided (or denied) hospital days are more than $50,000 per week, so the expense of hiring the nurses is certainly justified. You and the medical director discuss the expectation of your sponsor that you will get NCQA certification. This will require some quality monitoring as well as the utilization monitoring currently being done. You agree to allow the hiring of three more nurses —one to work on quality issues and two more to help handle the concurrent review workload.

You accompany your elderly mother on a visit to her neurologist early in the month. He asks you how your new medical plan is doing. You tell him the story of the unnecessary hospital utilization. He counters with a story indicating that most of the patients he sees with migraine headaches have had at least one and sometimes two or three unnecessary imaging studies done by primary care physicians before the referral is made.

Later in the month, you accompany your father on a visit to his urologist. You swear the neurologist and the urologist must be in cahoots—because after hearing about your hospital experience, he tells you he is seeing patients with prostate cancer in apparent remission being followed with imaging studies when a PSA blood test would be more accurate and more sensitive—not to mention less expensive.

The neurologist visit didn't alarm you, but after the urologist sings the same song, you decide to talk with your medical director. He agrees to call both physicians, settle on an auditing technique, run the audit, and report back. Near the end of the month, he reports that the neurologist is right. Many typical migraine patients are receiving not only an MRI, but also CT scans and a few PET scans. The chance of any of these being abnormal in a patient with migraines is about the same as in someone with no symptoms at all. Therefore, it does not seem reasonable to be incurring this expense. Your father's urologist, on the other hand, is mistaken, or at least is not talking about your patient population. All of your prostate cancer patients are being followed appropriately with PSA tests.

The medical director suggests that all PET scans (which cost about $2,400 each) be subject to preauthorization. In addition, he suggests that medical criteria be applied to CT scans and MRI scans of the head. If he can implement this process, some cases will be paid automatically and others will require review, depending on the diagnosis. You hope this will put the brakes on some very expensive unnecessary tests.

Your working population is now more than twice what it was in January. Your IT manager needs help, and you allow him to hire an assistant. With all of the claims adjustments being processed, the claims payment pro-cess is lagging and the number of claims in pro-cess has increased. You agree with your claims manager to hire another claims processor. Customer Service and Provider Relations are both having trouble maintaining good telephone response times, so you hire one more provider relations representative and two more customer service representatives. In doing so, you realize you are now paying almost $200,000 per month for salaries even though you only bud-geted $125,000. You also note that your postage costs have increased monthly because of in-creased communication with providers due to claims reprocessing and care management activi-ties. (See Figure 5 on page 49.)

May: Quality Contin-ued, Unnecessary Ser-vices Revisited

You continue to be concerned about your ability to end the year with money in the bank. The high April claims number is alarming.

In your conference with the medical director early in the month, you

April Cash Summary	
Income	$12,500,000
Medical Cost	
Jan	$300,000
Feb	$1,430,000
Mar	$4,440,000
Apr	$5,062,500
Total	$11,232,500
Net of Medical	**$1,267,500**
Med Exp Ratio	**89.9%**
Operating Costs	
Salary	$192,083
Benefits	$67,229
Other	$738,058
Total	$997,371
Cash Flow	$270,129
Bank Balance	
opening	$10,623,788
closing	$10,893,917

Figure 5: April Cash Flow

learn that the weekly savings continues and is now trending toward $80,000 a week. That's the good news. The preauthorization process for head scans is causing additional work and friction. In addition, the medical director thinks there are other interventions being over-utilized. He notes that the hysterectomy rate for women in the plan is almost three times the national average. Hip and knee replacement surgeries are being done twice as often as the national average. Laparoscopic cholecystectomies are being done as inpatient procedures nearly 75% of the time, but the literature suggests this number should be closer to 5%. You agree to expand the preauthorization program. He will hire two more nurses.

The IT manager complains that the medical director has been badgering him for reports and statistical analyses. You recognize that the analyses you have been asking him to do are data-intensive. This is a change for the IT department. You instruct the IT manager to hire two data analysts.

The claims supervisor notes that the increasing load of claim adjustments is continuing to slow down claims processing. You decide to hire two more claims processors.

In spite of adding two new customer service representatives last month, the average time-to-answer increased to more than 90 seconds and the call-abandonment rate climbed to 15%. You decide to hire five more customer service reps. The provider relations area is also mildly over-loaded, so you hire a fourth representative. You now have more than 50 employ-ees, and you need help with hiring and discipline, and with tracking benefit programs. You hire a human resources manager.

Your monthly salary schedule is now more than $100,000 over budget. The extra expense is well justified, however, if it is needed to support the nurses in producing $80,000 per week in cost savings. This comes to about $350,000 per month—a net savings of almost a quarter of a million dollars a month.

In May, your ending bank balance is $11,884,371 —up almost a million since last month. You might make it through the whole year after all! (See Figure 6.)

May Cash Summary	
Income	$12,500,000
Medical Cost	
Jan	$100,000
Feb	$220,000
Mar	$1,560,000
Apr	$4,162,500
May	$4,400,000
Total	$10,442,500
Net of medical	**$2,057,500**
Med Exp Ratio	**83.5%**
Operating Costs	
Salary	$232,500
Benefits	$81,375
Other	$753,171
Total	$1,067,046
Cash Flow	$990,454
Bank Balance	
opening	$10,893,917
closing	$11,884,371

Figure 6: May Cash Flow

June: Double Billing and Overpayment

You meet with the medical director, as usual, on the first Tuesday of the month. He reports that the preauthorization program for head imaging studies seems to be slowing down utilization. It is hard to be certain just what the cost savings might be, but it seems to be on the order of half a dozen studies a week—something in the $10,000-a-week range.

He has some bad news, however. In looking at quality measures, his nurse discovered a prevalent pattern of double billing. The gynecologist or primary care physician doing the Pap smear was charging for reading the Pap smear, but Utopia was also receiving and paying a bill from a cytologist for reading the same smear. The reading was being done once and paid twice. The medical director suggests recouping the excess payments and looking for a way to block this in the future.

When he looks into the system to find out why it did not stop such double billing, the medical director finds that a number of editing functions had not been activated in the initial set-up of the system. As a result, it didn't catch such things as reducing the payment for a secondary surgical procedure by 50%, denying payment for incidental procedures, rebundling unbundled procedures, and denying payment for surgical facility and anesthesia fees when the surgical procedure is not covered. You have been paying claims at a higher than necessary level of reimbursement. In aggregate, this represents a sizeable expense—probably as much as the concurrent review at the hospital.

You decide not only to put the edits the medical director suggests into effect, but also to go back and recoup overpayments. Your contracts allow you to go back 180 days to recover payments made in error. You consult with IT, Claims, and Provider Relations and discover it will require additional help in all three departments to complete this process—and you should probably forget about having it up and running in time to recoup much from January. You start hiring again. Two more data analysts and a computer technician will be required to make and monitor the system changes. Two claims processors and two provider relations representatives will be needed, in addition to two more nurses to review appeals. Since you have started denying services, appeals are becoming more and more common, distracting nurses from their primary jobs.

Your CFO tells you that the increasing complexity of the business, especially the recoupment process, is making accounting more difficult. He needs another two bookkeepers to keep up with the business.

By the end of the month, some recoupment from February and March is apparent in the net payment numbers, but the numbers for more recent months are high, and the total payment is the highest so far. You hope that all of the processes you have put in place are helpful. Care costs are above budget, and you now have more than three times as many people working at the medical plan as you had anticipated. (See Figure 7.)

June Cash Summary	
Income	$12,500,000
Medical Cost	
Jan	$100,000
Feb	$55,000
Mar	$360,000
Apr	$1,462,500
May	$4,400,000
Jun	$4,950,000
Total	$11,327,500
Net of Medical	**$1,172,500**
Med Exp Ratio	**90.6%**
Operating Costs	
Salary	$263,333
Benefits	$92,167
Other	$775,315
Total	$1,130,815
Cash Flow	$41,685
Bank Balance	
opening	$11,884,371
closing	$11,926,056

Figure 7: June Cash Flow

July: Fraud!

Well, just when you thought you were getting your arms around the process, new things begin to happen. During the last few days of June, there was a meltdown in the Customer Service Department. Calls were suddenly taking longer to be answered and longer to complete. You make the decision to hire an experienced manager for this area, and she will start right after the Independence Day holiday. Also, one of the bookkeepers noticed an irregularity in claims payment. An investigation reveals that one of the claim examiners has been hiding claims in her desk drawer—more than $400,000 in claims she had received credit for processing. As you fire her, the claims supervisor suggests building an audit function into the department.

Amazingly, this month the medical director does not suggest hiring more personnel for his department. However, he has discovered claims for brain surgery and open-heart surgery submitted by a psychiatrist. He is investigating. Cost savings from his department are no longer as crisp as they were when they were all hospital days avoided. However, his nurses are now also picking up some case management activities in which they are assisting members in finding and receiving care, directing traffic to preferred providers, and helping members stay out of the hospital. The medical director estimates weekly savings at $150,000 in hard dollars (denials) and another $250,000 in soft dollars (costs avoided by arranging alternative care).

One by one, the managers in IT, Provider Relations (your "contract manager" is now Director of Provider Relations), and Accounting come to you to indicate that the increasing activity of the medical managers is causing ripples that their people have to manage. More employees are called for.

In mid-month, the new Customer Service Manager comes wanting to hire one additional rep. Two troublemakers are being fired and will be replaced. Medical Management needs another person to answer their telephones. Things are improving: average speed-to-answer is below 40 seconds and the abandonment rate is below 10% again.

The monthly summary of claims paid indicates a net payment for January of zero. This brings January to a total of $10 million, which is a million below budget. However, February, March and April are all at or above the $11 million budget. Your ending cash balance is $11,927,817, unchanged. But with the leveling off of the early months of the year, this may not be so bad. You do not yet have a full month of revenue in reserve, but you are getting close. The cash flow for July, with a year to date column added this month, looks like Figure 8 on page 55.

Figure 8: July Cash Flow

Cash Summary		
	July	YTD
Income	$12,500,000	$87,500,000
Medical Cost		
Jan	$0	$10,000,000
Feb	$55,000	$11,000,000
Mar	$120,000	$11,880,000
Apr	$337,500	$11,025,000
May	$1,650,000	$10,450,000
Jun	$4,070,000	$9,020,000
Jul	$4,950,000	$4,950,000
Total	$11,182,500	$68,325,000
Net of Medical	$1,317,500	$19,175,000
Med Exp Ratio	**89.5%**	**78.1%**
Operating Costs		
Salary	$302,083	$1,400,417
Benefits	$105,729	$490,146
Other	$907,926	$5,356,620
Total	$1,315,739	$7,247,183
Cash Flow	$1,761	$11,927,817
Bank Balance		
opening	$11,926,056	$0.00
closing	$11,927,817	$11,927,817

August: The Fraud Story Continues

You meet with your medical director as usual early in the month. Things are stable. You hear that the psychiatrist who has been billing brain surgery and open-heart surgery to your plan has been doing this with other plans as well. It appears you have paid him almost $50,000 in what appear to be fraudulent bills. The State Board has revoked his license, and the DA is investigating whether to press criminal charges.

Cost savings appear to be stable at between $350,000 and $400,000 per week, counting both hard-dollar and soft-dollar savings. He explains that soft-dollar savings are an estimate made when there is no way to know how much money has actually been saved by an activity. He explains why he believes his method of estimating this money is conservative, but admits he could easily be off by 30% to 40%.

This month, it is your claims shop supervisor who comes to you with what appears to be fraudulent billing. Some providers seem to be billing for services not performed. The local version of the process is that the provider gets the member to share billing information by offering a bounty of $500. They then bill the medical plan for tens of thousands of dollars in services, and the plan pays the claims. The claims shop has noted large payments to several providers at the same address. In collaboration with the medical director, they have asked for medical records. They have asked provider relations to arrange an on-site visit. The claims supervisor believes you have paid claims amounting to more than $100,000 to this bogus provider for services never rendered—and that you will probably not recover the money.

In response to the discovery of unpaid claims last month, two claims processors have been retrained to perform claims payment audits. The claims supervisor has found it necessary to hire two new claims processors to replace them. Customer service has improved its response times, but not to a level acceptable under your contract with your client. Three more customer service representatives must be hired. With the additional work of auditing providers, two more provider service representatives are needed. And of course, accounting must track all of this activity from a financial standpoint, so two more clerks must be hired.

Although you are not yet aware of it, you have hired all the people you need to continue smooth operations. Your payroll has now reached $330,000 per month. As you consider this number, you realize you only need a small amount of the promised $350,000 per week of care management savings to justify the whole payroll—to say nothing of the improved services you are rendering to members, providers, and your client by controlling costs and providing a relatively transparent set of rules for doing so. Your cost for equipment has risen because your number of employees has far surpassed all anticipation. If your projection of 88% medical expense ratio is correct, your margin for August will be about $112,000, or less than 1% of your $12.5 million monthly income. Your margin, which was budgeted at 5%, has been shrinking.

Claims paid for August show no net payments related to January or February dates of service. In actuality, medical plans are often still receiving claims and adjusting claims for up to a year or more after the date of service. For the purposes of this exercise, I have limited that time to six months. By examining the pattern in which claims reach the plan, you may be able to project the total cost for a month based on the claims received in the first two or three months. For the first time since May, your total cash flow to claims paid is less than $11 million in the month. Your ending cash balance is $12.57 million—just over one month of revenue. Cash flow for the month and year to date look like Figure 9 on page 58.

Finishing Off the Year

The rest of the year is uneventful. Things continue on a stable course. Gradually, the number of preauthorization denials and appeals is decreasing. Your customer service department is doing such a good job that your client has called to compliment you. Your medical management department has not only curbed the escalation in costs, you note that the estimates for the last few months are trending down below your 88% budget.

As you approach the end of the year, you estimate that you will have $12.8 million in the bank on December 31 and just under $10 million in payments that will eventually be due from claims not

Cash Summary		
	August	YTD

Income	$12,500,000	$100,000,000
Medical Cost		
Jan	$0	$10,000,000
Feb	$0	$11,000,000
Mar	$120,000	$12,000,000
Apr	$112,500	$11,137,500
May	$330,000	$10,780,000
Jun	$1,430,000	$10,450,000
Jul	$4,070,000	$9,020,000
Aug	$4,395,000	$4,395,000
Total	$10,457,500	$78,782,500
Net of Medical	$2,042,500	$21,217,500
Med Exp Ratio	**83.7%**	**78.8%**
Operating Costs		
Salary	$328,750	$1,729,167
Benefits	$115,063	$605,208
Other	$956,150	$6,312,770
Total	$1,399,962	$8,647,145
Cash Flow	$642,538	$12,570,355
Bank Balance		
opening	$11,927,817	$0
closing	$12,570,355	$12,570,355

Figure 9: August Cash Flow

yet received (in the business this is called IBNR—incurred but not received)—for a total margin of $3.2 million on the year. Most of this 2% margin was accomplished because of reduced overhead early in the year. Your current run rate of about 0.1% will not be enough to sustain you if you have another catastrophic case. Your challenge for the final months of the year will be to negotiate a higher monthly payment from your sponsor to reflect what you believe will be the rising cost of medical care during the coming year, plus a larger operating margin.

If you cannot achieve that negotiation, you will have to arrange for some transition out of business. You cannot close out operations over the five months it will take to receive and pay all of the December bills with the reserves you have in hand. Either you will need additional payments to cover your administrative costs during the transition, or a new third-party payer will have to assume responsibility for paying residual claims from your year of operation —a responsibility you did not have at the beginning of your operation.

Congratulations! You have made it through a year of operating a medical plan. And you emerged with a profit—although it was not as large as you had anticipated. You believe your idealism and service ethic continue to be evident in how your plan is run on a day-by-day basis, although not all of the enrollees and not all of the physicians share your views on that subject. The numbers and ratios I have used in the scenario are realistic, though simplified. Frequently, the Medical Expense Ratio is lower and overhead higher— we have not considered the need for a legal department. And if we are to be commercially successful over the long term, we will need an underwriting department and a marketing and sales department.

Lessons Learned

You reflect on the year gone by and what you have learned. First, you learned that your business started the year totally out of control—not because of what you were doing, but because of the business model. All of your health care expenditures are determined by two strangers, neither of whom is an employee of your medical plan, and both of whom have an ulterior motive at odds with yours. The patient, your member, wants you to pay for all desired care because it costs too much for the member to pay. The doctor wants you to pay for it because it is much easier to collect from you than from the patient.

You have also learned that when you are in the business of handing out money, people will line up for it whether they have earned it or not. And even those who are earning it may try to increase the amount you give them. Determining how much you should pay each recipient is not an easy task.

To do the job well, you found you must intrude into the relationship between the physician and the patient. In doing so, you regain some control over how your money is being spent. Your members object to this, especially when it slows down access to tests and procedures, and most especially if you decide not to pay for something. Physicians object to this because they perceive it as "second guessing" how they practice medicine. They see you as telling them what to do, interfering with their business, imposing unneeded restrictions, and requiring them to do a lot of paperwork you aren't paying for. All you want is to be sure that when you receive a bill for services, the bill is correct and the services were medically necessary and appropriate as called for by the physician's contract and the member's coverage documents.

Welcome to the World of the Third-Party Payer

This is where we are now. Physicians frequently behave as though the third-party payer is their enemy. There is a side they do not see, though: if there were no third-party payers to foot the bill for their services, patients could not afford them and either could not have them or would not pay for them. If there were no third-party payers, doctors would have much more trouble collecting, and would probably not be able to collect nearly as much money as they get from a third-party payer.

In fact, it is the advent of the third-party payer—with funding largely from employers at first, and now from employers and the government—that has paid for the amazing expansion in the availability, variety, and effectiveness of diagnostic and treatment techniques. If it were not for third-party payers, how many cancer patients would be able to pay $4,000 per dose for chemotherapy? If it were not for third-party payers, who would pay $200 for an X-ray, then $500 for a CT Scan, then $1,000 for an MRI, then $2,000 for a PET scan—all to look at the same piece of anatomy to refine a diagnosis and prognosis?

To a very real extent, the indications for diagnostic and treatment procedures change not only with refinements that make them safer and more accurate; the indications also change with a change in the amount the patient must pay out of pocket for them. In the classic world of health insurance, this change in indications (or frequency) is known as "moral hazard" (see Chapter 14 for a more detailed discussion of moral hazard). The suggestion in the economics literature is that this represents waste. I believe that some of it is indeed waste, but much of it is merely closing the gap between what we can afford now and what we could afford if we had another million dollars or so available to pay for our own medical care. The true measure of the waste of moral hazard is how much the patient would be willing to pay if the money were available and the only choice the patient had to make was how to spend it. We have not yet figured out how to study this issue.

Conclusion

In wandering into the world of the third-party payer, we have shared some of the angst of trying to make a few dollars stretch across an entire year of medical care. We have seen some of the obstacles and crises facing the third-party payer. This is not an idle exercise. There are only two alternatives: either we get rid of all third-party payers and make everyone pay for medical care out of pocket, or we have at least one third-party payer. The former solution seems recidivistic and unlikely, making the latter all but certain.

Chapter 7

Safe and Effective Care

"Although the world is full of suffering, it is full also of the overcoming of it."
—Helen Keller, deaf-blind author, activist, and lecturer

What is quality? Is quality in the eyes of the beholder (as the consumer advocates would have us believe)? Or is it a professionally defined parameter, artfully described in arcane terms understandable only to the professional (as most physicians believe it should be)? I believe it to be both of these, but it is also something much more important—the assurance of safety and efficacy.

In fact, I am convinced that the consumer-versus-professional standards of quality come in so many iterations and such intricate layering that sorting them out may not be possible. Take, for instance, some of the aspects of quality from a consumer's perspective:

- How accessible is the system? Do my phone or e-mail inquiries receive a response within an acceptable period of time?

- Am I able to schedule a timely appointment?

- How long do I have to wait when I show up for my appointment?

- Do the physician, staff, and other providers treat me courteously?

- Do they see me as a person as well as a patient? On the other hand, do I feel the doctor is prying inappropriately into my personal affairs?

- Am I given an adequate explanation of the cause of my symptoms and of the proposed treatment?

- Are follow-up appointments within an interval I can understand and at a time I find convenient?

This list is not intended to be exhaustive, but it is illustrative of a set of consumer expectations that are gaining acceptance not only from consumers (patients) but from many health care professionals as well. There is another set of consumer expectations, however, that will not receive such ready acceptance from health care professionals and those responsible for funding health care:

- Did the provider I saw give me the referral I wanted?

- Did the provider I saw give me the prescription I wanted?

- Did the provider I saw order the tests I wanted done?

- Did the provider I saw recommend the surgical procedure I wanted done?

- Did the provider I saw do everything—up to and including insurance fraud—to get the insurance company to pay for a service the provider and I both know is not covered?

While these questions may represent quality to the patient, they beg the question of whether the referral, prescription, test, or surgical procedure was necessary or appropriate. If we are to control costs, we must build a system that provides only necessary and appropriate care—which, in itself, may be a source of dissatisfaction to the patient who wants something else.

Health care providers want to define quality in a very different way. For them, quality means doing the right things for people from a practice standards viewpoint. Practice standards are defined as what everyone else is doing, or what is generally accepted to be the standard. This is rarely articulated well enough to be measurable, and even when it is, the data are difficult to collect, and the providers object strenuously to the process of data collection, analysis, and publication.

In its own special way, this approach boils down to voodoo quality. This will not satisfy me, nor should it satisfy the public.

Sam's Garage

In your community is an auto shop. Sam's Garage is convenient to your home. When you call in with a problem with your car, they always offer to schedule an appointment the same day, usually within a couple of hours. When you arrive, you are well treated. They offer free beverages and snacks and a comfortable waiting room. Your car always seems to be in the shop being worked on within a few moments of your arrival. The clerks and mechanics are all friendly and polite. They explain what they have found on your car and what they have done to fix it. They are nice people and you really like them.

What is not clear is that they have a high error rate. On one of every twenty cars, they mistakenly put brake fluid or antifreeze into the car instead of oil. On another one in twenty, they use the wrong type or weight of oil for the car. The first mistake can be lethal for the car. The second only makes the car's engine wear faster.

They also do not take some basic safety precautions. When the car is on the lift, they leave the car in neutral and do not set the parking brake. As a result, once or twice a year a car rolls off of the lift and crashes to the ground. So far, none of the mechanics has been injured, but the cars are destroyed. They also never lock cars when they park them after they have finished. Two or three cars a year are stolen from their parking lot.

They have a high omission rate. Half of the time when they are doing a routine "lube job," they forget at least one of the steps —which include changing the oil, changing the oil filter, checking coolant levels, checking the windshield washer fluid level, checking the transmission and brake fluids, and adding grease to appropriate joints. Most of these errors do not cause immediate problems, but they increase the wear and tear on the car. Last year, Mrs. Jones was driving away from the shop after a lube job and was unable to stop at a red light. Her brakes didn't work because there was no brake fluid in the system.

The mechanics have a tendency to do more than asked. Almost every lube job is accompanied by changes of light bulbs, windshield wipers, air filters, air conditioner fluid, rotation of tires, or a recommendation to replace tires with marginal wear. Their advertised price for a lube job is $19.95, but the average actual bill is more than $50.

Would you go to Sam's? From a classic customer-service definition of quality, they are a high-quality shop. From the standpoint of safety and efficacy, they are a disaster. They are very nice, but they are not doing a good job of what they are supposed to be doing, and they are charging way too much for it.

Exit "Quality." Enter "Safety and Efficacy."

The problem with all of the above customer service issues is that they really are trivial compared to the REAL quality problem in our healthcare system. The real problem goes somewhat like this:

According to the Institute of Medicine report,[1] errors in the delivery of care account for about 80,000 deaths per year. According to the Institute for Healthcare Improvement, failure to implement six processes to protect and care for patients result in one potentially preventable death per year for every two hospital beds in the country—a total number of preventable deaths that numbers more than 150,000 per year.

Currently, here are the officially listed[2] most frequent causes of death in the United States:

- Heart Disease: 696,947

- Cancer: 557,271

- Stroke: 162,672

- Chronic lower respiratory diseases: 124,816

- Accidents (unintentional injuries): 106,742

- Diabetes: 73,249

- Influenza/Pneumonia: 65,681

- Alzheimer's disease: 58,866

- Nephritis, nephritic syndrome, and nephrosis: 40,974

- Septicemia: 33,865

If the preceding is true, then failure to institute appropriate safety measures in the care of patients is the fourth leading cause of death in the United States today, and medical errors are the seventh leading cause of death. (Medical errors would be sixth on the above list since it doesn't include the "failure to implement safety measures" figure.) Seen in this light, the healthcare system is directly responsible for both the fourth and seventh leading causes of death —which if combined would be outpaced only by heart disease and cancer.

This represents a crisis in the safe functioning of the healthcare system. Even if the two numbers above are twice as high as they should be, it only moves the healthcare system from third place to fifth. A safe and effective healthcare system should not appear at all in the top ten causes of death!

Three things are clear. First, the system needs a major overhaul to bring it up to acceptable safety standards—and we need to define those standards. Second, all of the things shown to improve outcomes should be done in a high percentage of cases (certainly better than the current 50% to 60%).[3,4,5] And third, unnecessary interactions with the healthcare system could be dangerous and should be avoided.

So what do we put in place of the mundane and confusing quality issues at the beginning of this chapter? Regardless of what we decide, safety and efficacy should be foremost:

- Injury or death should not be a side effect of whatever we do to or for patients. Interactions with the healthcare system should always improve the odds of healthy survival of the patient.

- The system should use all diagnostic and treatment modalities clearly shown to be necessary for the diagnosis and treatment of the condition at hand. Failure to spend the resources to do the job right the first time has downstream costs—either in money or in the life and health of the patient.

- Whatever we do should have a reasonable and documented chance of resulting in improved health or life expectancy for the patient. Not only does unnecessary intervention waste resources, it is also dangerous to the patient.

Safety—The Relentless Search for Error Reduction

To me, high quality means "safe." As one of the top ten leading causes of death in the U.S., our current healthcare system is manifestly not safe. (I will present reasons and ways to make safety-related corrections later in Chapter 20.) For the moment, it should suffice to note that our current healthcare system should be searching relentlessly for ways to reduce errors and improve safety (and therefore quality).

Before I'll be satisfied that we have designed a high-quality system, I will need to be assured we are building in strong incentives for a relentless Quality Improvement system.[6]

Efficacy—The Establishment of National Standards

We need national performance standards. Variation in treatments and results from one community to another is not acceptable.[7] We are all Americans, and we all deserve the best care available in the United States.[8,9] There are sincere and serious people working very hard to establish national standards and protocols.[10] To the extent we can, we need to make adherence to these standards measurable—and we need to measure and publish the results. Providers (doctors, hospitals, physical therapists, etc.) will all see how they compare to their peers. That in itself will create pressure to change.

Unfortunately, it will not create an equitable formula consumers can use to figure out who is the best doctor or which is the best hospital.[11] The measures will be many, and there will be many rankings on many scales. One hospital in town might be the best at treating pneumonia and another at treating bronchitis, but how is the patient to know which illness he has before choosing one hospital over the other?

It will take a concerted effort to create some amalgamated summary or overall ratings. We need something the average layman can look at when choosing a health plan and see that the hospital system included on one plan is rated 85 and the hospital on another is rated 75.

And What of Customer Satisfaction?

I find the problem of sorting out the threads of what satisfies and dissatisfies people these days to be too difficult to manage in the expectations I place on a national healthcare system. One of the consequences of a universal system will be some restriction on the scope and breadth of services available, so until we as a society are able to adjust our expectations, I suspect we will have some VERY dissatisfied patients on our hands. On the other hand, making health care more available for the many uninsured will certainly result in a large number of grateful patients.

One of the consequences of a pluralistic system is that there will still be competition between delivery systems, which may well show up in how "user friendly" different clinics are. Customer service may follow form in this case. If we build a monolithic system, we may instead have to do something about building in customer service.

In Summary

I believe we need to build a system that is safe and effective. A safe system puts forth a constant and tenacious effort to find problems in the system that create errors and fix those systemic problems. An effective system provides the services we know from scientific evidence to have a beneficial effect on the process in question. An effective system does not provide services we know will not enhance the outcome of the diagnosis and treatment process. We are failing in all three realms at present, and we must build a system to do better.

Chapter 8

Availability

Location, Location, Location

Health care should be available to everyone. By available, I mean it should be offered in both physical and temporal proximity to the patient. Having high-quality care available 250 miles from home is not very comforting. Having to wait until next week to be treated for today's emergency is equally inappropriate.

Such may be obvious. What is not obvious is that this is a difficult problem that has been defying solution for some time. Many proposals for organizing health care have promised geographic redistribution but have fallen short of this goal.

It has proven difficult to entice physicians to settle and practice in rural communities, and many communities large enough to support several physicians have none. To some extent, this maldistribution of physician manpower is a result of economics: the pay is lower for practices in a rural community than in a suburban one. To some extent it is a social phenomenon: physicians spend many of their young adult years in urban settings—in cities large enough to support a college or university for four years, in cities large enough to support a medical school for four more, and in cities large enough to support a residency training program for an additional three to seven years. In other words, "How you gonna keep 'em down on the farm after they've seen Paree?" Clearly, the combination of social and financial disadvantages to a rural practice will keep many physicians from considering it.

It has proven equally difficult to staff inner city areas. Here, though the pay from private payers may be the same as in the suburbs, the combination of low-pay Medicaid patients and high overhead tends to assure a lower income. In addition, there is a significant socioeconomic barrier between the provider and the patients that creates some of the same sense of isolation a rural physician feels.

At the base of the economic forces pulling physicians to suburban practices are two issues, both based on our free-market system. First, the price is "whatever the traffic will bear"—which happens to be more in more affluent areas. Second, reimbursement from government programs, especially Medicaid, tends to be lower than a physician can expect to collect from his cash-paying patients or their insurance companies. As a society, we tend to believe in equal pay for equal work, and standard pricing for standard products. Remember how appalled we were as a nation when we learned what the Armed Forces were paying for tools and equipment? Because health care is so local, it defies this rationality, and prices can vary significantly within small geographic areas. To some extent a national health plan should overcome this.

But regardless of the reasons for the maldistribution, I would expect a healthcare system to expend consistent effort to pull physicians into rural communities. I don't expect a full range of specialty care, but basic care should be available everywhere there is a certain basic population, and specialty care should be available in accordance with consistent population or disease prevalence standards. If the distribution fails to meet these criteria, there should be ongoing efforts to correct it. And as a way to improve care in smaller communities, we may expect to see more rural physicians linking to distant medical centers via video feeds and the Internet for "telemedicine" consultations.

Access Time

Time can also be a problem. In the United States today, time is seen as a quality issue more than a barrier issue—one waits too long in the emergency room or physician's office and is dissatisfied with the experience. Time becomes a barrier issue when a resource is so constricted that the waiting time begins to cause people not to receive the services they need. In other countries, it may work to ask people to wait six months or a year for a CT scan, or an MRI, or open-heart surgery. I do not believe such a system of restricted access will—or should—satisfy the American public or the healthcare system.

This isn't to say there isn't a rationale for the waiting time. If one doesn't have enough CT scanners, for instance, and does not wish to spend the money to purchase more of them, then people will have to wait in line to have a CT scan. This line does not, however, continue to increase in length indefinitely. Not only do people leave the line because they get their scan, they leave for other reasons. Some die. (Some will die from the disease for which the scan was ordered, others from other causes that just got there first—like an automobile accident.) Some get better and no longer need a scan. (It would, of course, be preferable to detect those who will improve spontaneously in advance and not put them on the schedule, but a long wait is another way to detect them.) A third group will become acutely worse while waiting, and the option of waiting will no longer be available. These will be admitted to a hospital and will have the study expedited. And finally, there will be the remainder who will continue to wait in line until their turn comes.

"Reasonable" availability suggests we may not eliminate the waiting period, but at least it will not be "excessive." The term "excessive" can be defined by the patient or by the physician or by national standards. The advantage of national standards is that it provides a uniform measurement system across the country, which helps planners identify where additional resources need to be mobilized. The waiting time is different for different tests and for different diagnoses. National standards should recognize this.

At the other extreme is a standard calling for instant availability: no matter what the test, if the doctor orders it, it can be done today. While this may seem expedient, striving for this standard often results in excessive spending on capacity. The problem with excessive capacity, especially in a profit-driven system, is that capacity pushes demand. After all, the machinery is making no money while sitting idle, so we should run more patients through the machine to increase the revenue stream. This tends to sponsor unnecessary utilization, which is both a quality (safety and efficacy) issue and an affordability issue.

Currently, much of the machinery of medicine is in use only during "normal business hours," and rarely if ever after 5:00 p.m., or on holidays or weekends. It is clearly a waste of a resource for it be idle 120 hours each week. In a well-run system looking to eliminate waste, operating hours ought to extend to more than eight hours and to all seven days of the week. Fewer CT scanners, for instance, working longer hours, can produce the same number of CT scans, of the same quality, at less cost. For some people, such scheduling may mean waiting an extra day or so, or until the weekend, to have a test or procedure done, but such delays usually are not consequential. And where they do have serious consequences, delays should not be allowed.

Our current system is filled with inequities in the distribution of resources, which will require some management. The goals are that we make an appropriate level of care available to everyone within reasonable distance and time, and that we utilize our resources to the optimum.

Chapter 9

Comprehensive

"Every human being has a responsibility for injustice anywhere in the community."

—*Scott Buchanan*

Comprehensive health care. That certainly has a nice ring to it. But what, exactly, do I mean by "comprehensive health care"?

By comprehensive, I do NOT mean that coverage should be provided for anything that anyone could want. And I do NOT mean that coverage should be provided for anything having anything remotely to do with health. I will explain both of those NOTs presently. What I mean to convey is that no scientifically, demonstrably valid healing technique should be categorically excluded from coverage because of the discipline or style of healing or where it is delivered.

This is to distinguish from old-style indemnity coverage that covered care provided in a hospital, but not care provided in a doctor's office. It is also to distinguish from Medicare, which offers hospital care in part A and outpatient care in part B, but nowhere offers comprehensive coverage for pharmaceutical or preventive care.

One of the mistakes with the Medicare program is that it was modeled on the then-dominant form of health insurance—major medical. Major medical covered hospital costs, but that was all. The authors of Medicare recognized that seniors might want coverage for outpatient medical costs as well, and Part B was added to take care of that. No one remotely considered that pharmacy would ever be a significant portion of health care cost, so it was not included. All of that made great sense in the mid-1960s when the law was passed. The problem is not how the program was structured. The problem is that the program is locked into that structure in a way that makes change very difficult.[1,2]

The importance of the comprehensive nature of the coverage is that a categorical denial of coverage for any particular pathway of care may be politically expedient at one time and financially disastrous at another. We need to accept that health care is a fluid medium and that the things for which we pay the most money today may be irrelevant tomorrow. To lock the system into paying for things we no longer need and keep it from paying for the things we now do need is silly. Let's open the gates and let various treatment modalities prove themselves to be cost-effective (or not) and be accepted (or rejected) based on evidence rather than legislation.[3]

Balancing Act

As I indicated, comprehensive coverage does not mean paying for anything anyone could want. We must achieve a balance between comprehensive care and affordable care. The care covered and paid for by the plan must be generally and specifically effective, safe, and of reasonable cost for the benefit provided. There may well be many things not covered because they are not effective, or because they are not safe, or because the cost is too high for the benefit.

One can think of many examples of each of these. Krebiozen, for instance, is an anti-cancer nostrum available in Mexico that has no effect on cancer. We should not, as a society, be willing to pay for people to go to Mexico to receive it. Some treatments have such high complication rates that the average life expectancy of the victim is shorter with the treatment than without it (such as with high-dose chemotherapy and bone marrow transplant for advanced breast cancer, for example). Some treatments are effective, but one wonders about the price versus the benefit—a heart transplant in a 95-year-old may well restore cardiac function, but most 95-year-olds do not have sufficient life expectancy to make the expenditure of several hundred thousand dollars seem reasonable.

Could such "non-covered" treatments be available "outside of the system"? I don't know of a way to prevent it, short of imposing adherence to the criteria of the plan as a requirement of licensure, but even so, people with the resources to do so can still travel to Mexico, England, India, or China to receive treatment.

I also indicated that by comprehensive I did not mean everything related to health should be covered. The problem with "everything related to health" is that it becomes an endless list—food, shelter, a job, less stress in life, and a number of other things most rational people would not include in the rubric of medical coverage. Yes, it is desirable for people to have adequate food and shelter, but I would not ask the healthcare system to provide those.

Common Sense Comprehensiveness

Comprehensive, therefore, does not prevent us from establishing definitional lines around what varieties of needs are considered to be "health care" needs. However, within those boundaries, any safe, effective, cost-efficient method of care should be covered. Thus we include hospital and ambulatory care, care offered by physicians, podiatrists, psychologists, social workers, chiropractors, dentists, and many others. Some of it falls within the realm of "alternative" or "complementary" care.[4] Much of it is in the mainstream. Restrictions may be placed on who is eligible for certain interventions, based on reliable outcome studies or on underwriting data. There may be specific reasons for not covering some specific interventions, such as cosmetic surgery.

The point is that no safe, effective, cost-efficient method of care should be generically denied for coverage to the entire population.

Chapter 10

Personal

"The difference between a lady and a flower girl is not how she behaves, but how she is treated."
—Audrey Hepburn as Eliza Doolittle in "My Fair Lady"

Health care, at its best, is personal. For the patient, the transaction is always personal. One of the potential problems in delivery systems is that the episode of care—the illness—may not be treated in a personal way by the caregivers. This is especially problematic as the care delivery system becomes larger and more bureaucratic.

The classic one-to-one relationship between a patient and a solo primary-care physician is often the paradigm against which all medical care is compared. At one time the doctor did everything personally. Somehow, this one-to-one delivery of services represents what we think is best and most pure about health care. There is a certain nostalgia about it. In many ways, we look back on that style of delivery as being "the good old days" in healthcare. Is this really just nostalgia? Or is there something about this we should seek to retain or regain?

Healthcare today is no longer a solo activity. I am not sure that the system for educating physicians has caught up with that fact yet, but it is nonetheless true. Even at a time when most physicians still practice solo or in groups of fewer than six, the trend toward healthcare being a team sport is irreversible. The physician is assisted by a laboratory and an imaging center. In the hospital, the patient's "regular physician" is often not the one in charge of care. Patients do better when care is directed by a "hospitalist"—a physician who does nothing but care for hospitalized patients. The attending physician used to be the "captain of the ship" with a crew that was small and had very little latitude for independent judgment. Now the attending physician is often one of several physicians seeing the patient, and there are teams of nurses and therapists with considerable independence who also affect the care of the patient in one way or another.

The addition of more people with independent professional judgment has improved the quality and safety of the care provided. Of the six initiatives proposed by the Institute for Healthcare Improvement[1] to save one life per two hospital beds per year, several involve bringing more people with more independent judgment to the patient's bedside. It is hard to argue with the approach of including these other people when the results are better.

But we still yearn for the one-to-one relationship with an identified "personal physician" who is with us through thick and thin. And, actually, it is not the "being in charge" part that is important to us as patients. It is the "being with us" part that is so important. It is, in fact, the personal relationship that is important. It is the confidence we feel when someone cares about what happens to us. Even the best hospital team cannot give us that sense of confidence, because, after all, we just met them when we came to the hospital. But we know that our personal physician, whom we have known for years, cares about us—not just in the sort of vague way that caregivers care about the people they are paid to care for, but in the personal way that can only happen in the context of a long-term relationship. There is a warmth and comfort in this relationship that is of value to the patient.

Is this "warm and fuzzy" relationship enough to justify building a system to accommodate to it? Probably not. But this relationship has actually been studied. It seems pretty clear, based on studies by numerous psychologists, that the caring relationship we develop with a personal physician has a very powerful influence on our health. There are a lot of reasons why this is so, but let me start with the one I think is the most important and the least studied: placebo effect.

A placebo is an inert treatment—a substance with no known value in the treatment of the process under consideration. Sugar tablets for pain, for instance. The "placebo effect" happens to the subject who takes a placebo. One would expect that a placebo would produce no effect whatsoever. This, however, is not true. Placeboes frequently have effectiveness rates that rival active medications. Fully half of people given a placebo will get as much pain relief as from morphine. Please understand that I am not suggesting that the doctor says "here, take this sugar pill and see how it does." I am talking about studies in which neither the physician nor the patient knew whether the patient was receiving the active medication or the inert tablet.

What we do know about this effect is that it is greater when the doctor says "this will work for your problem" than if the doctor says "this probably won't work, but let's give it a try." It also works better when the person providing the placebo is a trusted intimate as opposed to a stranger. This is very important. When a trusted resource prescribes a course of treatment with a sense of confidence, it is much more likely to work. This is true regardless of whether that treatment is a placebo or not. The effectiveness of active treatment is greater when it comes from a trusted source. What better trusted source could there be than the personal physician?

Is this a "sham"? Am I talking about something that is not "real"? I don't think so. When I am ill and I need help, I not only want the best care science can provide, I want it delivered by someone in whom I have absolute confidence and with whom I have a warm long-term relationship. I think it is appropriate to offer solace to my psyche as we offer active treatment to my body.

That relationship with the personal physician is important even in the context of the whirl of activity in the hospital—activity over which that personal physician may have no control at all. The mere fact that my doctor came to visit, sat at my bedside, held my hand, and expressed confidence in all the people taking care of me —that action would make a great deal of difference to me.

There are a number of other aspects to a long-term, trusting relationship that are also important:

- Communication gets better the better we know someone. This is true in the doctor-patient relationship as much as it is anywhere else in our lives. I will communicate better (both in the telling and in the listening) with my personal physician of many years than with a new doctor I have just met. This will always mean I get more appropriate care from my personal physician.

- Feeling like a person is important to me. I like to be me, not "the appendix in 402." Because I have a personal relationship with my personal physician, I always have confidence that I am who I am to that physician. This helps mitigate the impersonal nature of institutional care and the sense of "loss of self" I get when I am ill.

- I have personal desires about how I would like to be cared for. I may have expressed these desires to my personal physician. I would expect my personal physician to have some clue about what I would want—to be able to connect with me and my desires as a person. I know that many of the people in the hospital will not be able to do this, and my personal physician is a buffer between them and me. It also means that when my personal physician is treating me, I can confidently expect that the treatment suggested is recommended with some consideration about me and my desires.

The Physician's Point of View

That is quite a testimony about the one-to-one relationship from the point of view of the patient. It seems that the comfort, the confidence, and some of the effectiveness of the treatment are dependent upon the patient's relationship with the physician. Yet this aspect of healthcare is disappearing. There must be a reason why. Is this relationship bad for physicians?

As noted, for many patients, that personal relationship is crucial to appropriate care. For many physicians, that relationship is what makes the practice of medicine rewarding. Those physicians find comfort and reward in the personal nature of the relationship and the act of caring for another person. A number of years ago, an outsider challenged me to find happy physicians. I did. And each of them talked about their relationships with their patients as being the thing that made it all worthwhile—as being the thing that sustained them.

If personal care is critical to the recipients of care and rewarding to the providers of care, why is it going away? There are many reasons, but the important ones, I think, boil down to the following:

- It takes time to form these relationships. Many physicians feel they cannot take the time to do it, and that frustrates them.

- Lifestyle is an important issue for many physicians, and they are not willing to commit the time and effort required to form personal relationships with patients.

- Personal income is an important driver in healthcare today, as it is in all aspects of our society, and physicians pay a financial price in committing the time and effort to form personal relationships with patients.

- More and more physicians practice in large organizations. These organizations are designed to maximize efficiency. This often means the patient is seen by the next available physician, rather than the same physician repeatedly. This makes it harder for any one doctor and any one patient to build a personal relationship.

Summary

Efforts to provide universal coverage will increase the bureaucratization of health care and increase the number of multiple-physician organizations. We must work to safeguard—indeed to encourage—the personal relationship between patient and physician at the point of care.

Chapter 11

Professional

"Reputation is what other people know about you. Honor is what you know about yourself."

—Lois McMaster Bujold

The members of a profession distinguish themselves as a special class in society. In turn, they are granted special status. There is, in essence, a covenant between the profession and the society in which it exists. This generalization is true of all professions, but it is especially true in the context of the "caring professions."

The characteristics of the covenant between the caring professions and our society deserve examination. A profession establishes its own standards for entry and continued participation. A profession sets its own ethical standards. A profession offers a service not easily mastered or understood, the quality of which may not be readily apparent to the recipient, so the assurance of the professional stature of the provider may be the best guarantee the recipient has of quality. These three characteristics apply, to some degree, to all the caring professions.

All of the caring professions require certain education and training before conferring professional stature. The ability to practice is codified in law. The participation of members of the profession on licensing boards is everywhere assumed to be appropriate.

The caring professions also have their own self-announced ethical standards. First proposed by the medical profession as the Hippocratic Oath, such ethical standards persist and are the subject of considerable commentary at many levels in the profession. The fact that the ethical requirements of a physician or other caring professional are frequently misunderstood does not negate their importance. It only stresses the need for further education about their true nature.

These standards include beneficence, non-maleficence, and self-effacement (charity) as three distinct underpinnings of the profession. Beneficence means, in essence, "doing good." What is done must be to the benefit of the recipient. Non-maleficence means, in essence, the old dictum in medicine *primum non nocere*—first, do no harm. It may actually be that this is more important than beneficence as a principle, since it is more basic. For much of our history, the caring professions have had little of benefit to offer supplicants, so the minimum caution was at least not to do things that were harmful to the recipient.

The third principle is perhaps even more important. Self-effacement means that the benefit to the recipient is the only benefit to be considered in the caring transaction. The personal benefit of the provider should not be a consideration. To a significant extent, we have moved away from self-effacement, both in our society and in the caring professions.

These ethical standards are very important. They are what assure us that our caregivers will attend to us and our needs. The traditional view in the medical profession was that if the physician did a good job of caring for patients, financial success would follow. Today, it often seems that financial success is a primary goal, and taking good care of patients is fine as long as it does not interfere with achieving financial success. While this may sound like a gross exaggeration, the mere appearance of self-serving decision-making is enough to cause concern.

There are good studies to indicate how a small conflict of interest can interfere with impartial consideration. Pharmaceutical company representatives use this regularly. When they offer pens, writing pads, and lunches for office staff, they create a sense of obligation that obscures, in however small a way, the judgment of good physicians. If this is true, how much influence on judgment should we expect if the physician owns the surgery center, the laboratory, the x-ray unit, or the hospital, and every referral results in income to the physician? What if the physician draws the blood for lab work and sends it out to a reference laboratory, then charges the patient (or his/her insurance company) a significant mark-up on the lab's fees? What about the physician who stocks medications in his office to administer to patients at a large mark-up? Might this influence the physician to choose to administer medications in his/her office rather than having the patient fill a prescription and take them at home? Might this also influence the physician to choose a medication with a greater profit margin over another medication that might be better for the patient? Might this decision be made at such a subconscious level that the physician is convinced he/she is making the right choice for the patient?

We do not develop ethical standards because conflict is impossible. We develop them precisely because guidance is needed. Ethical standards help avoid situations that place the provider in a conflict of interest. The public has a vested interest in the professionalism of the health care providers with whom it deals. Trust is an extremely important part of the therapeutic relationship.[1] The restoration and continuation of high ethical standards is crucial to the professionalism of the caring professions. Our caregivers should understand and behave according to high ethical standards or be removed from practice.

Health care professionals live in the same world the rest of us do, and their behavior will reflect the values and standards of our society as a whole. When society values financial success more than spiritual or ethical success, adherence to ethical standards, especially those related to financial issues, will tend to wane. As a society, we should recognize that health care providers who do a good, caring, and ethical job ought to be rewarded financially for the job they do. We must not only support access to adequate income through ethical practice, we must also support the idea that our health care professionals deserve recognition for their ethical behavior. Such recognition is important precisely because it must be a substitute for the additional financial rewards available to the unethical.

Today, the profession has largely relinquished the requirements for a professional standard to other organizations—to the universities to train new professionals, and to the licensing boards to license and discipline them. Breaches of ethical standards rarely seem compelling enough for disciplinary action by a licensing board. This loss of responsibility for developing and enforcing standards has resulted in a general decrease in the sense of responsibility for maintaining and abiding by those standards. It would serve both the profession and the public to restore both the responsibility and the authority to the profession, with an accompanying accountability to assure performance of the expectation.

Professionalism, most especially as manifested by the enunciation and enforcement of ethical standards by the profession, is the key to restoring a better relationship between health care practitioners and the public. Both providers and patients long for the relationship of trust that can only be built on a strong ethical base. The stature of the professional and the independence of the profession are based on this professionalism. The confidence we can have in our healers is entirely dependent on our confidence in their professionalism. For the sake of all parties, the underpinnings of professionalism must be supported.

Part Two

How Can We Build a System to Do This?

Chapter 12

Introduction

"Dreams come true; without that possibility, nature would not incite us to have them."

—*John Updike*

In Part One, I outlined my personal expectations for a health care system:

- It should provide universal coverage—all Americans should be covered.

- It should be affordable to the individual and to society.

- It should provide safe and effective care.

- It should be uniformly available across geographic differences.

- It should be comprehensive and designed to accommodate new technology.

- It should provide personal care.

- It should promote professionalism in the providers of care.

There is room for debate on the validity and relative importance of these expectations. Perhaps some should be dropped or more added. I would encourage a vigorous national debate on this

91

subject because we cannot build the system we need if we cannot agree on the basics of what we need. If you don't know where you are going, no road will get you there.

That said, it is comforting to have a set of expectations. (Without this set of expectations, there would be no more book to write.) Is it possible to design a system based on these expectations? Certainly, none appears to exist in a form we could copy and import to the United States. Can it be done? Frankly, I don't know—but I don't think that should stop us from trying, especially if we can figure out a way to design a set of circumstances and incentives that will reward the system and its participants for fulfilling our desires.

The next task is to start designing. What would it take to do these things? The easy issues are usually the first ones in the lineup, because they can be addressed without interfering with other issues on the list. However, intellectual honesty requires us to take all seven expectations into account as we discuss each one, so I shall attempt to do so.

The list above is mine, but it need not be yours. There are undoubtedly other answers to the issues I raise, and there are certainly other answers if you construct a different set of desirable characteristics.[1] I have chosen what I have chosen because it is pleasing to me. If it is pleasing to you also, I am heartened. But it is not so much that the solution is crucial as that the method of deriving it is crucial.

The best way to illustrate that point is with a quick hypothetical scenario. Let us say that the country adopts my seven principles and my suggestions for implementation. As I have already pointed out, the health care system is a complex system, and systems theory predicts there will be unforeseen consequences to the forces we put into play. Let us suppose we are exceedingly fortunate, and we are five years or so into the implementation of the plan before we notice anything unforeseen happening. But then, there it is. A wart on the nose of our best laid plans. What do we do? We cannot go back to this book and reapply my plans, because we have already done those things and they resulted in the unforeseen wart.

The only rational course is to perform the whole analysis again. Maybe we want to change our goals. Maybe we have learned something new about the implementation of the goals that makes my vision no longer seem rational. Or maybe we need to conduct another gap analysis and reassess where we are and what needs to change. No matter which is required, we will only discover it if we follow the process through again from beginning to end. The process is what is important here, not my ideas of what may flow from the process.

I know of no way to draw a map other than by putting pencil to paper to draw. So here we go.

Chapter 13

Universal Access

"Each time someone stands up for an ideal, or acts to improve the lot of others, or strikes out against injustice, he sends forth a tiny ripple of hope."

—*Robert F. Kennedy*

Universal access, or universal coverage, can be accomplished in several ways. No matter which we choose to pursue, the federal government must assume a significant role in both the financing and the implementation of the system.[1] For the federal government to play a significant role will mean legislation, which implies the necessity to develop sufficient political momentum for change—something we do not currently appear to have. I think that political momentum will appear late in this decade,[2] after having been delayed by the events of 9/11/01 and the subsequent wars in Afghanistan and Iraq. While I cannot see the future, I continue to believe that the pressure for change will build to the point where action will be taken.

I can envision three basic mechanisms by which universal access could be accomplished:

1. A single-provider system—in other words, federalize health care and the whole provider system[3]. This federalization would involve

one or more of the following actions, each dependent upon the previous one:

- The Federal Health System condemns and purchases all hospitals.

- The Federal Health System condemns and purchases all other health care facilities, including physician offices.

- The Federal Health System employs all those involved in the provision of health care services.

2. A single-payer system—presumably a federal single-payer system (choose one of these):

- With all functions internal to the federal government.

- With a single private subcontractor to handle the payment system.

- With multiple private subcontractors to handle the payment system.

3. Mandatory insurance—a pluralistic system, with payments coming from some or all of the following:

- Employers—under the current "rules" plus some "play or pay" provisions

- Individuals—with significant tax incentives to self-purchase insurance, but with the government providing it to those who do not purchase it themselves

- Federal government

- Federal/state partnerships

Universal access can be accomplished under any of these three basic mechanisms—as has been either done or proposed elsewhere. The first is a classic European model, best exemplified by Great Britain. It also pertains in Canada, where hospital ownership and operation have been taken over by the government. (The physicians were not nationalized when the facilities were, however.) The second system mirrors the Medicare program in the United States, with multiple private subcontractors handling the payment system to providers. The third system was proposed by President Clinton during his first term.

Single Provider—Federalization:

Federalization of the healthcare system provides some advantages and some disadvantages.

Among the advantages are simplicity and directness. Because the health system becomes non-competitive (there being only one owner—the federal government), some redundancies can be eliminated, and resources can be allocated according to need rather than according to profitability. The federalization solution, well executed, would probably be the least expensive for these and other reasons.[4]

Among the disadvantages of such a system are the loss of the independence of the providers of care.[5] They may have some distaste for working for the government. It will also deprive them of some flexibility to be individualistic. Some of the special idiosyncrasies that most endear our providers to us are largely dependent upon their independence, meaning that each provider can decide what is important, and each patient can choose a provider based on the match between the personal judgment of the patient and the style of the provider. The flip side of this disadvantage is the gain in quality and safety from standardization of processes and expectations.

The professionalism of individual providers becomes more tenuous in the more regimented single-owner system—something I think represents a loss to the consumer (patient). Centralized planning would help to standardize expectations, but it would also need to accommodate regional variations required by real differences in the populations being served.

Federalization could be accomplished at intermediate levels. It would be possible to federalize all hospitals (or all residential care facilities—places where patients stay overnight) and leave much of the remainder of the system in private hands. This has been done with some success in Canada. However, it leaves a gulf of poorly matched motivations between the non-federalized outpatient facilities and the federalized inpatient facilities. Conflict is especially likely when inpatient care is optional or marginally indicated—if the cost of care is high, physicians will tend to push the care to the more expensive inpatient place of service because it moves the cost out of the accountability of the physician. Partial federalization also potentially leaves federally owned outpatient extensions of its inpatient facilities (such as laboratory and x-ray facilities, physical therapy and occupational therapy departments, and outpatient surgery facilities) in direct competition with freestanding, privately owned, community-based equivalent services.

Interestingly, the VA Health System is a federalized system co-existing with our otherwise pluralistic system here in the U.S. Despite its bad long-term reputation, the VA is currently providing some of the highest quality care being offered anywhere in the country.[6] Obviously, a clearer picture of this alternative may not emerge without significant study of the VA and its current success.

Single-payer System:

A single-payer system sponsored by the federal government is exactly what Medicare represents to its enrollees.

The Medicare system has a number of administrative service providers interposed between itself and the providers of care. They receive, review, and pay claims. The more administrative agents there are, the more variation will exist from one geographic area to another. Currently, there are a number of diagnostic and treatment processes for which coverage determinations have not been made by the Center for Medicare and Medicaid Services (the federal agency in charge of the Medicare program), and for which coverage is provided in some areas of the country and not in others.

An advantage of single payer, rather than single provider (the federalized system) is that it leaves the direct provision of services to the providers, allowing for the persistence of professionalism and differences between doctors and clinics based on the preferences and perceptions of the providers.

To date, the federal government has exerted little effort to manage the processes or outcomes of care. There has been considerable interest and activity related to managing the unit cost of services—resulting in annual congressional activities on behalf of providers to avoid reductions in per unit payments. There have been some dramatic efforts to find and prosecute fraud. There are the first inklings of movement toward quality control. For the new, universal coverage system, the historical interest of the Medicare program in per-unit cost control is not going to be adequate, though it will be a needed component in the cost-control system (see Chapters 18 and 19).

The final problem with the Medicare system as it exists is its lack of comprehensiveness. The recent addition of prescription coverage is both an example of what I mean as well as a partial resolution of the problem. The fact that it took an act of Congress to correct a coverage oversight is very discouraging. If each adjustment in the program is going to require an act of Congress, the program will be mired in inertia. To be effective, the management of the details of coverage must be delegated to an independent group with the authority to manage the coverage of the plan within a budget.

In summary, then, the Medicare system is an interesting example of a single payer system, but there are compelling reasons not to adopt it as a model.

The Pluralistic Solution

The pluralistic solution is the easiest to conceptualize, the hardest to realize, and the most fraught with pitfalls.

In the pluralistic solution, the "who pays?" question is resolved by multiple means, with those employed by "qualifying" employers obtaining coverage (as they now do) through the employer (or via an employer contribution to a funding pool). For those who are indigent (meaning unable to afford the cost of an insurance premium), there would continue to be state, state-federal, and federal programs to provide coverage. Adding means testing and graduated premium participation, or tax credits and/or rebates, might expand these. And for those who are not employed by "qualifying" employers and who can afford coverage, there would be a mandate of self-purchased coverage that might be either a legal requirement or a set of tax incentives or tax penalties.

Conceptually, this is the easy part. From a functional standpoint, it is still the easy part, and many people have proposed "solutions" which are nothing more than funding mechanisms. The problem with inaugurating a funding mechanism in the absence of system changes is that nothing about cost or quality will improve. If we are to have an affordable system, we must also change the delivery system.

The pluralistic solution requires some restructuring of the relationship between the fiscal intermediary and the delivery system. Nationalized premium structures, perhaps together with price controls, might combine with risk sharing to produce provider networks aligned with fiscal intermediaries in an effort to compete in cost-effectiveness, safety, and customer satisfaction with other networks in the same geographic area—which was part of the descriptive language involved in President Clinton's proposal in the early 1990s.

It is precisely the restructuring of the fiscal intermediary-provider relationship that is the difficult part and is liable to missteps. In concept, the description is too close to the current system —which may lead to a false sense of security that we are close to where we need to be. This is a dangerous presumption. Getting to where we need to be to control costs will require fundamental changes in the forces being applied to providers, and perhaps some additional regulation. Providers must be rewarded for doing what we want and penalized (or not rewarded) for failing to accomplish those goals. Customer service, safety, effectiveness, and cost control are all possible as aspects of the same system, even though much of the health care delivery system does not believe it. Not only will the belief system need to change, but so will the external forces, including the tort liability system and the mechanisms by which we organize and pay for health care services.

The advantage of the pluralistic system is that it is best-suited to the American personality. We love choices (although no one likes too many choices). We believe that different people should be allowed to have different values and should be allowed to seek vendors (delivery systems) that provide the best value to each individual. The flexibility inherent in the pluralistic system allows for that individualization. We must not allow that flexibility to perpetuate the vast differences in the amount, type, and cost of services provided to similar people in different parts of the country, though—differences that may be justified as "pluralism" but that may result in higher cost care, and less effective and more dangerous (less safe) care.

Evaluating the Options

To summarize, let us consider the effects of the three financing systems on the other six goals I have set for the system (see Figure 1, page 104).

My conclusion is that the financing pathway most compatible with my goal set is a pluralistic system, with heavy emphasis on practice changes and moves to assure that the rest of the goals are under control.

- I believe that affordability is something one builds into the system in a number of ways, regardless of the payment system.

- In a similar way, one may build in systems to assure safety and effectiveness. In this case, however, the more independent the providers of care continue to be, the greater the challenge to provoke the necessary changes in practice and business patterns.

101

- Availability—the geographic issue—is another solution one builds into the system. It can be done with less attention to the personal preferences of the providers in a federalized system, and must be done with somewhat more attention in a pluralistic system.

- Comprehensive coverage must also be built into the system; it will also require that the rules be rewritten from time to time due to the expansion of health care into unforeseen areas. It is much more likely that this change of rules will happen smoothly and rapidly in a less centrally controlled system, or at least a less legislatively controlled system.

Criterion	Single provider	Single payer	Pluralistic
Affordable	Yes	Yes	Yes
Safe, effective	Yes	Probably—will require changes in practice modes	Probably—will require changes in practice modes
Available	Yes	Yes	Yes
Compre-hensive	Threatened by the general inertia of federalized systems	Probably—the risk of inertia is intermediate here	Yes
Personal	Threatened by the imperson-ality of large bureaucratic systems	Yes	Yes
Professional	Threatened by the imperson-ality of large bureaucratic systems	Yes	Yes

Figure 1: The varying effects of the three healthcare financing systems

- Personal care can be delivered in any system, but the federalized system poses an inherent threat because of the level of bureaucracy involved. The more independent the provider, the higher the likelihood of a truly personal approach to care.

- Professionalism can also be delivered in any system, but is much less likely in a highly bureaucratized system, and rather more likely if the profession has a greater sense not only of its ability to police itself, but also of the necessity to do so.

Building a Pluralistic System

What kind of pluralistic system must be built, then, to accomplish universal financial access to care?

First, we can continue the current system of employer-sponsored medical coverage. I think that with some standardization of procedures and prices, the general cost of that insurance will abate somewhat without imposing financial hardship on the providers because they will receive payment for what is currently "uncompensated care." This insurance could, like current insurance, provide higher benefits than the minimum standard set by the basic government medical coverage program, but could not provide less.

Second, any employer whose characteristics indicate it should be offering medical coverage will either do so or pay sufficient tax to support the basic government medical coverage program for its employees. These employer characteristics would include number of people employed (and I would suggest a fairly small number, certainly less than a dozen, as the threshold) and the average wage paid. (The wage threshold should be something above, but not much above, minimum wage). There are two competing calls here—first, not to handicap a VERY small business from being able to get started, but second, not to give a smaller competitor an unfair economic advantage over a larger one that must pay for medical coverage. The tax could be used in either of two ways: to enroll the employees in the basic government medical coverage program, or to purchase medical coverage directly for the employees of the non-compliant business.

Third, everyone whose income is below a certain level will be covered by a government program (similar to the way people become eligible for Medicaid today). This "basic government medical coverage program" would also cover any foreign national with health care needs while in the United States for any purpose other than obtaining health care services, as well as the uninsurable, employees of companies not providing medical coverage, the elderly, and anyone else not otherwise covered.

Fourth, the elderly would continue to have a health care program, but it would be integrated either into one of the three above or the one below.

Fifth, anyone not covered by an employer plan (under options one and two above) or the basic government medical coverage program would be offered two options: purchase a basic medical coverage policy or be enrolled in the basic government medical coverage program (or have the government pay premiums to a medical coverage plan to provide coverage). These people would be subject to a progressive tax, based on income, that would start at zero for those who qualify under the third provision above and would rise enough to pay the full premium for those whose income is sufficiently high.

I envision the basic government medical coverage program to be somewhat more than the word "basic" might imply, but limited carefully by underwriting and an imposition of society's cost-benefit assessment of any particular application of any particular technology. Thus, I would expect that visits to a primary care physician would be covered, and so would most visits to a specialist—though visits primarily for cosmetic purposes would probably not be. The benefit would include a variety of approaches to healing that have evidence to support their benefit (such as, perhaps, chiropractic and acupuncture). The benefit would also include diagnostic testing and hospital care. However, the benefit almost certainly would not include cosmetic surgery and would probably not include a number of other interventions. For example, we might weigh high-cost interventions for the extreme elderly against the potential benefit and decide not to cover them.

The question of exactly what should and should not be covered is a discussion for another time and place. While I might have much to say on the subject, this is a discussion for our entire society, which must decide how it wishes to spend its money. Certainly, we will want to consult experts in the field, but the decision does not belong to them; it belongs to the people who pay the taxes.

On the other hand, I believe there is the potential for a significant secondary market in insurance to cover things not covered by the basic government medical coverage program. This clearly means that the rich will be able to buy insurance for care that will become inaccessible to the poor—but that is inevitable in any case. The availability of secondary insurance will, however, reduce the push to expand the benefit package and will offer an option to those who find it important. Depending on what benefits are sought, the cost might be relatively minimal or relatively high. In any case, two things are clear to me:

- The same contracting and system management tools that apply to basic coverage would have to apply to secondary coverage in order to permit such coverage to be offered at a reasonable price.

- Whatever co-payment, co-insurance, and deductible rules apply, there should not be insurance that would take these responsibilities away from the insured individual. (This will be discussed in greater detail in Chapter 15.)

Conclusion

In summary, then, here are the points I have covered:

1. Universal financial access can be arranged in a number of ways.

2. A pluralistic solution seems to be the most likely to produce the desired results and the most acceptable to the American people.

3. A pluralistic system would incorporate the current delivery system, but would have to impose controls to assure affordability, safety, and professionalism.

4. A pluralistic system would use a combination of public and private funding mechanisms to provide coverage, with employers, private individuals, and governments paying. Tax incentives and/or penalties would compel participation.

5. The system would enhance affordability by limiting the scope of services available based on cost-efficiency determinations. A defined, basic level of coverage would apply to all medical coverage regardless of funding source.

6. Secondary insurance could be obtained on a self-pay basis for those who wished coverage for things not covered under the basic program.

Chapter 14

Affordability to Society—
Adding 45 Million Americans

"The good neighbor looks beyond the external accidents and discerns those inner qualities that make all men human and, therefore, brothers."
—*Martin Luther King Jr.*

You will recollect from Chapter 4 that by affordability, I mean the system should be affordable to our society and also to each individual who needs care. These two subsections of affordability deserve separate discussion. Furthermore, there are several aspects of the societal affordability issue that need separate discussion. In this chapter, I will focus on the potential impact of adding 45 million Americans to the population covered by a medical plan. In the subsequent chapters, we will take up other issues related to the affordability of a revised healthcare system.

Adding 45 Million Americans to the Insured Population

As a society, can we afford to provide economic access to health care to all of our citizens? We are currently spending 15% of GDP and failing to provide that access to 45 million (45,000,000) Americans.[1] If we extend access to those 45 million, does that mean we will be spending 20% of GDP on health care? To cover this many people at a premium cost of $250 each per month would come to $135,000,000,000[2]—which is about 10% of what we spend annually on health care. So the increase might rise from 15% of GDP to 16.5%—but is the change likely to cost even that much? Most commentators on health care financing do not seem to think so.

The amount being spent in this country on health care has to be considered to cover all care being provided, including the cost of the care provided to those who are uninsured. The total amount currently being paid to providers is what they see as income. Many of the services that providers render to the uninsured and under-insured may go uncompensated. In effect, this drives up the cost to those who actually pay for services. In some arenas, this is referred to as "cost shifting," but I don't think we need fancy titles to understand what is going on.[3]

"Shrinkage"

You are in charge of an emergency room. Your rent (an allocation of floor space costs from the hospital of which you are a part) is $20 per hour. Your capital equipment amortizes at $10 per hour, and you consume an average of $20 per hour in disposable supplies (and utilities) for which no charge is rendered. Salaries for the two receptionists, two clerks, five nurses, and two physicians, plus an allocation for your time as the administrator, come to $350 per hour. (This is an average staff. It is actually heavier in the evening and lighter between midnight and 6:00 a.m.) So, your basic cost is $400 per hour. You also know that your average cost for billable supplies—injectibles, sutures, and so forth—is about $25 per patient. On the whole, half of the patients you see are uninsured, so you expect no payment from them. Of the remainder, half are on Medicaid, which pays a flat fee of $50 for an ER visit. You contemplate seeing 12 patients an hour. How much must you charge in order to break even?

Answer: Your basic cost is $400 per hour plus $300 per hour for chargeable supplies for twelve patients. Six patients pay nothing. Three yield revenue of $50 each. To this point, you have spent $700 and received $150; you need $550 in order to break even. You divide that among the remaining 3 patients and discover you need to charge them enough to result in $184 in income for each. Most insurance companies pay you 20% over cost for billable supplies, so you can bill and recover $30 each for those supplies. The remaining $154 must come from payment for the services rendered in the ER. Now you know what your charge structure has to look like.

As noted, some writers refer to this as "cost shifting." What they mean to reflect is that the cost of operating the ER is being shifted from those who cannot or do not pay to those who do. And this is true. However, this is much the same problem that a store plagued by shoplifting faces. If a quarter of the vegetables and fruits disappear or rot without anyone paying for them, the store must raise the price on the remainder to come out even. All retail stores have "shrinkage," but no one talks about this as "cost shifting." It is just a cost of doing business. For health care providers, the cost of providing care to the uninsured is a cost of doing business.

The point is that the uninsured are seeking and receiving care when there is no other choice, and the cost of rendering that care is being calculated into the cost of doing business by all of the providers involved. An occasional provider may go bankrupt because of the volume of unpaid services rendered, but most providers make up the deficit by charging more to everyone else (or at least wherever prices are elastic enough to permit increasing the charge).[4]

It is true that the uninsured—because they are uninsured—are not seeking or receiving some services they would no doubt seek if they were insured. On the other hand, they are seeking services because of crisis or urgent need—and the providers ask others to pay for those services by adjusting charges to reflect their increased overhead. One way or another, the services actually being received by the uninsured are included in the $1.5 trillion accounted to the health care sector.

Demand for Services

If those 45 million uninsured people were brought into the system, would there be an increase in demand for services that would increase the total cost to the system? Probably, but only a relatively small increase, and only in the short run. We know those 45 million people are a mixed lot.[5,6]

- Some are young and healthy, and are not insured because they have no immediate medical needs, so they feel no need to seek insurance. They will not increase demand or cost if enrolled. In fact, they will disproportionately contribute to the financing of the system (which they are not currently doing).

- Some are in the early stages of illness, when access to care and intervention would make an immediate difference and would avoid more intense care later. Early treatment of many diseases is much more cost-effective than rescue care late in the process. Although there is an initial increase in cost of care for these people, by avoiding crisis-care costs later, we stand to save money on people in this category.

- Some are sick and in need of services—and receiving crisis services but not the routine services that would help them avoid the crises. It is likely that if maintenance services and medications were available to these people, the costs related to their care would actually decrease. There is excellent evidence in the disease management literature to show that improving interval care cuts overall costs for diabetics, asthmatics, and patients with heart disease. This happens in the short run— within a year of intervention.

- Some are ill and are not receiving rescue care. Some may die of their current illness. These people, given access to care, may

require large amounts of expensive care, and may die anyway
—or they may not die. In either case, they will significantly increase the cost of care over the short haul. In the long term,
fewer and fewer people will reach this point of extremis without having received care, and the increase in cost will abate.

Adding 45 million currently uninsured people to the insured
pool will increase costs in the short run, but it is likely that this will
be a short-lived phenomenon. Costs for crisis care will decrease as
costs for routine care increase. Crisis care is generally MUCH more
expensive than routine care, so the shift out of crisis mode into routine care mode should alleviate the increase in the overall cost of
care.

Public vs. Private Cost

Adding 45 million people to the pool of those insured by the
federal government (or by a federal/state combination) will certainly
increase the amount spent by the government on health care. Some,
probably significant, amount of this should be offset by reduction
in the cost of private insurance. Private insurance costs would be
expected to decrease, as the providers no longer need to pass costs
to private insurers to make up for lack of payment from the uninsured.[7]

Think back to the ER operation outlined earlier in the chapter.
For 12 patients seen, we figured the total cost at $700. Because of
"shrinkage," the cost to be recovered from privately insured patients
was $184 each. But if the world is restructured and we now receive
reimbursement for billable supplies at cost on all patients seen, the
$300 in supply cost is covered. Our service charges for 12 patients
need to produce $400—or about $34 per patient instead of $154.

Would we voluntarily reduce our prices, or would we eagerly
accept the extra $120 per patient as a "windfall?" I think private
employers will want some assurance that the redistribution of the
payment profile will result not only in a reduction in provider charges,
but also in medical coverage premiums. Federal laws will be needed

to assure large employers that their costs will go down as a consequence of the federal program. Clearly, if we are to reverse cost shifting, we must at the same time ensure that those who have been supporting the system by paying higher costs are rewarded by decreased ongoing costs.

Infrastructure

Adding 45 million people to the pool of those insured will also increase the demand for primary care services in many communities. We are in the awkward position of having under-funded primary care for a long time. There are not enough primary care doctors right now, and an increase in demand will overload the primary care infrastructure that is available. I will discuss later the quality benefits from a good primary care base. Suffice it to say at this point that we cannot wait for more primary care physicians to become available, but we can begin the push at the time we institute universal coverage. We will do that by preferentially paying primary care physicians more in relation to what we pay specialists, and by augmenting the pay for primary care physicians who are in underserved or difficult-to-serve areas.

In Summary

There is a cost to covering an additional 45 million people who are currently without medical coverage. This cost will appear in the new coverage program. The magnitude of the cost increase should be mitigated by a shift to less expensive care and by a reduction in provider charges that currently reflect significant "shrinkage." In addition, as total program costs are more explicitly attributable at the individual recipient level, costs for private insurance should go down.

As a society, I think we can afford to provide medical coverage for the 45 million uninsured, but we must pay attention to the two issues noted above: assurance that prices will go down for private insurers and provisions for more primary care physicians.

Chapter 15

Affordability to Society—
The Cost Trend

"Every gun that is made, every warship launched, every rocket fired, signifies in the final sense a theft from those who hunger and are not fed, those who are cold and are not clothed."
—*President Dwight D. Eisenhower, April 16, 1953*

You will recollect from Chapter 4 that by affordability, I mean the system should be affordable to our society and also to each individual who needs care; in the last chapter, I alluded to the complex nature of affordability to society. One of the major issues surrounding the affordability of health care is the cost trend. In this chapter, I will focus on the cost trend and how we might construct a healthcare system to reduce that trend.

Cost Trend

The overall cost of health care is increasing in double digits annually. Even in a time of very low inflation rates, medical costs are going up 12% to 15% per year.[1,2] At this rate, costs double every five to six years. This rapid increase in cost is a major contributor to the problem we have with the affordability of coverage. Merely changing the payment mechanism will not decrease the cost trend.

113

In fact, there is evidence to indicate that it is the existence of insurance coverage that drives the spiraling cost. In some way, we must understand and deal with this cost escalation.

Why is the cost of health care increasing so quickly? There are several reasons, among them:

- New technology

- New medications

- Wasted resources due to unnecessary testing

- Wasted resources due to unnecessary treatment

- Wasted resources due to nonstandard practice

- Inefficiency in a system with little motivation to be efficient

- The increasing average age of the population

Let us sort these out.

New Technology

Part of the reason heath care costs are increasing is the advance of technology. This brings both blessings and curses.

On the blessing side is the probability that better treatments will become available. Some of these will treat medical problems that were not amenable to treatment before. Some will offer more effective treatments or treatments with fewer complications or side effects. All of this is good. Some of it may even save money on a per-case basis. But, as we have seen with laparoscopic cholecystectomy (telescopic or "minimally invasive" gall bladder surgery), the reduction in side effects and complications changes the balance of indications and contraindications for the procedure. The result is that more gall bladder surgery is done today. This may be a good thing, but it is not a cost saving.

There is a danger from untested or unproven technology. Each new intervention, whether for diagnosis or for treatment, should undergo careful testing before it receives any use outside of the arena of research.[3] Too much money and too many lives are wasted on untested technology that turns out later to have been ineffective. Within the past decade, we have seen examples of this:

- High-dose chemotherapy with bone marrow transplant for breast cancer: Formal testing was short-circuited by a general insistence on this form of treatment. Ten years later, there is still no evidence that it is superior to routine care. In fact, this treatment appears to reduce rather than lengthen the life expectancy of the average woman receiving it. Currently, use of this treatment has declined substantially. Studies are in progress to determine if there is any subgroup of breast cancer patients for whom it offers an improvement in outcome.[4]

- PSA testing for prostate cancer: After a decade or more of PSA testing, we still do not know whether the PSA test is adequately accurate, nor do we know that the cancers detected by the PSA test are ones that need to be treated. Prostate cancer is an incredibly common finding in the autopsies of men who have died from other causes, reaching almost universal occurrence in men over age 90. Most of these prostate cancers never pose a threat to the life or health of the man harboring them. We find ourselves in the odd position of being able to detect and treat prostate cancers without knowing if that detection and treatment is actually helpful in many cases. The most recent conversation in the literature indicates that we may be losing interest in PSA testing, not because it has been replaced by something better, but because it never was as good as we thought. Another recent study indicates that many men with low-grade prostate cancer are still well after twenty years without treatment.[5-8]

There is no single agency setting standards for the evaluation and use of new technologies.[9] For medications (see below), there is the Food and Drug Administration (FDA). Despite all of the problems with the FDA and how it regulates drugs, at least there is a single entity making the decision as to the licensure of medications.[10] With technologies, there is no such agency; new technologies are introduced and spread without the objective evaluation of a single, reputable organization. If such review were available, then such tests and treatments would never receive wide distribution until the scientific evidence was sufficient to support their use and help us understand the consequences of their use.

Some initial steps are being taken within the Medicare program to create both the administrative structure and the practical underpinnings of a technology evaluation process. A uniform payment system could make this process truly compelling (see Chapter 22).

Make no mistake. New technologies offer treatments where none existed before. New technologies offer improvements in treatments and outcomes for other diseases. The issue is certainly not how to curtail the development of new technology. It is to delay widespread use of new technology until we are sure it actually works and when it should be used.

New Medication

Like new technologies, new medications may allow or improve treatment of serious diseases—often at a high price. Like new technologies, they may also be abused.[11] Unlike new technologies, new medications spring into being via the approval of a central agency —the FDA.[12] To some extent, this protects us against dangerous or ineffective drugs; to some extent it slows the introduction of new medications and makes them much more expensive to introduce. Because a drug manufacturer, eager to market the new drug, supports the research on each new medication, there is money available for that research. One of the failings of the system is that there is little or no money available for testing older drugs.[13] This is a potential added role for our government or the new medical plan.

To find several examples of medications cleared by the FDA and subsequently removed from the market does not require going back far into history. Some of these are fascinating sagas. It may be that the FDA functions need to be split so that the initial licensing falls into one arena of operation, and subsequent monitoring of the utilization and side effects falls into another. There is some movement in this direction even as I write this chapter.[14] Examples of interesting discoveries that might have been handled better:

- Tysabri—a new treatment for multiple sclerosis was introduced in late 2004 only to be removed from the market in early 2005 when it was discovered that it caused a lethal complication.

- Vioxx—a COX2 anti-inflammatory medication, similar to aspirin and ibuprofen in effectiveness, was introduced onto the market with the hope that it would reduce the incidence of stomach bleeding in comparison to aspirin and ibuprofen (and other older medications). There is no evidence that it was ever more effective than aspirin, and even the evidence that it reduced bleeding was less than compelling. In 2004, it was removed from the market because it increased the risk of heart attacks and strokes. The evidence for this complication was not new—I first saw it published at least three years before Vioxx was taken off the market.[15,16,17]

- Zomax—a non-narcotic pain medication introduced in 1980 that seemed to be very effective. It caused serious allergic reactions in six people and was removed from the market in 1983.[18]

Another problem with medications is that their use is not restricted to the uses for which the FDA has approved them. For instance, Vioxx was introduced as an alternative to aspirin or ibuprofen in people who experienced intestinal bleeding from aspirin or ibuprofen. Because of the vast disequilibrium in promotion between Vioxx and aspirin and ibuprofen, Vioxx came to be used by many physicians as a standard, first-line, mild pain medication and anti-inflammatory. Because Vioxx was a patented, branded, exclusive medication, its manufacturer had every motive to promote its use[19] —the manufacturer made a profit from each prescription written.

Aspirin and ibuprofen, on the other hand, are both available over the counter as generic medications. You may still see ads for Bayer or Motrin—brand name forms of these two medications. This is nothing like when Motrin was new, on patent, and available by prescription only. I had a pharmaceutical representative in my office monthly telling me why I should prescribe Motrin. They never come anymore. No one tells you to use generic ibuprofen. It is the same stuff as Motrin—but it is cheaper than Motrin and very much cheaper than Vioxx. Profit margins are very thin on these generic medications. They are cheaper BECAUSE there is no advertising campaign. But without constant promotion, they lose ground. One cannot count on the Vioxx salesperson, after all, to tell us ibuprofen is just as good—even if that is true.[20]

The point is, regardless of what the FDA said the use of Vioxx should be (and it is just a handy example), once it is licensed and available, there is nothing to prevent the manufacturer from promoting it (perhaps not publicly, but quietly in doctors' offices) and nothing to prevent physicians from prescribing it in instances where neither its effectiveness nor its superiority to existing medications has been demonstrated.

Compounding this effect is the direct-to-consumer advertising of prescription medications. The mass media ads are enticing, laden with emotional messages, and almost devoid of usable factual information. These ads induce patients to pressure physicians for prescriptions, which are often written whether the medication is appropriate or not. At the very least, this drives up the cost of care by the cost of the ads. At worst, it also adds the cost of a significant amount of unnecessary use.

In reality, the FDA is doing its job pretty well. The expense of getting a medication through the FDA gauntlet is an issue, and it raises the cost of introducing a new medication—and therefore the cost of the medication once introduced. On the other hand, the

FDA is only the ticket-taker letting medications into the arena; once they are in, there is no control over their use. This process is somewhat analogous to paying admission to a theme park. They make you pay to get in, but once you are in, they have no control over which rides (if any) you go on. At a theme park, however, the ticket you buy is a general admission ticket; the ticket given by the FDA for a medication is for a specific use. But the FDA has no power to enforce use patterns. It is sort of like buying an admission ticket to the theme park that is supposed to allow you to go on only three of the fifty rides, but because no one checks your ticket once you are in the park, you may actually do anything you wish.

Does this produce waste? I believe it produces significant waste. When there are much cheaper drugs on the market that do the same thing, why should people be receiving a more expensive brand-name drug?[21,22,23] A recent example comes to mind:

Prilosec, the original "purple pill," is not only generic; it is available over the counter (without a prescription). Prilosec OTC 20 mg is exactly the same strength of the same medication as Prilosec 20 mg and omeprazole (the generic name) 20 mg. The costs of the three preparations at the drugstore are substantially different. A month of Prilosec 20 mg costs about $120; a month of omeprazole 20 mg is about $65; six weeks of Prilosec OTC 20 mg is about $25. If we were paying for this medication out of our own pockets, I suspect we would choose the last alternative.

What is more interesting is that there is a NEW "purple pill" whose brand name is Nexium. Nexium is esomeprazole. It turns out that omeprazole has two mirror-image versions—call them right-handed and left-handed. They occur in Prilosec and generic omeprazole and Prilosec OTC in equal amounts. The left-handed version is more potent than the right handed, though both of them work. Esomeprazole is exclusively the left-handed version. So, it stands to reason that 20 mg of esomeprazole is more potent than 20 mg of omeprazole. But two 20 mg tablets of omeprazole contain as much esomeprazole as a 20 mg tablet of Nexium, plus an equal weight of the right handed omeprazole, which also is effective. So two 20 mg tablets of Prilosec OTC are better than one 20 mg tablet of Nexium. To take two tablets a day of Prilosec OTC raises the cost to about $35 per month; Nexium costs about $150 per month.

The final issue about new medication costs and pharmaceutical house profits relates to immunizations. How much better is it to treat everyone once with an immunization to prevent a disease rather than to treat it once it happens? But where are the drug company profits?[24] We must work to ensure that preventive strategies are good business opportunities.

Wasted Resources Due to Unnecessary Testing

Running tests seems to be a significant part of what physicians do. There are, of course, reasons to run tests—but I think (and I am not alone) that the trend has gone too far. In medical school many years ago, I was taught that a good history provides the majority of the information needed to make the diagnosis, and a good physical examination provides most of the rest. Tests, I was taught, are to confirm the diagnosis the doctor has already made. Such an approach would lead to very austere use of testing—and might be inappropriate given the technology and more sophisticated treatments available today.

However, it sometimes seems that physicians are using testing instead of taking a thorough history and performing a complete physical examination. It is certainly quicker to do so, but it bypasses opportunities to interact further with the patient, an interaction that may not only be beneficial, but also may be enjoyable for the physician and the patient. One of the pressures of modern practice, especially emergency room practice, is the sense the physician has that he/she has only this one chance to make the diagnosis and start the correct treatment on this patient. This leads to doing ALL of the tests one can think of NOW, rather than following a more rational thought process to the diagnosis.

For example, if a patient complains of fatigue, and there are few other clues in the remainder of the history or physical examination, what should the physician do? The range of diagnoses includes a number of immune disorders (from lupus to AIDS), hepatitis (A, B or C), any number of cancers (especially lymphomas and leukemia), anemia, several congenital blood disorders, and a veritable host of other diagnoses. To check for anemia is very simple and quite inexpensive, but if we find it, we must take more blood to move on to the tests that will tell us what kind of anemia, which may suggest the cause. Similarly, there are specific tests for hepatitis A, B and C, but if the initial tests for hepatitis show no evidence of hepatitis, there is no point in doing them. The tendency is to order the whole battery of anemia and hepatitis tests at the first blood draw. Since the cause is very unlikely to be both hepatitis AND anemia, at least half of the tests are wasted—they could have been eliminated by attention to the result of a screening test. The bill for the initial blood tests in this situation may run to several thousand dollars, much of which need not be spent.

Who is to control this and how is it to be controlled? Currently, neither the physician nor the insured patient has a preference about how the tests are done, except the convenience issue of one blood draw versus several. The laboratory is being paid on a piece-work basis for the tests and has no interest in limiting a profitable line of business. Only the payer has an interest—and that interest is characterized as being crass. The payer is the "bean counter" telling the doctors how to practice medicine.

And, to some extent, it is. But when we initiate a national health care program, we all become payers and we want the "bean counters" doing their jobs. We do not want them telling our doctors HOW to practice medicine, but we may want them telling our doctors how not to waste our resources in the process of practicing medicine. We may expect laboratories to exert protocols so that no definitive test may be done without a positive screening test; or we may want to have carefully developed clinical pathways in place to guide the choices of laboratory tests to be done. What we must be careful not to do is to allow the doctor and the laboratory to run up the bill without regard to the likelihood that the test results will assist in the care of the patient.

Wasted Resources Due to Unnecessary Treatment

Amazingly (or not so amazingly, if you think about it), the same kind of thing is happening in the realm of treatment.[25] It happens in a number of ways. A physician may prescribe a more expensive medicine than needed, or a more expensive form of the medication than needed—an issue I covered above in the discussion of medications. A physician may choose a different set of indications for a surgical or medical procedure that result in performing more of such procedures than would be the case if the standard indications were used—which I will discuss in the next section. A physician may order a different selection among several alternatives, based not on any particular criteria about what is best for any particular patient, but based on what is financially most advantageous for the physician. A physician may choose to use a treatment that has been shown to be unnecessary or outmoded out of habit or because people ask for it or because the physician has not yet heard that the treatment is no longer necessary. It is the latter two circumstances I will address in this section.

Physicians may choose to recommend treatments that offer them financial advantage over those that do not. This should not surprise us, despite the professional ethical standard against physicians doing it. In fact, most physicians who seem (to a third party) to be doing this will declaim loudly they would never make a treatment decision based on their own economic advantage. Yet who can doubt that when a surgeon recommends surgery, he will be paid more for doing the surgery than for not doing it? Who can doubt that the medical oncologist who recommends a chemotherapy regimen to be administered by IV in his/her office stands to make more money on the mark-up on that medication than if he/she wrote the patient a prescription to have the same or another treatment administered by someone else?

It is hard to quantify the effect of recommending surgery in the practice of most surgeons (See further discussion in Chapter 18). It is easier to talk about the income-related effect of chemotherapy administration in the office of the medical oncologist. When Medicare began to talk seriously about reducing the reimbursement to medical oncologists for the cancer treatments they administer, the fact that some oncologists achieve half of their take-home pay from the mark-up on the medications they administer came to light. The issue here is not how much medical oncologists should be paid. It is, how could that magnitude of financial involvement not have an effect on the decision-making process of the physician?

Even if the mark-up on medications had no influence on the medical oncologist, do we really believe that physicians should be making their money not from the use of their hands, hearts, and brains, but from the mark-up on medications? In many states, there are laws that prohibit physicians from owning and operating pharmacies, just because of this concern. Please be clear: I am not saying that medical oncologists make too much money; I am only saying that this is the wrong way to make money. In any case, it makes no sense for the payer to pay more for the medication when administered by the medical oncologist than the payer would have to pay to buy the same medication from someone else (like a pharmaceutical supply house). If the oncologist is to receive income from administering medications, let it be for the act of administration. The point is that care must be taken in how medicine is practiced when there are strong financial motivations toward a particular form of treatment.

As to the issue of physicians ordering unnecessary treatment, one might think this a relatively infrequent happening. In my observation, it is not infrequent at all.[26] Long after it became clear in the scientific literature that much more stringent limitations should be applied to the performance of tonsillectomies, too many of them were still being done. Long after it was clear that penicillin has no role in the treatment of a cold, doctors were still treating colds with penicillin, "because it works." Of course, treating colds without penicillin also works—and just as well.[27,28] It is now clear that most cases of "ear infections" in children do not require treatment with antibiotics, much less tonsillectomies, adenoidectomies, and ear tubes. The surgical procedures are on the wane, but antibiotic use continues.

Two of the examples above focus on antibiotic use. This should not be a surprise because antibiotics were the wonder drugs of the 1950s and 1960s. Thanks to antibiotics, a number of previously serious or fatal illnesses were tamed. It was thought that antibiotics would be the miracle that would wipe out all disease. This has clearly not turned out to be the case. However, physician use of antibiotics is not in any way cynical. We physicians also believe in the effectiveness of these medications, and we do not hesitate to use the latest and the best when we think an antibiotic might help.

This costs the system money in several ways. The first is the cost of an unnecessary prescription. The second is the added cost of "the latest and greatest" antibiotic, when an older, less expensive one would do just as well. The best example of this is beta strep—the cause of strep throat and tonsillitis. It is still uniformly sensitive to penicillin—but is all too often treated with newer, more powerful, more expensive antibiotics because we believe something more powerful will do a better job. There is no evidence that the newer, more powerful drugs do a better job on beta strep.

The third cost of the overuse of antibiotics is the emergence of resistance to those antibiotics among disease-producing organisms. The more antibiotic we distribute into the world, the more we select for organisms that resist the antibiotic. Resistance is not a minor problem. For some organisms, more and more powerful antibiotics are needed; and for some, we are running through old antibiotics faster than we can invent new ones. There is a real risk that the unfettered use of antibiotics will lead to a return of the untreatable infections of the past. There are studies showing that decreasing the use of antibiotics can lead to a decrease in the prevalence of resistant bacteria.

For a number of reasons, we need to reduce antibiotic use. Some education and arm-twisting from the Centers for Disease Control and Prevention (CDC) has helped, but only a little. The implementation of a national health plan will provide us with an opportunity to establish and enforce criteria for the use of medications and other treatments so that practice will be more in accord with science.[29]

Wasted Resources Due to Nonstandard Practice

It has been very difficult to establish standards for medical practice. It is common knowledge now that there are vast regional differences in the rate at which some surgical procedures are performed—differences that cannot be explained in any other way than variation in how the doctors think things should be done.[30] These variations do not have any scientific validity; they are not based on demographic, disease, or physiologic or anatomic differences between the treated populations.

If you have a ruptured disk in Boston and you need surgery, you are much less likely to have a spinal fusion than if you are in Portland, Oregon. This is only one example. There are many others, such as the likelihood of a woman with a particular complaint having a hysterectomy, someone with chest pain having bypass surgery, or a man with prostate trouble having surgery to open the prostate passage. I do not want to enter the debates about which is the right way to treat a particular problem. I do want to make the point that there is only one way that is the most cost-effective treatment.

If the person with a ruptured disk should have a back fusion, then it is inappropriate to operate and not perform the fusion because it produces an inferior result; if the person with a ruptured disk should not have a fusion, then it is an overuse of resources to perform an unnecessary surgery. These issues can be studied and we can know which is the better treatment—and everyone who needs that treatment should receive it. We can even discover whether there are particular reasons—characteristics of the patient or the disease—to make an alternative choice.

This is a cost issue; it is also a quality issue and a safety issue. It is a cost issue because it always costs more to do the job wrong the first time and have to do it again. It is a quality issue because doing the job wrong the first time is always a quality issue. It is a safety issue every time someone is subjected to more risk than necessary to treat the presenting disease—and more surgery than needed (whether it is adding an unnecessary spinal fusion or having to do the spinal fusion later because the surgery without it was inadequate) is always riskier than less surgery.

Sometimes, we know what the standard of care ought to be, but some physicians either choose not to believe it or to adopt a different standard. This happens for a variety of reasons. Commonly, this is what the physician was taught and it has worked so far for his/her entire career—and he/she honestly believes the announced national standard is wrong. Another reason for a different interpretation is monetary—if you know how to do coronary bypass operations and you make good money from doing them, you are less likely to tell a patient he does not need a bypass than you will be if you do not do the operation.

Sometimes, we honestly don't know what the standard of care ought to be.[31] And there is plenty of room for different groups of physicians to approach the same problem in different ways because no one knows which way gives better results. In such instances, we need an established, orderly way of assessing the results of the different approaches to determine which gives better results so we can adopt a national standard (more about this in Chapter 22).[32]

Regardless of the reasons we don't adhere to a national standard, there is no current mechanism for enforcing a national standard of care in any meaningful way. I think we all deserve the best care the science of medicine can supply. We need to develop good ways to establish the standard, good ways to test it, and good ways to enforce it.[33] A national health plan will allow us to do that.

Inefficiency in a System with Little Motivation to be Efficient

What does it mean that one hospital is able to contract, at a profit, to care for patients at a cost of $1,500 per day, and another hospital is losing money being paid $3,000 per day? What does it mean that patients cared for by one family practice group cost the health plan an average of $120 per patient per month for care, and those cared for by another group cost $300 per patient per month —even after adjusting for how sick the patients are?

Of course, there are lots of explanations.[34] I am certain that the physicians in the second medical group would explain that their patients are sicker than those of the first group—whether there is any evidence to support that contention or not. In talking with physicians about comparative cost of care, I have never heard a physician explain his lower cost of care by stating that his patients were less sick than those of another physician—but I have often heard the reverse. It is a special variant of Lake Wobegon, where all the children are above average—only here, all the patients are sicker than average.

Of course, that explanation won't work for long. There are now excellent ways of adjusting for risks in groups of patients so that the cost per level of disease burden is comparable. The disparities still exist, and we still have a hard time explaining them.

What motive does the physician have to work hard at controlling the costs engendered by his pen? Essentially none, unless the physician is being paid per patient, and not per service rendered. This is called capitation and was the preferred method of contracting in the early years of the HMO movement. Physicians were given the money and the responsibility to pay for the required care. The theory was that this would encourage those physicians to engage in more preventive care and in more care designed to reduce the risk of complications from chronic illnesses, and that this would help to keep the cost of care down.

This worked in some areas with some physician groups. The perception among some publics and among other physicians was that these successful physicians were achieving cost reductions by depriving patients of the care they needed. This, too, probably happened in some instances, but not nearly as often as our legislators were led to believe. In some parts of the country, capitation contracts are still common, but in most of the country they no longer exist.

What prevails is fee-for-service contracting, in which a health plan may receive a reduction from the "retail" price (presumably for sending a volume of patients to that physician or hospital). If I am being paid for rendering services, the easiest way to make more money is to render more services. And if I have no responsibility for the overall cost of care, it is a sure bet I won't pay much attention to how much anything costs when I order it. The person who is most likely to pay attention is the patient, and if the patient has a medical plan that covers the service in question, even the patient does not care about the cost.

The most interesting twist to this is that if the physician or hospital does a bad job of providing care, and there are complications, the patient stays in the hospital longer and receives more services, and the health plan pays extra for all of the extra services necessitated by the complication. The payment system provides no motivation for quality care—in fact, it provides quite the opposite motivation. The issue of compensation and appropriate motivation to providers of health care services is so important that I will discuss it in some detail in Chapter 18.

Most health plans do not have the ability to take care of their enrollees outside of contracts with independent physicians and hospitals, so they must negotiate contracts with those providers of services. The health plan then writes medical coverage based on the contracts in force. When a large group of physicians threatens to cancel a contract, the health plan may be faced with renegotiating a higher rate or paying retail prices for services. Clearly, while a higher rate was not calculated into the premiums charged for the policies, a higher negotiated rate is better than retail, so there is a motive to settle with the group for higher prices. Many hospitals in relatively uncompetitive markets have negotiated for pricing as a percentage reduction from retail, which leaves them in the position of being able to raise prices and increase income whenever they want. Where is the motive for efficiency if I can drive the amount I get paid by raising prices and adding on unnecessary services?

This does not mean physician offices are often inefficiently run. In fact, the efficiency in the organization and operation of physician offices took many hospital administrators by surprise fifteen years ago when they bought up physician practices, offered the physicians a salary in excess of what they had been making, and tried to squeeze efficiency into the practice. Most hospitals lost money doing this.

Hospitals, on the other hand, seem to have a lot of leeway for inefficiency—whether it is in how they are organized and run or how they render care. If there is no one available to perform diagnostic tests on the weekend, then patients merely remain in the hospital for two more days (for which the hospital charges) waiting for the test to be done.

I remember poignantly the transition of Medicare payment from cost-based reimbursement to Diagnosis Related Group (DRG)-based reimbursement in the 1980s. Our hospital's administrator looked at the amount of reimbursement the hospital was receiving and what was proposed under DRGs for the same business the hospital was then doing. He calculated that the change would result in a significant decrease in reimbursement—enough that the hospital would go from making money on its Medicare business to losing it. The transition to DRGs was phased in over several years. By the time we got there, our care was efficient enough that the hospital had a larger margin on Medicare under DRGs than it had had under the cost-based reimbursement that preceded it.

Here was a way to motivate the hospital to efficiency, and it worked to the extent that the hospital could motivate the medical staff to join it in being efficient. Since the physicians control the application of resources to patients, they also control the cost per episode of care. There was movement to the point required by Medicare; then the motion stopped. Over time, Medicare reimbursement went up. The drive to further increases in efficiency stopped.

If we are to avoid the cost-creep caused by inefficiency and inattention, we must have ways of comparing costs from one hospital to another, from one region to another, and we must expect that hospitals, and the physicians they work with, can and will be motivated to operate efficiently and to provide care efficiently.

The Increasing Average Age of the Population

Last, but not least, is the aging of the population. It is the signal of success for a good job of taking care of people, but also the dark warning of increasing costs to come. It is difficult, though, to compare what it cost to take care of a 65-year-old ten years ago and what it will cost to take care of a 65-year-old ten years hence. The average 65-year-old these days is healthier than the average 65-year-old of ten or twenty years ago, and therefore costs less to care for. On the other hand, if that 65-year-old lives to 85 today and only lived to 75 ten years ago, we have ten additional years of care to pay for on the way from here to there. During those ten years, we will be caring for the chronic conditions that are inherent to aging—something we do not do well and must improve.[35]

It still remains true that the last year of life is likely to be the most expensive, and the last six months more expensive than the six preceding them. We Americans have, as a group, a harder time letting go of life than people in some other cultures. It is noteworthy that we often spend large sums on essentially hopeless care at the end of life trying to restore unrestorable function or extend a life that cannot be extended for long. It makes me sad to see people still receiving noxious chemotherapy treatments during the last week of their life when the inevitability of the outcome is clear to see.[36]

I don't know how to confront or change this penchant to choose maximum last-ditch treatment. I don't think we should count on changing this pattern in planning for our national health plan. I do think we should count on our longer-lived, older population consuming proportionally fewer resources (on the average over large populations) per year at any age than their predecessors of a few years earlier did at the same age. This does not mean there will not be a trend of increasing cost as we have a trend of increasing age in the population; it does mean that it will not be directly related to historical costs at that age, but some amelioration of that.

In Summary

There is a trend toward increasing cost. This trend is a complex mix of different causes. Some of these causes are appropriate, and some are not. We must recognize the trends and plan for ways to control the portions we can control so we will have the funds available to pay for the cost trends resulting from desirable changes (like the aging of the population and the advent of appropriate new technology). Before we explore some of those possibilities, we need to take a look at another cost driver—the patient.

Chapter 16

Moral Hazard

"I've been rich and I've been poor; rich is better."
— *Sophie Tucker*

One of the cost concerns of any insurance (or benefit) program is a phenomenon known as "moral hazard."[1] In brief, moral hazard is the tendency of people who have insurance to use more insured services than they would if they did not have insurance.[2] This is a concept of the insurance industry, adopted and codified by economists, with an interesting set of mathematical equations to demonstrate how it works.

As I understand the concept of "moral hazard," any expenditure on health care in the presence of medical coverage that would not be made by that individual in the absence of medical coverage is considered "waste" or moral hazard. I think this probably represents one piece of the truth, but not the whole truth.

One of the issues I have already dealt with—the fact that we really are not talking about insurance in the normal sense of the word when we are talking about medical coverage. The second issue is that, when it comes to things at the more expensive end of health care, almost all Americans are indigent. A single episode of illness can cost more than our home, perhaps more than we will earn in a lifetime. It is hardly fair to ask someone whose total net worth is under $100,000 if he would spend $250,000 on a liver transplant if he did not have insurance. Of course, the answer will be "no." Not only does he not have $250,000, there is no way he can raise such a sum. If he could borrow it, it is unlikely he could ever pay it back. But if he had insurance that covered the liver transplant, he would have it done. (All of this assumes that we are dealing with someone with end-stage liver disease for whom a transplant is indicated and reasonable.)

In such an instance, the classic economic theory would declare that the expenditure on the liver transplant is "moral hazard" and "value reducing" because it is not an expenditure this individual would have made if uninsured. That theory essentially ignores the indigence of the recipient. Here is a better question to pose: "If it would cost $250,000 for a liver transplant, would you prefer to have the liver transplant or the $250,000?" The question of "If I had the money, would I spend it on this care?" is a much different question from "Given that I don't have the money, would I spend it on this care?"

This is not to say that there is no such thing as "moral hazard" in health care and medical coverage. There certainly is; it just isn't quite so cut and dried as many economists believe. It is my intent to use the term "optional care" to indicate choices that increase expenditures (above the minimum necessary) made by the patient by virtue of having medical coverage; I will use the term "excess care" to signify increased expenditures (above the minimum necessary) made in the process of care for insured people but without making any judgment about who made the choice to spend the money or whether it would have been spent in the absence of medical coverage.

Everything we buy has a certain degree of price sensitivity. Offered a particular car for $10,000, you would be more likely to purchase it than if offered the same car for $20,000. The economist statement is that there is "elasticity in the demand" that reflects changes in price; in some way, as the price decreases, the demand increases.

The Utopia Vehicle Club

If we think in the same analogy about how medical coverage works, it goes somewhat like this. We are offered membership in the Utopia Vehicle Club. For an annual dues payment, we become eligible to access vehicles. The vehicles we access don't ever belong to us (they belong to the Club), so we cannot sell them at a profit, but we can use them for as long as we want. Whenever we tire of our current vehicle, we can turn it in and obtain another, subject to the same rules (no trade-in value is allowed). Dues can be paid in two ways: Happy Motor Options (HMO) where each vehicle is subject to co-payments and coinsurance, and Major Motor (MM) where all vehicle acquisitions are subject to a single deductible.

- The dues we pay are the equivalent of medical coverage premiums.

- Club membership entitles us to obtain new bicycles, motor scooters, motorcycles, golf carts, cars, speedboats, private planes, recreational vehicles and luxury yachts subject to certain rules.

- The HMO co-payment is a fixed cost which we must pay, but for which we are entitled to any product on lists A, B and C.

  * List A requires a co-payment of $100 and includes a wide variety of bicycles and motor scooters.

  * List B requires a co-payment of $250 and includes a wide variety of motorcycles and golf carts.

  * List C requires a co-payment of $1,000 and includes an exhaustive list of automobiles and speedboats.

  * A coinsurance of 40% is applied to products on list D —we are required to pay 40% of the club's cost; the club will cover the rest. List D includes private planes, recreational vehicles, and luxury yachts.

- Major Motor membership is available in three dues amounts, with deductibles of $50,000, $100,000 and $250,000. Under the MM50K plan, we can access all of the club's vehicles, but we must pay the first $50,000 of the price of whatever we want.

What is the effect of such an arrangement? First, my decision to pay dues or not will relate to how much the dues are and what is the likelihood I think I will want to acquire something included on one of the lists. I will be less likely to pay dues if I do not think I will need something listed. I will be less likely to pay dues as the dues amount increases, especially as that increase is significant as related to the cost of the item I might need. Thus, if I think I will probably only need a new bicycle, and I know the price of the new bicycle I would probably buy is about $500, as the combination of the co-payment ($100) and the dues approaches $500, I will become less and less likely to pay dues, since the economic advantage of doing so is decreasing.

But, once I have paid HMO dues, my price sensitivity for anything on one of the four lists is changed. The decision to buy a new car is essentially a $1,000 decision. And it remains a $1,000 decision whether I buy a Honda or a Rolls Royce. I don't know offhand whether Rolls Royce is looking to sell more cars, but under a financing arrangement like this, I would expect their business to boom— and if they wanted to keep output limited, they could just raise prices. In either case, profits at Rolls Royce go up.

Similarly, my decision to buy a luxury yacht is no longer a $1,000,000 decision; it is now a $400,000 decision. And my decision to buy a less expensive yacht reflects in less cost to me. On the other hand, if I don't have $400,000, the yacht is still out of reach.

But suddenly the MM50K plan looks more attractive. I pay the first $50,000 and the club pays everything else—so the million-dollar yacht is now a $50,000 decision, and therefore a much more attractive one, even though I will have to pay full cost for my bicycle, my golf cart and my new Toyota.

The point of this exercise is that all purchasing decisions are price sensitive as well as value sensitive; but in a situation where a third party assumes a large portion of the cost, the only price that influences the consumer is the price seen by the consumer. If I have the HMO plan and decide I really want a Ferrari, do I care what the club pays for it? No. The only influence on my decision is the $1,000 I pay for it.

From the point of view of the economist, there is waste in this system to the extent that, if it were all my money, I would have selected the Honda instead of the Ferrari. This is moral hazard personified.

Back to Health Care

One of the things that medical coverage does very effectively is to reduce the personal cost of care to the recipient. This certainly changes the attractiveness of the purchase to the patient, as well as reducing the patient's sensitivity to price above the level of the patient's commitment. The decision to see a physician is a co-payment decision of $25 (for example); there is complete insensitivity to the fact that the actual cost of the visit may be ten times that. And the decision to have an MRI may also be a $25 decision to the patient —though it looks to the payer like a $1,000 decision.

Is there any wonder that payers and patients look at medical necessity decisions differently? As long as the patient is looking at the decision as being a $25 decision and the payer regards it as a $1,000 decision, they will not see eye-to-eye. Very different criteria apply to a $25 decision than to a $1,000 decision. If only $25 is at risk, the correct consideration may well be, "If there is any chance it will help and only a small chance that it will create additional problems, we should do it." In this case, even though there is a 1-in-20 chance that it will produce a falsely abnormal value (a minor nuisance), this is a small risk compared to the 1-in-100 risk that it might shed more bright light (provide a major benefit) on the diagnosis of the problem.

In the case of a $1,000 decision, considerably more discernment is warranted. We might, for instance, expect the chance of a significant benefit to be rather higher than 1-in-100. (At those odds, it would mean we would spend $100,000 for each unit of benefit, which seems a high price to pay. Couldn't we do something less expensive or more productive?) We would be much more likely to expect the risk of a benefit to be higher than the risk of a detriment (the falsely abnormal study). One of the purposes of having the patient participate in the cost of every portion of the medical process is to keep the patient aware that everything has a cost.

One of the major differences between health care and the Utopia Vehicle Club is that there are a number of possible solutions for any vehicle need, covering a wide variety of prices; in medical care, there may be only a narrow range of options to treat a given disease, and all of them may be quite expensive. The actual cost of care in many situations is not determined so much by the patient's desires or lack of price sensitivity, but by the medical challenge being faced.

As an example, a patient with kidney failure has only a small range of choices: peritoneal dialysis, hemodialysis, kidney transplant, and death. There is significant cost to each alternative, although the cost of not treating and facing early death is not monetary so much as it is personal. Is there a difference in cost among the other three choices? Yes, there certainly is. There is also a difference in lifestyle disruption and a difference in the risk of complications. Nonetheless, all three are expensive, and a patient without insurance may be unable to afford any of them.

I want to break healthcare services into three groups for the purposes of discussion. I make no contention that the three groups are comprehensive, or mutually exclusive, only that they are interesting conceptually as a way of looking at payment decisions and excess care. The first group is healthcare services aimed at severe illnesses for which there are few treatment options. The second is a group of healthcare services aimed at the treatment of some problem sensible to the patient for which there are many options along a significant scale of cost. The third group is preventive in nature—either purely preventive, or preventive in the sense that it is treatment for a condition not sensible to the patient now but for which treatment will avoid complications later in the course of that condition.

Severe Illness, Few Options

The patient with liver failure for whom liver transplant is the only option; the patient with kidney failure whose options include two kinds of dialysis or kidney transplant; the cancer patient facing a choice of some combination of surgery, radiation therapy, and medical therapy—these are all examples of severe illnesses with few treatment options. Admittedly, there may be many options buried in such large categories as "dialysis" and "medical therapy," but the basic status is that the patient is faced with an immediately life-threatening derangement and expensive treatment. Without a cash infusion of some kind, many of us are indigent in the face of such an event.

Given the gift of enough cash to cover the treatment, we will almost certainly buy it (though even here, there is room for some variation in choice having to do with the value system of the victim and that individual's perception of greatest good). If there is a question about different treatments, those questions will predominantly be answered by the preferences of the providers of care and the capabilities of the local provider network. In these cases, though there may be excess care around the margins (do we do an MRI every three months or every six months?), the benefit paid by medical coverage has a positive value.

The classical theory of "moral hazard" would indicate that, if we weren't willing to spend the money in the absence of medical coverage, everything paid by the medical coverage is "moral hazard." Under our new understanding, there may be excess care at the margin, but the core expense is value-adding and not to be denigrated with negative terminology. In fact, this is one of the major core roles of medical coverage.

Many Options, Wide Range of Cost

For much of what healthcare is all about, nothing life-threatening is going on, and there are myriad choices ranging from the sublime to the ridiculous. Perhaps two examples will suffice to demonstrate what I mean by this.

Migraine headache: There are two phases to migraine headache—evaluation and treatment. Evaluation may be as simple as taking a good history and eliciting classical migraine syndrome symptoms, followed by a complete neurological examination showing no abnormalities. There is, to date, nothing in the medical literature to indicate that any additional testing will significantly clarify either the cause or the nature of the headaches or give guidance to treatment. However, we see additional tests being done for migraine headaches all the time—spinal taps, CT scans, MRI scans, PET scans, multiple laboratory tests, EEGs (brain wave tests), and full sleep studies are done with this diagnosis. (This is not to say that an atypical history or an abnormal physical examination does not warrant further study—it does.)

Then there is treatment. Treatment is more difficult because the treatment that works for some people does not work for others, so it may be necessary to go through several treatments before finding the right one. Correct treatments run the gamut from over-the-counter pain medications, to narcotics, to sumitriptan and its relatives, to acupuncture (it has now been shown that "real" acupuncture and "sham" acupuncture are equally effective—and both are more effective than no treatment at all), to botulinum toxin injections. To the extent that any diagnostic study beyond the minimum necessary is done, it is excess care; to the extent that unnecessary, invalid, or ineffective treatments are given, it is excess care.

Eyeglasses: Eyeglasses come in many shapes and sizes, and are manufactured to meet the needs of the individual patient. Two things are worth noting. First, there are lots of options, so that the same prescription may end up costing vastly different amounts depending on the extra things done to the lenses and the frames chosen. When someone chooses fancy lenses and frames they would not have paid for "out of pocket," it is optional care. Second, many older people develop difficulty reading due to "presbyopia," a progressive farsightedness caused by hardening of the lens of the eye. Glasses are available in most drugstores that will offer many people satisfactory correction for less than $5.00. But many people are walking around with several hundred dollars of eyeglasses on their faces that are not a bit more effective than the $5.00 pair would have been. This is excess care.

Preventive Services

Preventive services are those things that we know, as a profession, we can do that will effectively prevent disease later. They are done to people who are, in essence, perfectly healthy, but who have the risk of acquiring a serious disease at some later time if the preventive is not administered. Once again, examples may be the best illustration.

Immunizations: we immunize our children for a number of diseases with strange names that most modern parents have never heard of, except in the names of the shots their children receive. These include diphtheria, pertussis (whooping cough), tetanus, polio, measles, mumps, rubella (German measles), hemophilus influenza b, hepatitis B, pneumococcus, varicella (chicken pox). Each of these was a "dread disease" before the immunization was introduced. The immunization process has largely eliminated all of them.

Treatment of asymptomatic disease: even though there are no symptoms, we know that treatment of high blood pressure and high blood sugar result in significant reductions in the rate of complications—heart attacks and strokes in the case of high blood pressure and kidney failure, and loss of limbs and vision in the case of blood sugar.

The problem here is not one of over-use. The problem, rather, is under-use, especially when the "victim" is expected to pay for the privilege of being treated for a disease that causes no ill effects. As a profession, physicians know how difficult it is at times to get people to come to the office and continue treatment for prevention. It is always something that can be put off to a future date without any sense of complications occurring because of the postponement. The concept of moral hazard in preventive care is topsy-turvy. The expense of preventive care might not be an expense the patient would undertake without medical coverage.[3] But when the patient has medical coverage and engages in preventive strategies, there is a health improvement for the patient and a long-term cost reduction for the payer. Preventive behaviors are to be encouraged, not classed as excess care.

The Challenge

The challenge, then, is to build a medical coverage process that encourages people to get preventive care, helps them afford very expensive care where few options exist, and puts on the financial brakes where there is a range of care and we want them to include the price of care in the calculation of how much or which care to receive. Remember that much of this analysis proceeds from the practical man's view of how the people he has cared for have confronted such decisions, mixed with the economist's view of "moral hazard" and the "excess care" that results from the mere presence of health insurance.

There are surely finer grades of differentiation between levels of care. There are distinctions that cannot be covered in the space of this short consideration. There are relationships that may be open to more scientific exploration once economists stop regarding the purchase of health insurance and the purchase of lottery tickets as being essentially identical transactions.

I used the term "minimum necessary expense" early in this chapter. The use of the term is necessary in talking about moral hazard and waste. The problem is that such minimum-data sets or minimum-treatment sets have not been established across much of health care. I discussed some of the implications of our ability to define minimum necessary care in the last chapter, in discussing overuse of lab and medications and in the discussion of nonstandard practice. I will deal further with this issue when I discuss quality and safety.

In the meantime, it will do to remember our goals:

- Support preventive care.

- Support catastrophic care.

- Instill some degree of price-sensitivity in the users of the system (both providers and patients).

- Never set barriers that preclude people from accessing necessary care.

Chapter 17

Affordability: The Patient's Perspective

"Everything depends on what the people are capable of wanting."
—*Enrico Malatesta*

The issues surrounding affordability from the point of view of the payer are complex and require a number of approaches to a number of "leaks" in cost. In Chapter 15 we discussed a number of these "leaks," and in Chapter 16 we explored why some of those leaks exist. The payer's view of cost control is very complex.[1] From the point of view of the patient, it is simple. Whatever the patient must pay out of pocket must be affordable—within the means of the individual.

One of the cost-control avenues open to the payer (or society as a whole) is cost sharing—the more of the cost of medical coverage that is paid by the patient, the less must be paid by the payer. Cost sharing is attractive to the employer because it reduces the employer's cost. In addition, many payers also think it will increase the sensitivity of the patient to the actual cost of the care, inducing patients to be wiser consumers of health care services. There are problems both in concept and in implementation.

The first problem is determining what is affordable to any particular individual. Cost-sharing techniques that might be implemented by society (to protect affordability to the society as a whole) will impact affordability to the individual patient. There is, therefore, some tension between what the system must pay and what the individual must pay. This is not unlike the tension between employer and employee about how the costs of employer-sponsored health plans should be shared.

Cost-sharing techniques that have been used in the past include sharing underwriting costs (premium cost sharing), sharing costs at the point of service (co-payments, coinsurance, and deductibles), and exclusions (definitions of coverage that shift the cost of some services completely to the patient). I will discuss these individually (and the discussion of exclusions will wait until Chapter 19).

Sharing Underwriting Costs

Premium Costs: The sharing of premium costs is an effective way to shift costs from the system to the individual. Whatever amount the employee pays for the premium is a share the employer (or the government) does not have to pay. In the current system, if the employee decides he or she cannot afford to pay the employee share of the premium (or that the potential benefit to be gained is not worth the expense), that employee drops coverage. In this case, the employer pays nothing, which is a significant saving for the employer—the effect on the employee is indeterminate.

Within the system as we envision it, however, dropping out will not be allowed. I foresee the need for laws to limit the maximum contribution any employer may collect from the employee. Perhaps the "play or pay" laws will do this job well enough. As a general rule, I expect the cost of employer-funded medical coverage to go down (see Chapter 14) in the new system, so the magnitude of employee participation should not be a major issue.

Theoretically, sharing premium cost might do something else —it might make the enrollee, the insured person, more aware of the actual cost of medical coverage. I indicate that this is theoretical because I have not seen this participation fulfill this expectation. My observation is that participation in paying the premium is much more likely to result in the enrollee having a greater sense of being entitled to every imaginable medical service—after all, "I paid good money for the premium; I want the care I paid for. I'm worth it!" I think if we expect to educate the public, we will have to choose another way to do so.

Given that everyone MUST be covered, we can have a single-payer system, or we can have a pluralistic system. I have announced in favor of the latter. Under such a plan, employers would pay the bulk of the premium cost for employed individuals. Cost sharing by the government or the employee would be based on the income of the employee, not on the desire of the employer to avoid cost. This is important to emphasize—the sharing of premium cost is a way wealthier people will contribute to the provision of coverage for the relatively impoverished. But it is not the only way of collecting funds for coverage—general taxes will also do this—so there should be a balance in fund-raising methods. It may be that this fund-raising mechanism will be more ceremonial than substantive.

For the self-employed, the alternative of self-insurance would be available. Those who choose to self-insure would receive some reduction in tax burden to cover a portion of the cost of the premium. For those who could not or would not take that option, the individual would be required to contribute toward the premium—less of a contribution for those with lower incomes, more for those with higher incomes. At every income level, the idea is to have every person with income contribute to the cost of the program, either directly in the cost of the premium, or indirectly in taxes, or both.

Think back for a moment to the Utopia Motor Club. In our discussion, I indicated that if I didn't plan to obtain a vehicle this year, I might choose not to pay the dues. The disadvantage is that I would not be eligible for the benefit of getting a vehicle, but that would be a small loss since I do not intend to do so in any case. The advantage is that I would not have to pay the (probably hefty) membership dues. As we have noted, holding everyone into the program is part of the way we keep cost-per-participant down. If everyone has to pay dues every year, then the people who don't need a vehicle help to pay for the vehicles of those who do. It works the same way in a medical plan. Everyone participates, and everyone pays; only those who are sick receive benefit. The larger the paying population, the more widespread the distribution of the expense, and therefore the lower the cost per person.

All of this is for the basic plan. I believe significant enrollee participation in "extra" coverage is warranted—anyone who wants to have more insurance than the basic plan should be prepared to pay the full premium cost for that coverage.

Cost Sharing at the Point of Service

Co-payments: A co-payment is a defined, fixed payment required of the patient per episode of care, regardless of the actual cost of the care received. For example, it might be an amount such as $10 or $15 to be paid by the patient for each visit to the primary care physician (PCP). It doesn't matter how much that physician charges the medical plan for the visit (which might vary from as little as $20 to as much as $250); the patient's participation is the amount of the co-payment, no more, no less. The co-payment may be different for different kinds of providers or different circumstances (for instance: PCP: $15; specialist: $30; Urgent Care Clinic: $50; Emergency Room: $100; Hospital admission: $500). The principle of co-payments is that this is the amount the patient pays regardless of the complexity of the care received.

There are studies to indicate that the institution of co-payments for some components of care can reduce unnecessary ("excess") utilization. This presumes the co-payment is small enough to be affordable yet large enough to cause the patient to think twice before accessing care. In the experimental models, people were clearly able to afford the co-payment imposed. No one knows, at this time, whether the same co-payment will have this effect on people across a wide range of wealth. If it becomes necessary to institute a sliding scale of co-payments, it will take a significant effort to derive a sliding scale that will work about the same on all economic levels.

It is clear that a fixed co-payment may inhibit access to the system, but it will not control the cost of the interaction when one happens. In the Utopia Auto Club example, the $1,000 co-payment for an automobile may reduce the number of cars I elect to buy, but once I have made the decision to purchase a car, there is no inhibition on my aspiration for how expensive a car I might decide to get.

It is equally clear that the poorest in our country cannot afford any co-payment at all, or only a very small one.[2] There are Medicaid programs all over the country exerting some care management to control utilization. We must look at them and their results in an organized way to get a better feel for how to manage the co-payment process for the most financially vulnerable members of our society.

In summary, co-payments work to decrease the frequency with which services are demanded, but not the magnitude of the services. They help…

- When they are of an appropriate size, and

- When they are a significant portion of the cost of the service, and

- When they are applied at the same level only to services covering a fairly narrow range in costs (if there is no difference in co-payment between a $50 office visit and a $12,000 ER visit, why should I, as the patient, care whether I am treated in the office or the ER?), and

- When the option of bundling large baskets of care into a single co-payment does not exist (if I can pay one $10 co-payment and receive one doctor office visit plus several thousand dollars worth of imaging and laboratory studies, the co-payment is set too low; another cost participation method needs to be chosen for the imaging and lab studies), and

• When the general nature of the care is such that the option of avoiding or postponing care is not a significant error of omission (as it would be in the case of avoiding appropriate preventive care or necessary ongoing services for a chronic illness).

Coinsurance: Coinsurance is a set proportion of the allowable payment to the provider that must be paid by the recipient. Unlike a co-payment, this amount will vary depending on the price of the service offered. In the example of the primary care physician visit above, a 10% coinsurance could range from $2 to $25 as the fee for the visit ranges from $20 to $250, instead of the fixed amount ($15 for instance) required by a co-payment. Requiring the patient to pay a fixed percentage of the allowable payment is a premium-reducing technique because it reduces the payer's risk from 100% of the cost of care to a smaller percentage.

Many medical coverage policies using coinsurance will cover either 60% or 80% of the allowable amount—the patient must pay the remaining 20% or 40%. Because the patient participates in the cost of care, coinsurance is seen by some as a way to sensitize the patient to the actual cost of the service. The risk is that it may price the service out of reach. A 40% coinsurance on a $140,000 kidney transplant is $56,000, a cost many would be unable to pay. On the other hand, if there is a choice between several different options to care which may be about equal in expected outcome but have very different costs, coinsurance will help motivate the patient to sort out which is the least expensive pathway to follow. One problem with coinsurance is that it has no inherent upper limit—if the kidney transplant patient develops complications, the costs may run to a million dollars, and the coinsurance escalates to $400,000.

Coinsurance is illustrated in the Utopia Motors Club example by the payment mechanism for a yacht under the HMO plan—the requirement is that the buyer pays 40% of the cost. While this increases our price sensitivity, the million-dollar yacht still only costs us $400,000. On the other hand, a $700,000 yacht would only cost us $280,000. Our sensitivity to that price difference will be preserved, though somewhat blunted, since it is only a $120,000 difference instead of the full $300,000 difference.

Some coinsurance requirements put a cap on the amount the insured will ever have to pay. If there were, for instance, a $50,000 "out of pocket" cap in the case of the kidney transplant mentioned above, the coinsurance cost to the patient would be $50,000 for the procedure and the patient would have no risk of incurring additional cost if there were complications. If the liability limit is set too low, the risk is that the medical coverage becomes 100% coverage too early in the year and all subsequent care during that year costs the patient nothing. If the liability limit is set too high, the medical coverage no longer protects the patient from financial ruin in case of a complication.

The role of such a fixed percentage of coinsurance in encouraging the patient to be a careful shopper is unknown. Unless it is applied with a cap (such as an "out of pocket" maximum), it is an unlimited liability for the patient, which negates some of the value of having medical coverage. As noted, if the cap is too high, the co-insurance becomes a barrier to care; if it is set too low, it may have little effect on consumer behavior. I have been unable to discover any studies documenting the effect of coinsurance requirements on utilization of "necessary" services or on changes in "shopper" behavior.

There are some plans now experimenting with coinsurance for prescription drugs, rather than the staged co-payments that have been common up to now. The idea here is that paying a proportion of actual cost of the prescription will sensitize the patient to the actual cost borne by the medical plan. Patients may be more willing to choose a generic medication when the cost to the patient of the generic is under $5 and the cost of the brand name medication is $20 or $30 per month. Here, the upper limit on cost is present; coinsurance may work well in this kind of application.

Deductibles: This is an amount the enrollee must pay for his/her own medical care before the medical coverage becomes applicable. Deductibles are floors under medical coverage. The patient must pay the entire cost of care until the deductible is reached, then the medical plan begins to participate in the payment. The classic "major medical" plan was a great example: the deductible was high enough that most people paid for most of their own care, but if they had a medical catastrophe, they would have effective insurance.

The idea behind a deductible is two-fold. On the one hand, it reduces the financial risk to the payer by shifting the first dollars of cost to the insured. The first dollars are the dollars most likely to be spent (after all, you cannot spend $100 without spending $50), so the payer avoids the most likely expenditures. This reduces premium cost. The higher the deductible, the more premium cost one avoids. On the other hand, shifting cost from the payer to the insured happens in a defined, limited way, which (theoretically) should make the insured a more careful shopper. After all, the insured does not want to spend $50 for a service she could get for $25 if she is spending personal, "out of pocket" money.

Deductibles must be of a rational size considering the budget of the patient or the family. Until the deductible is reached, the patient is effectively "uninsured." If the family deductible is $10,000 in a family making $25,000 a year, any episode of illness consuming a sizeable portion of the deductible will effectively render the family medically indigent. They do not have the financial strength to pay the $10,000. On the other hand, for someone with a $250,000 annual income, that deductible should not represent an insurmountable obstacle.

Setting the deductible is much the same challenge as setting any other level of patient participation in care. If the deductible is met too soon in the year, then all care is "free" for the rest of the year. If the deductible is too high, the patient will forgo needed care to conserve funds, just as an uninsured person will. In fact, the patient IS uninsured until the deductible is met.

Recall again the Utopia Motor Club MM50K example. During the first $50,000 of expenditure, we might be very frugal if we did not expect to reach $50,000 during the year. On the other hand, if we already know we are going to purchase the yacht this year, then we know the $50,000 is already spent. Might as well buy the Ferrari, the Maserati, two Rolls Royces, and a King Air airplane this year also while we are at it.

What is the difference between coverage with a $5,000 deductible and 100% coverage above the deductible, and coverage with 20% coinsurance but with a $5,000 cap on patient (member) expense? With the former coverage, the patient will be very concerned about the way the first $5,000 gets spent and will not care at all after that. With the latter coverage, the patient continues to participate in the cost until the total cost reaches $25,000. Therefore, under the coinsurance model, whatever motivation there is to be a savvy shopper continues for longer into the expense year. Admittedly, however, most people enrolled in a $5,000 deductible plan will never reach that threshold and will never achieve any medical plan participation at all. To a very real extent, the role of deductibles as techniques for encouraging patients to be savvy shoppers is untested and its effectiveness is unknown.

One option just coming into being to encourage this careful shopper idea is the "high deductible health plan." It harkens back to the classic "major medical" plan referred to above. The idea is that it costs less to purchase a medical plan with a higher deductible. So the premium cost is less. New federal regulations allow the employer and the employee to contribute money to a Health Savings Account (HSA).[3] With the lower premium, both the employer and the employee have money available to put into this HSA. To the extent the patient wishes, the money to cover expenses "under" the deductible (before the deductible is reached) can be taken from the HSA. The annual contribution to the HSA is not allowed to be enough to cover the entire deductible, except that any money left over in this account during one coverage year can be carried over into the next coverage year. Thus, several years of frugal shopping may result in an HSA balance in excess of the deductible. Continued frugal shopping may result in a sizeable savings account—which is tax-deferred money going in and tax exempt coming out, with no tax on the earnings.[4]

The problem is that no one knows whether this actually encourages frugal shopping any more than any other technique. It has not been studied in any organized way. It could turn out that people spend the HSA money just as freely as they spend the "found money" paid by their medical coverage; it could equally be that the frugal shopping will extend to not buying medications necessary to ensure long-term health. Or it may work exactly as advertised. Some very early results indicate that the early adopters of this kind of plan are not saving money by scrimping on needed services.[5] However, there is a significant level of dissatisfaction with the lack of information about necessary services and how to save money. We will certainly learn much more about how this kind of plan works over the next few years.

The "Savvy Shopper"

I have written several times about encouraging patients to be careful, cost-conscious shoppers. This is a reflection of the consideration about "moral hazard" in the last chapter. To the extent that lack of financial accountability encourages people to seek and receive medical care they might not have if it actually cost them something, putting some financial burden on the patient seems to be a reasonable technique to reduce excess utilization. The American medical marketplace is characterized by a lot of confusion between what "I want" and what "I need." To the extent there are not financial barriers, then every "I want" can be recognized as a need without qualm; to the extent there are financial obstacles, one hopes for a more informed decision. It is worth noting that the physician (or other provider) is also complicit in this—a role discussed in Chapters 18 and 19.

One of the obstacles to fully informed decisions is clear. The only way to have a million-dollar yacht seem to the purchaser like a million-dollar purchase is to have the buyer have to pay the million dollars for it. Anything we do to reduce the financial impact of the cost of health care will reduce the financial impact at the individual level. Thousand-dollar decisions will look like $50 decisions if all the patient has to pay is $50.

The high-deductible health plan with health savings account previously described is intended to make the purchaser of health care services more fully aware of their actual costs. It is unclear whether it will work. It is not clear whether health care consumers will treat the Health Savings Account as they would treat the money in their checking account. To the extent the HSA represents "found money," it may not be husbanded as the designers of the plans would hope. To the extent that the HSA represents "my money," it may not be spent freely enough on medically important treatment. The early returns indicate that there does not seem to be a problem with excessive stinginess, but the jury is still out.

There is another flaw in the High Deductible/HSA system. The fact that it has an absolute ceiling on personal expenditures in any calendar year means there is a limit to the personal responsibility inspired by the high deductible. In any year in which I know I am going to have expenses exceeding the deductible, I may as well spend freely and get all the services I can fit into that year. To the extent this pathway is chosen, the system will not work as predicted.

Information and Education

There is a second problem with helping consumers to be "savvy shoppers." The attempt to make patients into savvy shoppers will succeed only to the extent that patients have adequate information on which to base decisions.[6] Such information must include not only costs, but also likely outcomes, and the difference in outcomes between one choice and another—regardless of whether that choice is between one path of evaluation and treatment and another,[7] or between one provider and another.[8] That information is largely not yet available, or, when available, is rudimentary or wildly biased.[9] (Much of the "information" available on the Internet is about as unbiased and factual as "infomercial" ads on television.) We are just emerging from a period in which attempts to create such information were greeted with justifiable challenges to its accuracy or relevancy. Time will help us on this one, but it may take more time than we have available.

By and large, we choose our primary care doctor based on what family or friends recommend, and our specialists based on what our primary care doctor recommends. This is not a sophisticated shopping technique. What we need is a "consumer report" for health care, filled with information about individual physicians, hospitals, and other providers that will allow us to determine where we want to go.

Provider report cards either deal in things irrelevant to cost-effectiveness, or they are based in such narrow disease categories as not to be meaningful. If I have pneumonia, what do the coronary artery bypass surgical outcome results of hospitals mean to me? And even more, if I feel that I am completely well, what measure of a hospital could I use to decide which I should sign up for? How does one interpret overall disease-adjusted mortality and morbidity figures (if one can find them)? Does overall disease-adjusted cost of care look better when it is higher or lower (if you can find such a measure)? Crucially, how does one get such indicators measured in the first place?

This shows education is also important. Education can help people sort the information presented to them. It can help them understand and assimilate that information so they can use it better in making decisions. More than anything, we need to educate our nation on how to stay healthy. The current epidemic of obesity is an alarming indication of how poorly we all understand what is healthy for us and what is not. Of course, education will only help if people are interested and willing to take care of themselves. One sometimes wonders.

We also need readily available, accurate information about what care we should expect to receive, including why more tests may not be needed. To a great extent, that kind of information is also inaccurate, biased, or not readily available. There is an overwhelming amount of disinformation available on the Internet—enough to confuse a careful and skeptical reader, much less someone who is anxiously trying to find out what to do for an obscure and serious illness.

There is a significant effort by a number of third-party payers (insurance companies) to direct people to good information. However, the altruism of the medical plan, and therefore the accuracy of the information, is open to some question. In point of fact, it may be much to the financial advantage of the payer to have the member seek care from the right provider the first time—it saves going back and doing the things over again, which always costs more. In spite of this, many people regard advice from insurance companies as being self-serving in a way that will play to the disadvantage of the patient. Frequently, information from the medical plan is the most organized information available to the member; if one does not trust it, the mass of disorganized, disconnected, and sometimes completely fallacious "information" available on the Internet may be all that is left.

The real point is that the cost-sharing mechanisms designed to encourage the insured to be a careful shopper do so by putting financial responsibility back on the insured. The decision-making processes employed by patients have been studied to some extent, and the results are not encouraging for the cost-sharing philosophy. The best results are from Rand.[10] We also know that increasing co-payments on medications leads to people taking fewer medications, but the ones they stop may be the most important, not the least important, ones to take.[11-16]

It is not clear if imposing cost sharing may result in higher overall costs by pushing more people out of early, inexpensive care into late, expensive care for the same illness. Thus, these attempts to shift responsibility to patients are subject to some risk that they will be futile at best or counterproductive at worst. We must recognize our inability to get people to react to a $1,000 test as if it were a $1,000 test when all they pay for it is $50. We can do better with many people than to make them think that everything is free, but we will not be able to make people feel the pain that the medical plan feels any more than we can get the medical plan to feel the physical pain the patient has from his or her illness. Patient education, patient information, and even patient financial participation all have limits on their effectiveness.

Other Interesting Experiments

There are other interesting experiments now getting started. In Arkansas, the Arkansas Safety Net Benefit Program is a government-subsidized program for employees who are not eligible for Medicaid and are employed in businesses that do not offer health insurance.[17] It is designed to cover health care needs starting at the low end but with a low benefit ceiling which will cover all of the medical care sought in any year by 90% of the people of Arkansas. So, with small deductibles and co-payments, the plan covers up to six office visits with physicians, seven hospital days, two outpatient facility charges, and two prescriptions a month. It will be interesting to see both what the reception to this plan is, and how it changes the healthcare dynamic in Arkansas as its implementation proceeds. The first enrollees are to start receiving coverage in January 2007.

In Massachusetts, a different kind of program is starting up that will cover all of the uninsured in the state.[18] Massachusetts will form a state insurance authority to issue policies to those unable to get them elsewhere. The plan will charge applicants a sliding scale premium based on income; it will balance its budget through charges to businesses that do not provide insurance to their employees and through state general revenues diverted from other medical care payment programs to support this one. This program, too, is not yet operational as I write.

California is considering how to achieve the same result as Massachusetts. The California Healthcare Foundation[19] actually prepared a long evaluation of the Massachusetts program and concluded it would cost California between $6.8 and $9.4 billion in additional costs to fund the program. It is not yet clear what action will follow in California. In San Francisco, however, the mayor continues to promise universal medical coverage. Again, it is too soon to see either the details or the outcome.

In considering how to create an equitable plan, it will be important to consider the results of these experiments, or perhaps, to allow them to continue longer so that results become visible. At this point we have far too many options and not nearly enough information about the likely results of choosing any particular plan.

In Summary

I am far from certain that the goal of converting the American populace to a group of educated, cost-conscious health care shoppers can ever be accomplished. Until we know not only that these cost-sharing mechanisms work and how they work, but also how they work on people in different wealth bands, we must approach them with a certain amount of caution. I hope the next few years will allow us to gain enough additional information from the High-Deductible Health Plans with Health Savings Accounts to have some idea how this "solution" actually fares.

In the meantime, the ad hoc rule must be that no financial barrier should ever be placed between an ill person and the medical care he or she needs if the barrier would preclude the person from receiving it. While we do know that people may seek too much care when it is free (so we need to guard against that), we also know that if the barrier is too high, they will not seek care that could reduce costs and improve health in the long run. Individual responsibility is a wonderful thing, but we need to nurture the sick to the point that they can receive appropriate care. And responsibility is hard to execute adequately without appropriate decision-supporting information.

In summary, then, affordability of health care at the level of the individual takes in two concepts. First, the premium cost must be shared between the individual and the society in a way that assures everyone can afford to have medical coverage. Second, the cost sharing at the point of care should be enough to make the patient think twice about the need for care, but not so much as to drive people away from seeking or receiving the care they need. Which mechanisms will best accomplish this second goal are still to be determined, but they will be some combination of co-payments, coinsurance, and deductibles.

Chapter 18

Compensation and Alignment of Incentives

"The definition of insanity is doing the same thing over and over and expecting different results."
—*Benjamin Franklin*

Compensation is not an easy subject—and it is not openly discussed by most health care providers. Any constructive discussion of compensation methods must start with a look at how providers are, have been, and can be compensated, and how much they are compensated. Only then can we approach the question of how to align incentives to reward providers for the behaviors payers and society expect of them.

How do we compensate providers? It largely depends on the role of the provider and his or her employment status. For example, most nurses are employed by hospitals, physicians, health care delivery services, public health departments, or insurance companies. They are paid salaries for this work. To a large extent, this is also true for radiographic technologists, laboratory technologists, cytologists, and a number of other technical workers. Self-employment is more common among nurse practitioners, nurse midwives, nurse anesthetists, occupational therapists, physical therapists, speech therapists, opticians, audiologists, and others, but even among these professions, most of those who are independent of hospital facilities are still employed by the owners of the freestanding facilities in which they work.

The trend to self-employment is much stronger in physicians, only a few of whom work for a salary in the same sense as clerical workers do. Physicians on salary often receive a significant portion of compensation in the form of bonuses. I worked in a large medical group in which physicians were paid a salary, but the salary was adjusted annually to reflect "productivity." In essence, these physicians were being paid for productivity; it was just being adjusted annually. At the far end of the scale are dentists and chiropractors, who are rarely found in salaried positions. These are the entrepreneurs of the health care system whose compensation is based on how much work they can bill and collect for, less the overhead costs associated with being in business.

Since most of the cost of the healthcare system is driven by physician activity, I will focus specifically on physician compensation; however, one must remember that many other health care workers are compensated in similar ways, with similar effects on performance and productivity.

Physician payment should be divided into two levels. One level is how money actually reaches the pocket of the individual physician; the second is how money flows into the organization that pays the physician. In the one-physician, independent, entrepreneurial office, the two are the same, so no distinction need be made. The larger the organization in which the physician works, the more disconnected the physician's own compensation may be from the economic benefit of the organization.

The Monthly Paycheck—Salary—"Working Nine to Five"

Some physicians are paid a salary. By salary, I mean a monthly compensation based on a job description and the fulfillment of that job description. In effect, the physicians show up for work and are paid a monthly amount for whatever work they do or do not do during that month. Physicians working for many government programs are paid a salary. Military physicians are paid a salary. Many ER physicians are paid a salary. New physicians joining existing practices are often paid a salary for some initial interval. Many other physicians are paid a salary, but many also are subject to a bonus system that is intended to motivate performance.

If the physician underperforms the job description, for whatever reason, that physician may be fired. In the absence of a bonus program, if the physician outperforms the job description, the compensation is not changed, though it may inspire a salary increase in a subsequent year.

For the most part, salaried physicians, like all other salaried or hourly employees, come to work every day expecting to exert their efforts to do the best job they can. And, by and large, they do. However, the point of this discussion is "How do we provide financial incentives that align the interests of the individual physician with the interests of payers and society?" so we must consider how the existing financial incentives will motivate physician performance.

The salary motivates the salaried employee to show up and do at least enough work to keep from being fired. Or, at the very least, to do those things that can be measured which will result in the supervisor having the impression that the job requirements are being met. There is no specific motivation to go above the minimum job requirements. There is no motivation to provide quality or quantity above what is required in the job description. As rapidly as healthcare changes, it would be impossible to include in a contract specific language about innovations.

I recall an interaction I had with another physician while I was in the Army several decades ago. I was assigned to a small, remote post; there were only two physicians on post. When one of us went on vacation, we requested that a physician be sent from the much larger post about 100 miles away to fill in for the vacation period. On one occasion, this particular physician was sent to fill in for me while I was on leave. I later suffered from reprisals from him, which I did not understand. I learned from another colleague that this physician had sworn (for personal reasons) that he would not render direct care to any patient during his tour of duty after being drafted into the Army. My vacation, and his brief tour as my replacement, had required him to render medical care to patients, and had broken his, until then, perfect track record of almost two years without having taken care of a single patient—while drawing full pay as a physician.

I think this is not what we want as a motivational structure for our physicians. Recognizing that most physicians are not likely to behave as the one I encountered in the Army, we still need to choose a compensation structure that provides tangible rewards for physicians for something more than just "showing up."

Piecework—Fee for Service

Fee for service is the dominant mode of payment. The physician performs certain services—conducts a face-to-face office visit, removes a skin lump, performs major surgery, interprets an X-ray —and the practice bills for this service. There are tens of thousands of code numbers for services provided by physicians so the service can be characterized in a computer and paid correctly by the claims payment system of a fiscal intermediary. The history of medicine is the history of fee for service compensation. We have paid the physician for his or her time and/or the skill and knowledge necessary to attend to the ailment of the patient. In a sickness-oriented treatment system, this makes a lot of sense.

Fifty years ago, fees were generally set between physicians and their patients. The physician announced a charge for a service; the patient paid, bartered, negotiated, sought care from another physician, or did not have the service performed at all. The fact that patients paid out of pocket and would walk away from high fees had a significant effect on keeping fees down.

In the interval, as new procedures were developed, they were added at new, higher prices to reflect their novelty and the high degree of skill or training needed to do them. Frequently, these procedures were performed in hospitals and were covered by insurance. As each new procedure became more commonplace, the price was rarely reduced. In this way, the "procedural" aspect of medicine became progressively more and more expensive, while the "cognitive" side of medicine (office visits, making diagnoses, and prescribing treatment) remained relatively inexpensive. As physicians specialized, some specialties led to large concentrations of procedural services, and others led to a predominance of cognitive services. Physician compensation became skewed along this spectrum as well.

In the late 1970s and early 1980s, there was a movement to do something to equalize the earning potential between "cognitive" and "procedural" specialties. A major work was performed to create the Resource Based Relative Value Scale. The RBRVS creators worked to set a total value for every procedure code based on three components—how much overhead is associated with the service, how much malpractice risk is associated with the service, and how much time and effort is required to perform the service (with some modification for the length of training required). Each component was assigned a unit value (relative value units or RVU). This created a way of comparing the amount of work required to perform different services across the entire spectrum of medicine. Medicare adopted it with the intent of moving gradually to a completely level compensation system.

Conceptually, the goal was that a primary care physician spending a full day in the office should be able to produce about the same amount of billings (fees for services) as a surgeon spending the same day in the operating room. This goal was never realized, though there was movement in this direction. As a result, Medicare has taken a piecemeal approach to some specialties and some surgical procedures. Cataract surgery, as an example, is much less expensive now than it was fifteen or twenty years ago.

Roger Howe

How Piecework Looks to the Boss

After looking at how the medical group gets paid, one must consider how the individual physicians are paid. Some physicians are paid on production. Production may be measured by dollars charged in relationship to services performed; it may be measured in dollars received in relationship to the work of the physician; it may be measured in relative value units. The medium of measurement is of some importance.

If the measurement is by dollars charged, then the easiest way to increase production is to increase prices, or to provide a mix of services with a higher price per unit of time. As we have noted, this is precisely what has been driving physicians into high profile, interventional specialties. However, even within a small or single-specialty group, production measured in dollars charged takes no recognition of differences in payment schedules between payers, or of charges for services that are not compensated by any insurance carrier, or which may not be collectable from the patient.

If measurement is by dollars received, rather than dollars billed, the accounting may be somewhat more complicated, but there is accommodation for capitation payments (which represent a fixed income regardless of services performed) and some adjustment for payer (so there will be no compensation for charity care provided). However, the motivation is still toward charging as much as possible, doing as much as possible, and doing more of the high-price-per-minute things and fewer of the lower-price-per-minute things.

If measurement is by relative value units (from the RBRVS), this tends to even out some of the bumps. Payment is not received by relative value unit, so the disconnect between what the doctor says he did and what the practice is paid still exists. However, the option of increasing prices across the board no longer increases production, since the same service has the same number of relative value units regardless of how much we charge for it. It can also even out geographic differences, since the relative value units are assigned to services on a national basis. (Medicare adjusts them by regional modifiers to reflect differences in cost of living and cost of doing business.) There is also some leveling between specialties, since the Resource Based Relative Value Scale uses relative value units which are supposed to be based on the time, effort, and training actually required to do the work, not on traditional price—which should mean that a surgeon earns the same number of relative value units per hour whether he is in the office seeing patients or in the operating room performing surgery.

One of the advantages of payment for production is that it emphasizes the work that the physician does. The focus is on the individual physician. However, it ignores many side issues, such as overhead. One of the principal disadvantages is that it focuses entirely on how many services the doctor did—so it continues the process of rewarding the doctor for rendering services (whether needed or appropriate or not)—which is not always in the best interest of the payer, the medical group, or the patient.

Piecework Variant—Pay for Profit-Margin

Think of the solo physician. His personal income is whatever the income of the practice is, less what it costs him to run the practice. This is margin. This principal can be used in larger practices, although the allocation of overhead becomes progressively more difficult the more complex the group structure. Basically, one is able to calculate how much gross income resulted from each physician's efforts; one allocates the overhead to physicians based on some formula that allocates all overhead somewhere, and whatever is left over belongs to that physician.

The allocation of overhead is the key problem. The salary of the nurse who works exclusively with one physician is easy. The cost of renting the waiting room is not so easy, as it is not used by just one physician. The salary of the janitor is even more difficult. Some allocation method must be chosen, and any number of methods will work if all participants agree to a particular method.

The advantage of this method from a managerial point of view is that it keeps the physicians focused on both sides of the business—the income and the expenses. This makes it easier for the manager to keep the business afloat. It does not overcome the disadvantage of the pay for production scheme from the point of view of the payer, although it does sharpen the perception of the physician about which services to render. Instead of rendering services that produce billings (or relative value units), the physician will now render services that produce operating margin. While this is better for the practice organization, I do not suspect that it substantially improves the lot of the payer or the patient.

A Comment

Why is all of this so interesting? Because people will tend to do what you pay them for. If you pay better for doing surgery than for doing office visits, you will tend to push physicians to specialize in areas with surgical services rather than office visits, and you will influence surgeons to do surgery rather than to see and care for people in the office setting. How does this work? If you have aptitude and interest in both areas, and one specialty promises an average pay of $400,000 per year while another promises an average pay of $150,000 per year, which would you choose? And if you have once chosen that $400,000 a year specialty, and the lifestyle to go with it, when the cash flow for the month is lagging, you will be aware that if you can only do a few more surgical procedures this month, you can pick it back up again. No one should be surprised to find out that we get more of what we pay more for.

This particular weakness is inherent both in fee-for-service payment and in the way the compensation system is arranged. If we even out the compensation between procedural and non-procedural specialties, we will have people pursuing careers in those specialties more in proportion to need (or personal inclination) and less in proportion to compensation expectation. Also, if we even out the compensation between procedural and non-procedural services, we will remove the added incentive to do more surgery, as opposed to just increasing the count or RVU number. On the other hand, no matter how hard we manipulate the relationship among the codes, fee-for-service will always motivate physicians (and others paid in this way) to provide more services.

I pay my barber a fee for service—a certain amount for a haircut. If my barber wants to make more money, and the price for haircuts is pretty much set, he can make more money by doing more haircuts—either by working more efficiently so that he can do more in the same length of time, or by working longer hours. He could increase his business by offering beard trim or neck shave for an extra charge. If I had insurance for haircuts, he might be able to increase his business by convincing me I needed to have my hair cut every week; if I pay out of my own pocket, I may not be willing to pay for a haircut every week and may wish to postpone my next haircut until four or six weeks. The principle is the same in medicine, except that essentially everything is covered by insurance, so the customer is not the impediment to providing more services.

If we had good evidence that increasing the volume of services rendered, without paying attention to which services are being rendered, actually produced a healthier society, we would have good reason to want to pay more for more services. However, there is excellent evidence, discussed in many places throughout this book, that just doing more services is not helpful—in fact, it is probably harmful.

Retainer—"Prepaid Medical Care"—Capitation

Capitation refers to a compensation method whereby a medical group or healthcare delivery system is paid based on how many patients have chosen to seek medical care in that group or system. The recipient of the capitation payment accepts responsibility to care for all of a defined range of needs of all of the patients for whom capitation is paid, and to do so for the fixed amount of the capitation payment. It does not matter if the patient requires no services, or a lot of services during the month, the monthly payment remains the same.

Capitation is perhaps most easily understood at the level of the fiscal intermediary—the medical plan. The medical plan receives payments from its members or subscribers as a fixed monthly payment—in an amount determined in advance (usually a year at a time)—called the "premium." In essence, the medical plan agrees to provide (pay for) whatever health care services may be needed for this fixed monthly payment. This is exactly the circumstance of "Utopia Medical Plan" (see Chapter 6).

Some months, the member (family, if the premium is for family coverage) may receive no medical care. Other months, the member may have significant medical needs. The expectation of the medical plan is that, at the end of the year, the average member will have used services that cost the plan less than the amount of premium paid—by an amount that is sufficient to pay for the overhead of operating the plan, plus something left over. Some members will use up far more resources than they paid in; others will use less. It is not what happens in any individual circumstance that is important; it is what happens in the aggregate. In a sense, then, the health plan's job is to take medical expenses out of the realm of the individual and place them into the realm of the population—and to charge enough per person to be able to cover the whole population for the year.

This position in the payment chain should motivate the medical plan to do several things:

• Keep people healthy—provide preventive services that cost less than the treatment that will be avoided within the period during which the contract is likely to be in effect for the individual covered. There are two problems worth noting here: determining which preventive services meet the criterion of saving money in the long (or short) run, and determining how long any individual enrollee will stay with the same health plan. Clearly, if it takes five years for a certain preventive service to pay off, and I have a 90% confidence that the enrollee will no longer be with my plan in five years, it makes no business sense for me to pay for the preventive service.

- Provide services promptly in any case where a delay will increase costs.

- Provide all of the services needed for any particular situation where there is evidence that providing less will increase costs in the long run.

- Provide no extra or unnecessary services, since these increase the cost without providing added benefit or long-term cost reduction.

- Keep healthy people as happy as possible so they will stay enrolled longer and contribute for more years at a level higher than what they require in care.

- Select enrollees, both new and re-enrolling members, carefully to avoid enrolling a predominance of those whose costs are higher than their premium.

- Raise premiums in anticipation of increasing costs; if unsuccessful at this, raise premiums steeply to compensate for losses.

If we carry this to the health care provider, we get a somewhat different picture, but one that clearly flows in parallel.

If the provider organization is large enough and includes a hospital, it may receive "global capitation"—which would include the expectation that the provider organization would provide all health care services to the identified population for the amount of the capitation payment (no longer called a premium, since that term is exclusive to the medical plan). Some services may be "carved out," meaning that the organization is not expected to provide them under the capitation payment. Carved out services might include prescription pharmacy, or services provided out of the geographic area when the member is traveling, or some services the medical plan may be able to provide more economically than the provider organization (such as mental health services) or some services the provider organization might not be able to provide at all (such as organ transplants).

The organization that includes primary care physicians, specialist physicians, and at least one hospital has to resolve the internal problem of how the different providers in its organization are to be paid. The fact that members identify primary care physicians as "this is my primary care physician" drives the capitation process and drives value for primary care physicians. The degree of financial integration of the primary care and specialist physicians has an effect on individual physician compensation techniques.

Hospitals are another matter. In theory, if there is a single hospital associated with a global capitation contract, the hospital can be allocated a capitation payment. There are complications that arise if the hospital and the physicians are not part of the same economic unit. Physicians drive hospital costs through their utilization patterns; when hospitals and physicians are in different economic units, physicians are quite capable of driving expensive care out of the professional component (physician compensation) into the institutional component (hospital compensation) by admitting patients to the hospital for care they might have received in the clinic. Gain sharing programs between the hospital and the physicians were initially quite effective in motivating physicians not to do this. Later, rising hospital charges often drove the gain sharing pool to zero. Federal laws have pushed the gain sharing programs into the realm of being illegal, or possibly illegal, depending on how they are structured, who structures them, and what the relationships among the parties are. I will return to some of these issues presently.

Unified provider organizations including both a hospital and a large medical group are not the norm. It is more common for capitation contracts with large, multi-specialty medical groups to be for the professional component (physician services only). The medical plan is left to make a contract with the hospital. In this situation, the medical group's responsibilities do not include inpatient hospital care—and perhaps other services will be carved out of the professional component to be covered by the medical plan. The medical group can maximize the financial return on this payment method by pushing as much care as possible into payment areas for which it is not responsible (such as the hospital).

Perhaps the best way to illustrate this is to take capitation down to the least expansive level—primary care capitation. In this case, the primary care medical group would be bound by a contract to provide a defined "basket" of services for the monthly capitation payment. One problem is that different primary care physicians provide different baskets of services. One group may be able to provide flexible sigmoidoscopies, another may handle a lot of dermatologic problems, and still another may provide obstetric services, including management of labor and delivery. It is difficult to account for these differences in deciding on a fair capitation payment. This may result in some services being "carved out" of the capitation payment and being paid on a fee-for-service basis. Let us presume we have arrived at a fair capitation rate.

The key issue is what happens at the service margin. Let us say that I am a primary care physician with a mixed patient population—about half of my patients pay me on a fee-for-service basis (or their medical plans do) and about half pay me on a capitation basis. It is Friday evening at 5:00 and two patients have called in, each believing she needs an urgent visit. One is among the capitated, and the other is not. I have a dinner appointment—my wife will kill me if I am late—and so I have time for only one of the two patients. If I see the capitated patient, I receive no extra compensation, since I have already been paid for this month's care; if I send this patient to the ER, it costs me nothing because I am not financially responsible for ER care. If I see the other patient, I get paid a fee, which I lose if I send the patient to the ER. If I am paying attention to the financial consequences of my decisions, I will send the capitated patient to the ER and see the fee-for-service patient.

Consider that it is 9:00 a.m. on that same day, and I have a fully booked day. (It already looks as though I may be late for the dinner party without adding a single additional patient.) One of my capitated patients calls the office with gastric distress. We make an appointment with a local gastroenterologist (the plan pays him fee-for-service) who fits the patient in the same day. What has it cost me? Nothing. And I still may make it to dinner on time.

Both of these examples demonstrate the reason why primary care capitation has been a failure. Unless the primary care physician is in some way responsible for the whole health care dollar, the primary care physician has the ability to shift care to some other venue at no cost to himself, but at potentially high cost to the health plan. After all, the medical plan was counting on the primary care physician being available to both the late Friday patient and the patient with gastric distress. The medical plan probably thought the primary care physician had a 95% chance of making the correct diagnosis and rendering the correct treatment without help from a specialist. The medical plan has already paid the primary care physician for the care. Now, the medical plan is going to pay, on the one hand the ER and on the other the gastroenterologist, for doing work it thought it had already paid the primary care physician to do. There is not enough margin in health plans for this to go on for very long.

Preventive services are also an issue for a primary care physician. In much the same way the medical plan has a business interest in paying only for preventive services that reduce the plan's costs, so does the physician or medical group paid on a capitation basis. Many preventive services cost money but produce no reduction in medical costs over a several-year time span. Almost all preventive services rendered by primary care physicians eventually save costs that are billed by someone else (a specialist or a hospital)—so the investment by the primary care physician has no hope of a financial return. The fact that physicians frequently do not behave in ways that reflect their own self-interest is a credit to the profession—but if our point is to reward physicians for behaving in ways that support the needs of patients and payers, then we need to pay attention to this disparity.

So, from this we can learn that when an individual primary care physician receives capitation for his patients, his motivations (if he is seeking maximum financial reward) will be:

- To please the patients so they continue to choose him as their primary care provider.

- To provide as little direct care as he can manage.

- To refer the patient to specialists for as much care as possible.

- To do only those preventive services for which there is an obvious short-term return on investment to the primary care physician, either in money, or in "points" with the health plan, or in patient satisfaction (retention).

- To persuade the medical plan to pay extra, on a fee-for-service basis, for anything it really wants him to do.

Needless to say, this is not a recipe for a successful alignment of the interests of the primary care physician and the medical plan —or the patient, for that matter.

If we extend this to the larger medical group, paid on capitation for some portion of health care expenses, but "carved out" of others, much the same logic applies. There is a financial advantage to shifting the care anywhere so long as the care is provided well enough that the patient is satisfied and the medical group does not bear financial responsibility. The goal is to provide (or pay for) the least possible amount of care without incurring larger downstream costs.

Combinations and Bonuses

As I have already hinted, it is possible for a group to be paid both fee-for-service and capitation on the same patients under the same contract (example: when a primary care physician performs services that are "carved out" of the capitation contract, for which a fee-for-service reimbursement is expected). Combination compensation for the medical group can be arranged in a number of other ways as well, some of which are measurable as being related to head counts (capitation), others related to services rendered (fee-for-service), and still others related to performance on some other scale not directly related to either ("pay for performance"). A variety of such arrangements exist in the marketplace at this time. Some possibilities:

- The medical group is paid on a capitation basis for essentially all services they render, but on a fee-for-service basis for some services.

- The medical group is paid fee-for-service for most of what they do, but is paid capitation for an agreed set of management services.

- The medical group is paid fee-for-service for patient care services but is paid a bonus for achieving certain objectives related to quality and/or cost of care (a bonus based on capitation).

- The medical group is paid on a capitation basis to include defined services to patients but is paid an additional capitation "bonus" for achieving certain objectives related to quality of care.

The Dilemma

The problem with all of these is that one physician, in relation to one patient, makes each individual care management decision. If the compensation system is going to impact that decision-making process, it will have to impact the individual physician in a way that affects that physician's data processing and decision-making faculties. Go back to the list of considerations for the health plan. Think about what the patient wants and needs. ("Deserves" is perhaps too judgmental a word for this context. What I am advancing is a balance that includes what the patient desires in the way of care with what the science of medicine indicates will be found to be effective in that patient for prevention, diagnosis, or treatment.) How do we influence the individual physician toward compliance?

Physicians want to do a good job. Most physicians truly care about the people they minister to; they want good results. They want cost-effective results, but cost-effectiveness is secondary to clinical improvement. They want to provide timely service and to have happy, satisfied patients. They are often as frustrated as anyone else by their inability to deliver all of this—and they are as trapped in the system as the patients are. If we could only educate physicians in how to do a better job. If we could only teach them, lead them, to greater effectiveness. It would seem their innate drive to improvement would get us the improvement we seek.

The problem is that we have been doing this for years, for decades, and it has not worked. We know of multiple interventions that can be shown to be effective (forget the cost issue for the moment), and only half of the people who should receive those interventions actually get them. For example, there are three keys to the treatment of patients hospitalized with community-acquired pneumonia. They are crucial to a good outcome: a blood culture taken before any antibiotics are given, the choice of an appropriate antibiotic, and administration of the first dose of that antibiotic within two hours of the patient's presentation to the emergency room. We have known these things for decades; the scientific evidence has been incontrovertible for over a decade. Each of the three elements is accomplished in fewer than 75% of all patients presenting nationwide; only 25% receive all three elements. There are no cost controls here. There is only good medical practice. And only 25% of the affected population receives the care we know we should be providing every time. Clearly, something more is needed.

Combination Pay for Individual Physicians

What appears to be needed is a way of rewarding individual physicians for doing what patients, society, and the payers want to have done. It is clearly not enough to educate physicians as to what they should be doing—the information just above certainly demonstrates that. It is also not enough to reward the groups for which they work for doing a good job. If the individual physician does not feel the joy of the reward or the pain of not achieving the reward, the system will not be effective.

This is the basis on which a new breed of pay-for-performance programs is based.[1] What are the parameters available to use? The underlying payment method is of little importance, though it would seem that it ought to be chosen with deliberation to provide baseline motivation in the desired direction. Overall, this probably means providing a base compensation related in some way to production, because, after all else is said, we really do want to motivate physicians to take care of patients.

Then we need to add a significant layer of additional compensation based on the other behaviors we desire. Here are several examples:

- Maintaining the profitability of the practice organization.

- Making efforts to control the overall cost of care—to do the necessary things in a prompt and orderly way, and to avoid doing extra things.

- Prescribing generic medications where appropriate generic medications are available.

- Providing defined preventive services to defined sub-populations.

- Following prescribed care pathways (or having a good reason for not following them).

- Reducing complications (including deaths) from surgery or other high-risk procedures.

- Reducing rate of hospital utilization and the length of hospital stays.

- Improving patient access to the office visit—same day visits, shorter waiting times in the office.

- Improving patient satisfaction scores.

- Improving patient health self-assessment scores.

Adverse Incentives

There is a flip side to rewarding performance that has to do with the extent to which physicians can make a profit from the things they recommend to patients. Physician ownership of laboratories, hospitals, imaging units, surgicenters, pharmacies, and therapy centers creates conflicts of interest between what is best for the physician economically (more utilization leading to more profit) and what may be best for the patient or society (the optimum balance between good outcomes and lower costs). To the extent that these relationships drive utilization past the optimum benefit, they are counterproductive as regards societal goals. To the extent that these ownerships provide more financial reward than the pay-for-performance bonus, they will exert a more powerful influence on physician behavior.

I have already commented on two issues in this regard. One is the adverse effect that such financial rewards may have on physicians' ethical behavior. (To what extent do you believe your physician would be able to recommend against a treatment from which she would stand to gain a profit 10 or 20 times what you—and your third-party payer—are paying as a fee for the office visit?) The other is the issue of how we really think physicians should make a living. I do not begrudge anyone the ability to make a killing on the stock market or in real estate, but do we really want our caregivers making a living off the profit they reap from the things they recommend to us for the diagnosis and treatment of our illnesses? I think the answer is pretty obviously "no." I assure you, though, it is not obvious to many physicians who consider themselves to be very ethical.

Physician Income

Physicians complain about their eroding incomes and not being able to make a decent living. They complain that managed care companies ask them to see too many patients in a day and force them to provide superficial and impersonal care. They complain they spend so many hours practicing that they have no time to keep up with the literature. They tell us Medicare pays them so poorly they cannot make a living on Medicare fees.

I do not intend to portray the life of a physician as without challenges or problems. Far from it. But much of the complaining sounds like excuse-making to me. Physicians are under a lot of pressure, but much of that pressure is self-generated. At some point, the medical profession must take responsibility for its own contribution to the sorry state of affairs of the health care system in our country. Not that the medical profession is solely responsible—all Americans have contributed to the problem, some more than physicians. The problem is that the medical profession seems only too willing to play victim and too unwilling to accept any responsibility. For the moment, however, all I want to do is take a look at physician incomes.

What I intend to do is hold up the objective standard—let us look at what physicians say they are making. Then let us make some judgments about whether that is a decent living or not. Figure 1 on page 183 is based on a 2004 survey of physicians conducted by Medical Economics annually to look at physician income.[2] In this survey, they mailed questionnaires to 54,725 physicians and received 11,094 responses, of which 8,159 were usable and form the basis for the numbers quoted below. Many questions can be raised about the absolute accuracy of these numbers, but it would be reasonable to presume they are not off by more than 10%.

PHYSICIAN INCOME

Cardiologists (invasive)	$400,000
Neurosurgeons	$396,000
Orthopedic surgeons	$367,600
Thoracic surgeons	$325,000
Cardiologists (noninvasive)	$300,000
Gastroenterologists	$300,000
Urologists	$300,000
Plastic surgeons	$292,000
Dermatologists	$266,000
Ophthalmologists	$250,000
Pulmonologists	$240,000
General surgeons	$235,000
Nephrologists	$230,000
Allergists/Immunologists	$217,000
Obstetrician/gynecologists	$208,000
Rheumatologists	$197,000
All respondents	$180,000
Infectious disease	$160,000
Psychiatrists	$160,000
Endocrinologists	$150,000
Internists	$150,000
Family Physicians	$149,300
Pediatricians	$140,000
General Practitioners	$120,000

Figure 1: Medical Practitioners' Salaries

There are several observations to be made.

- First, several key high-paid specialties are not represented: cardiac surgery, transplant surgery, anesthesiology, and medical oncology. All four of these would add to the top tier of this array.

- Second, the four at the bottom of this array are the primary care physicians—general internists, family physicians, pediatricians, and general practitioners. If we really want to have more of these specialists, we must be prepared to pay them more on par with the surgical subspecialists.

- Third, none of the physicians represented in this survey are destitute. Even the lowest on the ladder is making a multiple of the average household income in the United States.

- Fourth, none of these incomes compares favorably to the minimum salary that must be paid to a professional football player in the NFL, or to the average salary paid to a professional baseball or basketball player. To understand the impact of this comparison, imagine you are a hard-working family physician. Counting all of your professional activities (keeping office hours, maintaining medical records, returning telephone calls, attending meetings at the local hospital, attending patients in the hospital, reading journals to keep up), you work about 80 hours a week. You are making about $150,000 a year. You realize one day, as you watch television on Sunday afternoon, that there are no players sitting on the bench of your favorite professional football team who are making less than four times what you make. You may or may not have the physique to be a football player. When you were in college, you chose to dedicate yourself to learning and continuing in school rather than playing a sport. Would you not wonder if you had made the right choice?

In our society, we make judgments about personal worth based on income. We do this in a very public way—the contracts of professional athletes are openly commented on and evaluated in the sports sections of every newspaper in the country; the income from a new movie tells everything about how good it is; professional golfers and tennis players are ranked according to their income for the year. All of these numbers are readily available. All of these deliver messages to the rest of us that we are not as good as these athletes, not as good as the actors and actresses in the movies.

There is comment among the "downtrodden" (the less well compensated) about the "obscene" salaries of the CEOs of the nation's largest corporations. Physicians are not immune from this bias toward looking at compensation as a stand-in for personal value, competency, and success. Is it any wonder, then, that there is a relative lack of interest in the specialties at the lower end of the list and a lot of interest in the specialties at the top of the list?

I must stop at this point and apologize—because I have spent a lot of pages writing like a financier and a businessman, not like a physician. Physicians generally want to do what is right, and will continue to do what is right no matter how they are paid, no matter how large or small their annual take-home paycheck. On the other hand, physicians will also be influenced by the biases of society. While some physicians choose low-paying specialties out of a true desire to practice in that clinical arena, or out of an idealistic representation of what it means to be a physician, not all do so. And while most physicians may work to do what is clinically and ethically correct every day and with every patient they see, every physician will also have chosen a specialty fully realizing what the potential income for a practitioner of that specialty would be—and the lack of interest in lower paying specialties reflects that knowledge. You will always tend to get more of what you pay for and less of what you do not pay for.

What is more alarming to me is the attitude among members of some of the more highly compensated specialties that the primary care physicians are not necessary. One wonders if this could be a reaction to having made the specialty choice they made. Some specialists feel they could be primary care physicians quite well enough for their patients. The problem with this thinking is that it takes both training and experience to be a competent specialist; if that specialist starts to spend most of his or her time being a generalist, then what happens to that infrequently exercised expertise?

Further, specialists are trained with special knowledge of a single organ system or a narrow range of treatment techniques—this is what distinguishes the specialty. There is a human tendency to interpret sensory input in the context of one's knowledge and expertise. Thus, a cardiologist will tend to understand a particular set of symptoms as being of cardiac origin, while a gastroenterologist will interpret the same set of symptoms as being of esophageal origin. Sometimes it takes a generalist to sort out what is happening with the patient in a way that is unbiased by a specific expertise, to understand that the problem is neither, but is related to inflammation or irritation of rib cartilages, and that the patient needs neither a cardiac nor a gastrointestinal workup to understand what is going on.

I think most people find their way to the right specialist, although the assistance of a good generalist may make that trip unnecessary, or may make it more efficient. What is more important about a generalist is having a personal physician who is an advocate for the patient within the medical system. I discuss this in greater detail in Chapter 23.

Suffice it to say that my bias is that we need MORE primary care physicians, not fewer. We probably need fewer of a number of specialists rather than more.[3] In general, we need physicians in training to choose specialties based on what we need, not on what will produce the best income—and the only way I know to do that is to make the income much less variable from specialty to specialty.

What about Hospitals?

Hospitals, too, can be paid in various ways.

Capitation: Hospitals are rarely capitated outside of very tight arrangements with a multi-specialty physician group and a payment resource. Kaiser-Permanente receives money on a capitated basis as premium payments from businesses and members. Kaiser-Permanente owns and operates hospitals and medical clinics, and has an exclusive provider relationship with the Permanente Medical Group for professional services. At least this is how it works in the more concentrated foci of Kaiser-Permanente in the western states. It is not clear from the outside how money is allocated within the Kaiser system, so it is difficult to comment at a level of finer granularity than their annual report, which discloses little detail.

Quasi-Capitation: When hospitals and medical groups are jointly paid on capitation, the actual division of the funds has often proved to be problematic. Among other things, physicians are the drivers of the cost vehicle in the hospital. The hospital's total cost of providing care for any particular population of patients will depend on the frequency with which the physicians admit patients to the hospital, with what intensity of care, and how long they keep the patients in the hospital. The hospital administration has a great deal of control over how expensive any particular intervention may be (within some constraints, like the need for personnel who have defined costs associated with them), but they do not control how often that intervention is applied.

This is akin to the situation where the hospital gets to choose which car the doctor drives, but the doctor chooses how many miles to drive the car. The hospital may choose a more or a less efficient car—that will affect the overall operating expenses for the car. However, the physician choosing how far to drive the car is the one who really determines what the operating cost will be. A person who drives a very inefficient vehicle six miles a day will produce lower overall operating costs than a person who drives a very efficient one 500 miles a day.

If I am a hospital administrator and I am party to a capitated contract with a group of physicians for the care of a particular population, I will want to have some lever to encourage the physicians to keep utilization down—to drive fewer miles a day. I may or may not be able to do anything about reducing the operating costs of the hospital from being high-cost-per-service to being low-cost-per-service, but if I cannot influence the physicians to reduce the number, intensity, and/or duration of hospital stays, I cannot bring costs under control. What will I do? I will want to have a pot of money set aside to reward reduced utilization. I don't want to get involved in judgments about individual physicians (general surgeons will admit more patients to the hospital than dermatologists will, no matter how efficient either is at his specialty), so the reward will be paid to the physician group based on total admissions/bed days/ costs of care for the capitated population.

Measuring by either admissions or bed days will make sense only if some standard allocation of resources is associated with every admission or every bed day. In general, the costs that can be ascribed in this manner are small compared to the more variable costs associated with what type of disease the patient has or what intervention is planned. Therefore, the key feature to follow is the cost of care. And how better to track the cost of care than to look at what the hospital would have billed a third-party payer for that care? So we pay the hospital out of the pool of funds available to cover hospital care, based on some formula relating to billings; what is left at the end of the year can be split between the hospital and the physicians.

The problem with this allocation methodology is that the hospital is not being paid on capitation at all. The hospital is being paid on fee-for-service. And the more services that are rendered, the more the hospital is paid up to the point where the pool of available funds is exhausted. The quickest way to increase income is to increase the charge per service, especially if the draw from the pool is based on some percentage of the rendered charges. Further, although the hospital is insulated from any decisions the physicians may make that would cost the hospital more money, the actual result is that the hospital's maximal financial return is from rendering more services rather than fewer, or charging higher prices. This is exactly the opposite of the intended motivation of the capitation payment, and is the opposite of the motivation provided to the capitated physicians. Clearly, a payment strategy that provides partners with opposite motivations will not work very well.

Per Diem: Sometimes, hospitals are paid on a per diem basis. This payment provides a fixed payment for each day a member spends in the hospital. There may be different payments for hospitalization on different units in the hospital; some services may be "carved out" of the per diem payment. For instance, there could be a higher payment for days spent in the ICU, or an extra payment for surgical implants (such as artificial joints).

A per diem payment rewards the hospital best for the least intense hospital days. So it will be to the financial advantage of the hospital to maximize the length of stay and to minimize the number of services performed per day. For example, if a patient hospitalized with chest pain cannot have a stress test until at least a day after admission, and it takes an additional day to get that same patient to the cardiac cath lab, the hospital will be paid for three days; if the patient can be admitted, have the stress test 12 hours later and go directly to the cath lab if needed, the whole process could be done in a day. There is no practical medical benefit in waiting; there is only a benefit to the hospital for having enough "red tape" to make the process take just a bit longer.

For an acutely ill person admitted to the hospital, the first few days are frequently the most intense in resource utilization. It is likely that the hospital being paid on a per diem basis will lose money on the first day or two of such a confinement. As the patient improves, less and less needs to be done to make a diagnosis and render treatment, so the resource consumption goes down, but the payment remains the same, so the hospital begins making a positive net margin on the care being provided. Clearly, the financial reward to the hospital is to extend the hospital stay. This is in the best interest of neither the patient nor the third-party payer. If the physicians are paid on capitation, it also puts the financial interests of the physicians at odds with the financial interests of the hospital.

Diagnosis Related Groups (DRGs): Virtually all hospitals are paid based on DRGs for Medicare admissions, and it is a common payment technique negotiated by commercial payers as well. The goal of this payment method is to put the hospital at risk regarding the efficiency of its own processes and the efficiency of its medical staff.

Basically, the process works like this: Every patient admitted is classified into a DRG based on the reason for admission and what surgical procedure was done (if any). The DRG will class patients with similar illnesses with similar acuity into the same group. There will certainly be some variation in cost from one patient in a particular DRG to another. The idea behind the DRG system is that it will overcompensate for some stays and under-compensate for others. The system should work out overall.

Anything the hospital does that reduces the length of stay, reduces the resource consumption, or reduces the cost of providing those resources will result in a better net return from the DRG system. In contrast to the per diem payment, if the hospital expends resources in the first day that allow the patient to be discharged on the second hospital day, the DRG payment is the same as if the hospital expends those resources over three days and the patient goes home on the fourth hospital day—except in the first instance the hospital has only had the patient in the bed for two days, which reduces the cost of the stay; further, the hospital is able to have another patient in the same bed for the next two days and earn another DRG payment!

Fee For Service: Fee-for-service payment for hospitals (often referred to as "percent off of charge master") is much the same as fee-for-service payment for physicians. The more identifiable goods and services the hospital delivers to the patient, the more it is paid. This encourages itemization of the smallest services ($10 for two aspirin tablets) and encourages raising fees. Hospitals are generally happy to negotiate with payers for less than 100% of billed charges. Their expenses are generally a fraction of what they bill. If the hospital's break-even point is 25% of billed charges, a reduction of 15-20% off of billed charges may reduce the profit margin a bit but does not threaten economic viability. The hospital would rather be paid less, but paid soon and reliably. Medical carriers are generally very reliable at paying and do so promptly. If the hospital has to bill the patient directly, it can take a long time to be paid (if the hospital gets paid at all), and it costs money to collect.

Hospitals in Review

Fee for service is not a payment system designed to align the hospital with the payer. Either per diem or DRG payments does somewhat better at creating the alignment. Per diem leaves a significant disagreement about length of stay. DRG leaves a disagreement about indications for admission. Capitation would be wonderful from the payer's point of view, but how to accomplish it is a significant issue.

In a typical multi-hospital community, the hospitals will be under different, competing ownership. There will be several medical plans, some associated predominantly with one hospital system, some with another, and some having several hospitals "in network." Generally, an exclusive contract between a payer and a hospital is at a lower rate of payment because it promises a more consistent utilization. However, when the hospital is busy, there is no qualm about turning away patients covered by the exclusive payer. These patients then end up in the "wrong" hospital, at considerable additional expense to the medical plan. Alignment fails completely at this point.

In Summary

Payment systems tend to encourage production of more of any behavior for which there is greater financial reward and to suppress any behavior for which there is no financial reward. We have looked at a number of efforts to create payment systems that result in more of the behavior desirable to the medical plan. In every case, there have been unanticipated results that have mitigated or reversed the benefits obtained. We need to keep working on this problem. If we are to have a successful system, all the parts should be pulling in the same direction. Significant rewards for cost reduction and efficiency are an important aspect of what must be built into the system. We should not reward inadequate care, nor should we reward a system that resists patient needs.

The ideal payment system is yet to be found. It will probably include some motivations for providing services—because we want physicians and hospitals to have a positive motivation to take care of patients. The ideal system should also have motivations for improvements in quality, however we choose to measure quality.[4] And the system should have rewards for efficiency and cost-effectiveness. Such a system may be in the early stages of formation for physicians. The development and implementation of such a compensation program must be a part of our redesigned system.

Chapter 19

Controlling Healthcare Cost

"If you fear making anyone mad, then you ultimately probe for the lowest common denominator of human achievement."
—*Jimmy Carter*

Over the last five chapters, I have discussed some of the drivers of the cost of healthcare in the United States today. I make no claim to exhausting the list of causes, but I think I have produced and discussed enough to make the point that cost control is neither simple nor easy.

One of the concerns of many people is the cost of adding 45 million new people to the insured population. In Chapter 14, I responded to that issue. We will not know what the effect is until we do it, but this, by itself, seems unlikely to end up being a significant issue.

Another concern is the cost trend. In Chapter 15, we looked at a number of possible causes of the cost trend—some desirable, some undesirable, some just facts of life. For some of them, I have already proposed ameliorations. For others, further discussion follows.

In Chapter 16, we looked at "moral hazard," the tendency of people with insurance to use more services than they would use if not insured. I have attempted to clarify the issue and separate the different threads, some of which reflect appropriate utilization, others of which reflect inappropriate utilization and wasted resources.

In Chapter 17, we looked at the patient's view of affordability, and the role of patient participation in the cost of care in efforts to control over-utilization of health care services. Specifically, we considered the roles of co-payments, coinsurance, and deductibles in helping patients understand the true cost of care. We also looked at patient participation in the payment of a premium—which is not so much a utilization-control mechanism as a cost-sharing method. And I promised a discussion of the role that scope-of-coverage limits might play in the affordability equation. That discussion follows.

In Chapter 18, we discussed provider compensation. It is clear that there are many methods of compensating providers. Since rewards predictably drive behavior, we must look carefully at the behaviors we are rewarding within any proposed compensation system to be sure we are likely to get the behaviors we need for a safe, cost-effective health care system.

In this chapter I will bring together threads from the last several chapters in addressing ways to control healthcare cost—an essential issue in assuring that the cost of a universal health care system is affordable to our society.

What Is "Basic Health Care"?

As I mentioned previously, one of the ways to look at affordability is to set priorities for the coverage of health care. Clearly, some medical interventions assume a higher priority than others. Some things we probably do not wish to cover. (How about face lifts?) Other things we may wish to cover at some ages and not at others. (How about a heart transplant in a six-year-old versus in a 95-year-old?) Some interventions are of a nature that, though we may wish to cover them to some extent, we may wish to expect more participation from the recipient than we would expect for other care. (How about infertility treatment?) And some things we will want to cover as a matter of routine. (How about treatment after automobile accidents or immunizations for babies?)

Once we accept that medical interventions (procedures and services intended to prevent, screen for, diagnose, or treat a disease) fall into different categories in terms of the urgency of coverage, we can begin to sort things into priorities. Once we have the spectrum of health and medical care defined, we can figure out how much money we have, and this will help us make the hard decisions about maybe not covering some things. These are tough business decisions —but they are made all the time in the medical plan world.

If I represent a medical plan and I am talking to an employer who tells me medical coverage is a priority but that they can only afford a certain amount in payment for that coverage, then I will have to set priorities and whittle away coverage until I bring the premium to what the employer can afford. If I don't get there, no one in that company gets any coverage at all. If I get there, the coverage they get may not be the best in the world, but it may well be better than no coverage at all.

The same thing must be true in our national health plan. We have to set the coverage baseline at something we, as a society, can afford. If we do a good job of controlling cost trends, maybe we will be able to afford a bit more. If the cost trends get away from us, we will not be able to afford as much. It would be wonderful to be able to afford unrestricted coverage for everything for everyone—and maybe we can. But we had better start off with some well-defined priorities so we don't break the bank before we prove we can do it.

I suggest the following considerations for a basic medical plan:

- It should have carefully described limitations to coverage, as I have implied above.

  * The plan should cover all of the things we all agree are "necessary" components of a decent medical plan—things such as care for accidental injuries, care during pregnancy and childbirth, hospital care for serious illness, coverage of medications to treat acute and chronic illnesses, and many others.

* The plan would exclude from coverage:

    —things people ought to do for themselves (over-the-counter medications, for instance)

    —things that are truly optional (such as cosmetic surgery)

    —treatments that cannot be shown to be effective

    —treatments with very low cost-effectiveness (such as the heart transplant in a 95-year-old)

* The limitations need to be carefully drawn—and I believe this needs to be done with significant public input.

• There should be at least two styles to the plan, based on income and/or assets.

    * The plan for the less affluent would be without co-payments, deductibles, or coinsurance because these would create a barrier to care.

    * The plan for the more affluent might include co-payments, deductibles, and coinsurance increasing on a sliding scale with increasing wealth.

• The premium should be paid through one of several methods:

    * Employer funding for the employed.

    * If the employer opts not to purchase insurance, there would be a tax on the employer, based on payroll, to subsidize coverage for employees.

    * For anyone not covered by an employer, a combination of employer tax, general tax revenue, and recipient participation in the premium—with the recipient's participation based on income and/or assets on a sliding scale.

        —The government might provide this insurance directly.

        —The government might pay premiums to a private carrier, or group recipients to choose and negotiate with a private carrier.

- The program would specify a maximum level of recipient participation allowable under all plans designed to fulfill the basic health plan requirement (as the government has recently done with the definition of a High Deductible Health Plan). Individuals and/or employers could negotiate with health plans for lower participant participation, but at higher premium costs.

- Any insurance policies for services not covered by the basic plan would be subject to competitive offerings from private companies, who could offer any combination of co-payments, coinsurance, and deductibles they thought would entice people to purchase their coverage.

Patient Financial Responsibility

I have discussed the financial responsibilities of patients in some detail in Chapters 16 and 17. Suffice it to note that, in the long run, recipient participation in cost is a two-edged sword. The magnitude of the participation may deter or preclude people who need care from seeking it. However, requiring participation in the cost will help assure that people do not abuse the system by requesting health care providers to take care of things the recipient should have handled.

A system designed to cut across all socioeconomic barriers must both offer access to those who need it and restrict access to those who do not. Anyone who has visited a busy emergency room will understand that the crush of not-so-sick people in the waiting room may actually interfere with the care of people with real emergencies—broken bones, automobile accidents, and gunshot wounds. Not only do the not-so-sick hinder the operation of the emergency room, they are receiving less than optimal care, because the people providing that care are distracted by the real emergencies. Our overall healthcare system must be designed, in a larger way, to discourage the not-so-sick from seeking care in the emergency room, but not to impede those with real emergencies (for additional discussion on this issue, see Chapter 21). This is what a carefully designed system of recipient participation should do.

The Physician

Patient-oriented cost-control efforts work (to whatever extent they work) only when there is choice and when the patient is in control. At best, they may not work very well. They do not work at all when there is a catastrophe and the providers of care are making all the decisions. This happens in emergencies of all kinds, and it happens when the magnitude of the illness clouds the patient's ability to be objective (as frequently happens with a diagnosis of cancer). When these things take place, we must accept that the patient, no matter how educated and informed, will not be in control. There is only one remaining player in the care process who can be held responsible—the provider of care: the physician and/or the hospital.

Provider Responsibility—Utilization Management

When the patient is not playing the role of "informed consumer" and is not value shopping—for whatever reason—then the job of value shopping falls to the provider of services (generally the "attending" physician). Unfortunately, the physician (the same issues apply to hospitals, labs, imaging facilities, physical therapists, dentists, chiropractors, and others) often has a conflict of interest in recommending or administering services to the patient. What that conflict is depends on how the physician is paid. It is difficult for a conflicted physician to provide objective information on the relative value of different treatment choices in which that physician has a financial stake.

In the last thirty years, the payer has stepped into the transaction to exert some degree of influence over how these decisions are made. As has been noted many times, the payer has an economic stake in the medical management decisions—but that stake is at the same time less clear and more complex than the stake of the physician.[1] The interest of the payer is in achieving the most cost-effective outcome. The payer wants the patient to receive all necessary care as promptly as possible so the disease can be controlled or resolved as quickly and efficiently as possible, and with as few long-term consequences as possible. (As I mentioned in Chapter 18, long-term consequences cost the insurer money just as prolonged acute care does). What the payer does not support is additional medical interventions that are not strictly necessary to achieve that result. In this, the payer is frequently at odds with the physician, who would like to do more "things"—whether for personal gain, for personal comfort, for additional assurance on the chosen treatment, or for patient request. The physician, in any of these instances, will accuse the payer of "cutting corners."

Admittedly, these characterizations of physicians and payers are to some extent caricatures of what really happens. There is no doubt in my mind that there are MANY physicians who are dedicated to providing cost-effective care, and on whom there is essentially no effective financial influence to do more "stuff." There have also been payers who have shortsightedly cut corners that should not have been cut in an attempt to reduce cost. Unfortunately, this decreases efficiency and increases costs in the long run.

Another element in this is that providers, especially physicians, are close to patients and are trusted by them. Patients form bonds much more frequently with doctors and even hospitals than they do with "insurance companies." Whether it is appropriate or not, as a society we are much more inclined to trust the judgment of our physician than the judgment of the insurance company's medical director.

How will we resolve our dual roles as corporate payer (as taxpayers) and patient? I suspect we will want to do several things.

One thing we should consider is to limit physicians' ownership in health care enterprises. They should only be able to own enterprises to which they cannot make referrals. Any time a physician has an ownership in a hospital or imaging center, there will be a tendency for that physician to refer patients to that facility. On the one hand, this is reasonable, especially if the physician considers this facility to be the best in his area. On the other hand, to the extent that these referrals are not needed, they drive up utilization and total cost. This is an unnecessary cost driver and needs to be addressed.

Another thing I suspect we will want to do is limit the number of things a physician can "sell" in his/her office for a profit. In many states, it is against the law for a physician or group of physicians to have an ownership share in a pharmacy, yet physicians in those states still purchase medications that they administer to patients in their offices at some markup. In the case of medications of nominal cost with nominal reimbursement, this may not be much of an issue, but where the medications are high in cost and the markup of some fixed percent is a large amount of money, this is problematic. In fact, the Medicare program is currently working to reduce the profitability of this activity in the program.

Ideally, physicians should be paid for applying their talents, knowledge, and skills to the care of their patients. There is enough hazard of overuse here already without adding other distractions. There should be careful evaluation of utilization trends, and careful work with physicians who appear to be overusing their more profitable skills.

Pay For Performance (P4P)

Another wrinkle is emerging in the physician compensation arena—pay for performance. This is another run at holding physicians responsible for their results, but in a new way.[2,3]

Historically, physicians have been paid fee-for-service, but when the patient was the one paying the bill, the physician had to exercise some control when results were not expected to be good. There was, in essence, direct accountability to the patient. With the advent of the third-party payer, this direct accountability went away. The experiment of the late 1980s and 1990s was capitation. When the entire delivery system is capitated (which happens in the Kaiser-

Permanente system in California, for instance), there is accountability for cost, cost-effectiveness, and efficiency.

In most parts of the country it is not possible to consolidate the entire delivery and payment systems as they are in Kaiser-Permanente. An alternative was to capitate physician groups and make other arrangements with hospitals. The physician group would assume risk for the provision of care, but clearly was better off financially if they could keep people healthy (hence they were called Health Maintenance Organizations). Ignoring the subtleties of the system, it cannot be applied everywhere because most physicians are not practicing in the large multi-specialty groups required for this to work. Loosely affiliated physician groups (Independent Practice Associations) do not have the financial discipline to do this job well, and most are dismal failures at anything relating to either cost containment or quality improvement. The American medical scene is sliding back toward considering that fee-for-service is the inviolate norm.

Pay for performance (P4P) programs are intended to modify this. Most are an add-on to fee-for-service payment, though some require a reduction in that payment to fund the P4P program. The idea behind P4P is to identify critical features of high-quality, cost-effective, efficient care, and reward the physicians who deliver those critical features more consistently.[4] The belief is that physicians who do this will provide lower-cost care. There are means available now to permit risk-adjusting even small populations of patients, so comparability between physician practices can be achieved to a reasonable degree of accuracy. Such a system could easily include criteria such as adherence to national standards of practice and the implementation of cost-control measures as reward criteria.[5] We are in the early days of the P4P programs' lives, so we do not yet know how effective they are likely to be.[6,7,8] We will be finding out over the next several years.[9]

Cost Per Unit of Service—Controlling Price and Value Disparities

Another cost driver in the American system is the cost per unit of service[10], which has escalated rapidly, driving the cost of insurance up with it. There are three drivers to cost: new technology, higher cost per unit of service, and more units of service. In a number of ways, we have covered new technology and more units of service, and ways to look at the process of controlling their adverse impact on the overall cost of care. It is time to look at the cost per unit of service.

During the HMO revolution of the late 1980s and early 1990s, one of the changes was to limit the total cost of care by passing the responsibility of allocating the cost of care to the physicians through capitation. Whatever the disadvantages of capitation may be, this had the effect of restraining the escalation of the cost of care. The simultaneous change was competitive contracting with physicians for particular reimbursement rates—physicians would agree to accept a reduction in payment for their services in trade for a presumed volume of business. As time has gone by, such contracting has become the norm, and in many communities, if a physician does not have contracts with several insurance companies, that physician cannot effectively make a living. There have been similar contracts with hospitals.

The evolution of this process has varied from one place to another. There are still places where the insurance companies have the dominant hand, where physicians who wish to stay busy must agree to low prices because that is the going rate in the market. In these communities, physicians try to make up for the low payment per unit of service by increasing volume. In other communities, the providers have had more influence. In some communities, the providers have effectively combined into de-facto monopolies and are requiring larger and larger payments from the payers. The consolidation of the hospital industry has done much the same thing for hospitals, which are now often requiring that health plans pay whatever the hospital is asking if they want the hospital to sign a contract.

On the one hand, it seems unfair for the payers to ask physicians (or hospitals) to take so little money that they cannot make a "good living." There is, of course, the option for physicians to refuse to sign abusive contracts—which may or may not end up with higher compensation systems depending on what their colleagues do, and what their patients demand. I recollect during my practice days that an insurer sold its policy at a good rate to the local county school system at a time when that insurer had no physician in the county willing to participate in the plan. The teachers came to our office, one by one, to ask that we sign up with the plan, and we did. The rates were not bad, so it was not really an economic issue for us at the time. We just preferred not to do business with the company. I think if the fee schedule had been too low, we might have been able to negotiate that issue.

On the other hand, it is not reasonable for a sole provider hospital or hospital chain, or a physician group, to be able to demand exorbitant prices just because they are in essence the only resource for care in that community. Forbidding the accumulation of groups of physicians is not the correct pathway to control this problem. For example, it may be best for the five endocrinologists in a community to be in the same practice. It allows them to share call, which is an advantage to both the physicians and the patients. It allows them to afford the practice infrastructure that makes a difference in quality and safety, such as electronic medical records.

The way out of the conundrum is to have a central price-setting process that applies to everyone. Medicare does this fairly successfully, though the process is subject to political manipulation. If we are to have a successful program outside of the "single-payer" environment, there ought to be a central price-setting process that is not subject so much to direct political control, but is responsive to provider input.

Of course, this raises twin issues. On the one hand, we want good providers to be successful financially. It is not reasonable for the payment system to drive otherwise adequate providers out of business in the name of keeping prices down. At the very least, providers who are so inefficient as to be financially threatened by a reasonable compensation mechanism need to be helped to increase efficiency and learn how to survive financially.

On the other hand, as the payers of the system, we are not interested in paying exorbitant fees to support physicians and hospitals in an opulent lifestyle. The question of what is a "reasonable" living for a physician (see Chapter 18), or what is a "reasonable" operating margin for a hospital, is not an easy one. Further, it becomes almost impossible to fathom how to institute proper price controls when dealing with pharmaceutical and device manufacturers. It will take a significant public discussion to reach a strategic set of statements about how we want to deal with suppliers whose desires for financial well being may be beyond what our society is willing to accord them.

When we discuss quality and safety (Chapter 20), we will further discuss "pay for performance" bonus programs, which are designed to give incentives to physicians (and could be applied to hospitals as well) to produce the desired outcomes. How do we calculate this income into our assessment of what is an appropriate income for the provider in question?

In summary, then, we need to look carefully at the price per unit of service. The goal is to compensate providers adequately but not excessively—and we need good definitions of what the terms "adequately" and "excessively" mean.

Optimizing Care—Case Management, Disease Management and Population Management

A final way of reducing the cost of care is through patient-focused care management. There are many ways to conceptualize this, but the easiest is to think about the advantages of having a knowledgeable, professional guide to help one get optimized care during an illness, whether a chronic or an acute one. Case management is typically related to an acute illness or the acute exacerbation of a chronic illness. Disease management is typically concerned with the management of chronic illness in the absence of anything acute.[11] Population management works to help people deal with lifestyle issues to reduce their risk of developing acute or chronic disease. Case management and disease management help people to manage their own care better. And many times, they help to arrange that management at lower cost than might otherwise happen. Briefly, they work like this:

Case Management: When a person is in the hospital, or has some other acute illness or a need for surgery, a case manager can help the person through the episode and back to recovery more quickly. For instance, the case manager can help arrange for physical therapy before a total joint operation to help speed recovery. Or the case manager can assist patients in receiving in-home care needed for an illness so they do not have to be hospitalized. Often, a little extra work can get people out of the hospital and back home sooner, without placing undue burdens or stress on the family. These may all sound like "shortcuts," but they are not. People heal faster at home than in the hospital and are often happier with the outcome. It is known that the longer the period of disability associated with an illness, the longer the recovery takes, and the less likely (especially in an older person) that the recovery will happen at all.

Disease Management[12]: Many people with chronic diseases do not know how to take care of themselves.[13,14] The problem with a chronic illness is that the majority of the process of taking care of the disease is in the hands of the patient. Often, physicians do not have the time to explain in detail how patients should care for themselves. There may or may not be educational resources in the community, and the patient may or may not be willing to listen and make necessary changes at the time the program is offered. Disease management programs, as now offered in most formal programs, provide a telephone "friend" to discuss the chronic disease with—a friend who knows a lot about the disease and is capable of being a guide and teacher. This friend provides a long-term relationship, so the education can happen over time, as the patient becomes willing to provide more and more self-care, or as the patient is more and more willing to learn.[15]

Both forms of management assistance are designed to help people optimize their current health status and overcome current health barriers. Of course, people who are healthier cost less to care for.[16] Disease management programs have a history of being able to reduce the number of hospital admissions and emergency department visits. At the same time, there may be an increase in the number of physician visits or medication costs. Overall, the cost is less, and the patient does better.[17,18] This is a hard combination to beat.

Population Management: A new approach to helping people stay healthy is emerging. The underlying idea is that if we can help people to understand how their current health and their lifestyles interact to cause health problems in the future, we may be able to help people to make the changes in personal habits that will propel them to a healthier life. This process usually starts with a health risk assessment and builds on what that assessment finds. The goals of the program might be weight loss, dietary change, use of seat belts, smoking cessation, reduction in alcohol consumption or increasing physical exercise—or a combination of these goals. The program then provides counseling or other assistance in helping the person to make the changes identified.

Case management, disease management, and population management are all styles of care supplementation that have not been embraced by the Medicare program. This is an oversight of Medicare that needs to be corrected (and they are running pilots of disease management programs now). They also need to be integral parts of our national health plan.

In Summary

Efforts to control cost will be an important part of any national health insurance plan if the plan is to be affordable to us as a society. The components of cost control will include many, if not all, of the following:

- Formal technology assessment by an unbiased, contracted organization or organizations (more about this in Chapter 22).

- Technology controls to ensure that the utilization of new technologies matches the recommendation of the technology assessment.

- Improved drug-utilization controls to assure that the use of drugs matches their licensure and/or the indications for which there is good evidence for safety and effectiveness.[19]

- Establishment of practice standards with some process of encouraging compliance and/or enforcing adherence.[20]

- A formal process for determining coverage priorities—and limits on the coverage of the "basic plan" to reflect those priorities.

- Careful consideration of strategies to encourage patient assumption of responsibility for care choices to assure that people understand and consider the cost of care in making decisions about their own care.

- Careful consideration of strategies—such as limiting physician ownership in health care processes that produce conflicts of interest—to encourage physicians to be honest in helping patients assess the cost-effectiveness of alternative care strategies.

- Some utilization review or utilization management functions to check on provider performance.

- Pay-for-performance compensation systems for providers.[21]

- Unit-cost controls for physician and other provider fees, as well as hospital charges and acquisition costs for medications and devices.[22,23]

- Patient partnering services to assist patients to self-care and decision making, to include case management, disease management, and population management services.

- Further education and training of physicians in the care of patients with chronic diseases.[24]

Chapter 20

Safe and Effective Care

"Nothing in all the world is more dangerous than sincere ignorance and conscientious stupidity."

—*Martin Luther King Jr.*

In chapter seven, I discussed the crisis of safety and effectiveness of the present healthcare system. Certainly, the system we put in place to support healing and encourage wellness should not, itself, be a ranking cause of death. Something must be done to correct this.[1]

And, indeed, things are being done, which we will come back to. However, I must start this discussion by pointing out that the problem is not entirely at the feet of the health care provider community.

The "Public" Problem

The American medical marketplace is characterized by a lot of confusion between what "I want" and what "I need." This confusion is both a cost and a quality issue in more ways than one. What is necessary is something we can ascertain through scientific investigation and can apply with the artistry of the wise physician, who knows how to follow the rules and when to break them. What the patient desires is often beyond what is needed. We Americans tend to think that more is better.[2,3,4] When "more" is more interaction with the provider system that is one of the ten leading killers of people in this country, that desire may be dangerous. Doing unnecessary tests, for instance, has three consequences:

- There is a cost of doing more in the first place. (Not only is there a loss of quality, but also an increase in monetary cost.)

- There is a cost involved in investigating the results of what did not need to be done in the first place. (This represents a further loss of quality, a further increase in monetary cost, and an increase in risk.)

- There is a cost in caring for the consequences—or complications—of the first two. (This cost represents not only extra monetary expense, but also a quality issue with potentially severe consequences for the patient, up to and including death.)[5]

The cost of doing more in the first place is obvious—if we order extra tests, a CAT scan, or an MRI, this costs money. As fully insured shoppers, it is not our money, so why should we care? But someone does pay, and in the context of universal coverage, that someone will be us, the taxpayers.

The cost of investigating the results is not so obvious, but a few examples will suffice. If you x-ray the backs of normal young people with no back injuries or symptoms, you will find that a significant number of them will have abnormalities noted on the x-ray. These abnormalities are congenital—they are there from birth and last a lifetime. They are NOT causing back pain. But if we take back x-rays on everyone with back pain and find these congenital abnormalities, then it becomes our job to prove they are NOT the cause of pain. (Almost never do we find the cause of back pain on back x-rays.) The consequence of discovering something on the x-ray is more tests, maybe a CT scan or an MRI. More cost, and more chance for something unfortunate to happen.

Similarly, if we run a chemistry panel of twenty tests on everyone for no good reason, we will see a certain number of abnormalities. The way normal values are established, 2.5% of normal people will be above the high end and 2.5% will be below the low end. Which means that, on the average, one of those twenty tests will be out of the range of normal in every perfectly normal person. Now we have abnormal tests we must, somehow, explain—which will require more testing, more cost.

The cost of caring for the consequences and complications is even less obvious. At some level, the "something else" we want will be a surgical procedure, or will be a test that leads to an unnecessary surgical procedure. In the case of back x-rays, it might be that the x-ray results suggest an anatomic defect that could be fixed by surgery. In this case, physicians may suggest that the surgery be done even though the anatomic defect may have nothing to do with the cause of the pain. If the surgery fails to address the real cause of the pain, then it is not only unnecessary, it produces damage to the back. Instead of reducing pain, it increases pain, and at considerable cost.

Every surgical procedure carries with it a risk of complications. While this may be very small and therefore not important when considered one patient at a time, when you look at 300,000,000 patients over a year, even a low-risk complication occurs frequently. People die of complications. A lot of money is spent treating complications.

To a certain extent, then, we push our own quality problem with our demand for more things to be done to investigate and treat, when further investigation and treatment may not be warranted. A change in our attitudes about "more is better" might help us save both money and lives. Fortunately, there is good evidence that when people are educated about the alternatives to the treatment on which they have focused, they are able to consider these alternatives and make choices that reflect their own value system. There is increasing evidence that one of the obstacles to the provision of that balanced information is the very physicians who get paid for doing more tests or more surgery. We will have to change those incentives.

Clearing Obstacles

In the meantime, we have the right to expect our caregivers to do a better job of keeping us safe from harm and delivering high-quality, effective care. To get the best results from this process, we must clear obstacles out of the way. If there are aspects of the system that tend to impede quality improvement, these aspects of the system need to be identified and changed. One of the obstacles to quality improvement in health care is the tort liability system.

Tort Liability

The classic approach to safety has been the tort liability system, which comes to us from English Common Law. The tort system works like this: if I sell an inherently unsafe product, people who are injured by my product may sue me. The presumption is that not only will I be forced to compensate those injured, I will also be highly motivated to improve the safety of my product. This "system" of encouraging improved safety has been in effect in health care for as long as the tort liability system has been in effect (hundreds of years). If one judges a system by its results (and what better way is there?), the tort system as applied to health care is a dismal failure.[6,7]

What is it about the tort system that is a failure? How can we correct the problems with the tort system? Can we do something to make safety a priority?[8,9]

The tort system manifests its failure because it has had decades in which to inspire a safer system, and it has not done so. When I tell attorneys that the tort system was not designed to make the system safer, but only to make individual people more careful, I often get no response. Instead, I hear about how the tort system helps to root out bad doctors and compensates injured patients. The tort system actually does neither of these things very well. And it has not brought us a safe system, either!

"Bad doctors" are much more likely to be discovered by their colleagues (especially if they are impaired by drug or alcohol abuse or by mental illness) than by the tort system. Currently, there are diversion programs in most states to help drug addicted doctors recover and return to productive practice. Doctors who are willfully abusing patients in any number of ways seem to be discovered more frequently by complaints to licensing boards and hospital credentialing bodies than by the tort system. In both of these instances, the tort system is not an effective way of rooting out "bad doctors" because it does not begin to function until someone is badly injured, and even then, it takes many years for a case to reach its conclusion.

Injured patients deserve to be compensated. Unfortunately, the tort system, though it compensates some injured patients extraordinarily well, fails abjectly to compensate the remainder.[10] The following statements all have statistical validity:

1. Some of those who receive compensation through the tort system either have not been injured at all, or their injuries were not caused by any action or inaction of the providers.[11]

2. Most cases coming to court result in a defense verdict—because the injury was not the fault of the medical system, or because the patient was not truly injured, or because someone bamboozled the jury—and therefore, no money goes to the injured patient.

3. Many injuries are not caused by incompetent doctors, nurses, or hospitals.

4. Most injuries are the result of poorly designed care systems that fail to support the doctors and nurses in the quality of work they know how to do and are capable of doing.

5. Some injuries are incurred as a consequence of the disease being treated or the expected risks of the treatment procedures, and have little to do with poor performance on the part of the providers.

6. Most injured patients do not bring lawsuits against the providers. The number of lawsuits brought in this country every year is miniscule compared to the number of patients injured each year.

Why don't people sue? Because they like their doctor. Or because they truly believe their doctor did the best he/she could. Or because they don't know they've been injured. Or because they believe that lawsuits are nasty, ugly, contentious, antagonistic, even immoral affairs, and they prefer not to behave in that way. Regardless of the reason, they do not sue.

The nasty, ugly, contentious, antagonistic aspect of lawsuits is not a characteristic lost on doctors. Most physicians feel personally attacked when sued. What is "business as usual" to the attorney is an affront to the dignity and sense of self-worth of the physician.[12] Frankly, I think it is a good thing that doctors react this way. It indicates how much they care about the work they do—and we will go into that in more detail again in a later chapter. Doctors are so sensitized, so horrified by the possibility of a lawsuit that they would rather hide a mishap than confess it.[13-17]

Whether this is wise or not in the arena of tort law is an issue I will not discuss. In the arena of industrial quality improvement, it is anathema. You see, industrial quality improvement starts with several basic assumptions:

- People want to do a good job.

- Given the right tools, people will do a good job.

- Most errors are caused by system failures, not personal failures.

- If you can fix the system to support people in doing the job well, they will do a better job.

- "Don't fix blame, fix systems" is the conclusion.

If you use this set of standards in automobile manufacturing, on electronics assembly lines, in steel mills, or in lumber mills, you can reduce errors, improve safety, and improve output. We should be able to do as well in health care. What are the obstacles?

The tort system is a system for fixing blame. To the extent that the tort system drives the detection of system errors underground, it actually prevents quality improvement.[18] There are some very brave institutions trying very hard to do good quality improvement in the face of the impediments of the tort system, and I applaud and admire them. Against all odds, some of them are actually making progress.[19]

But why make the job more difficult than it has to be? If we want an industrial quality improvement process, we need to know about all of the errors as soon as possible. We need to be able to investigate them as quickly and thoroughly as possible. We need to be able to publish what we are doing and what we find so everyone with the potential to have input to the process in question will know what is happening and can contribute to the solution. Then we need to be able to put the solution into practice. And if it works, we need to tell everyone so others can avoid the same problem. This is a very open, public, and publicized process.[20]

When a minor error happens in a hospital, generally we get just the opposite reaction. Everyone gets very quiet.[21,22] If someone asks the hospital attorney, his advice is not to talk to anyone about it except the attorney (since attorney-client privilege will at least keep those conversations secret). How can we gather everyone interested in the failed process to the table to work on a solution?

In conclusion, the tort system is an abject failure. Not only does it not compensate most of the injured patients, not only does it not do a good job of finding the "bad doctors," not only does it not do a good job of improving safety, it actually gets in the way of quality improvement efforts. I think we need to get rid of the tort system if we really want a safe and effective medical system.

Injured Patient Compensation

What we need to build in its place is a system designed to compensate injured patients without placing blame on any individual physician, nurse, or other person—in that sense, a "no fault" system. As such, it would function more like an insurance system than like the tort system. There would be a schedule of allowed compensation for defined injuries. The injured patient would apply for compensation based on the outcome of care. Some injuries, which are predictable based on the disease the patient presents, would not be compensable events. Most injuries would be compensated, but few at the levels typical for tort lawsuit settlements.

Who would pay the premiums? I suggest premiums should be paid by all interested parties. To the extent they are able to afford it, patients should contribute. Physicians, hospitals, and other healthcare providers should contribute. Medical coverage providers should contribute. The government should contribute. The amount of the premium would be based on losses, so the premium would be higher for doctors and hospitals with higher injury experience (the less safe hospitals) and lower for the safer doctors and hospitals. This should have the effect of compensating injured patients and motivating both hospitals and doctors to identify and correct systems that cause errors and produce injuries to patients.

Do I really think that changing from the tort system to a "no fault" patient injury compensation system would be all we needed to do to ensure rapidly increasing safety? No. But I do believe that changing the system from one that randomly punishes a few errors very heavily and most errors not at all to one that more uniformly compensates injured patients and offers incentives to improve safety will make a big difference.

What else can we do?

Practice Standards

Practice standards come in a number of forms. Some are standards related to the infrastructure, such as computerized order entry in hospitals and electronic transmission of prescriptions from doctors' offices. Some are related to the processes of care (such as hospital care pathways for critical patients and guidelines related to outpatient care). The history of practice standards is mixed—as to their derivation, their effectiveness, and the rate of their adoption.

Practice standards may be derived as consensus opinions or based on scientific evidence. A major advantage of evidence-based standards is that they transcend the experience of any individual and rely instead on results achieved over large populations of people. More and more, practice standards are based on scientific evidence.[23,24] One difficulty in basing practice standards on good scientific evidence is that we have no evidence either to support or to displace much of current health care practice. Clearly, at some point we need to expand our focus of investigation from the new and novel to the old and perhaps not so reliable aspects of health care to find out what really has been working and what hasn't. A second disadvantage of evidence-based standards is that it is currently hard to get physicians to adopt and use them. I will discuss this in more detail later.

Practice standards have been developed primarily to address the proper way to treat particular medical conditions. One of the weaknesses of the whole practice standards movement to date is that little has been done to develop practice standards that are designed to reduce errors or reduce the rate at which patients are harmed by medical interventions. We could use more of this. While it seems apparent that electronic order entry in hospital settings and electronic transmission of prescriptions to the pharmacy would reduce errors, there is not the large body of information on this subject that there is on many clinical issues, like the treatment of cancer. Until we have the evidence of what infrastructure changes can produce in terms of safety and accuracy, we are still in the "consensus opinion" days insofar as the standards for medical care infrastructure are concerned.

More About Infrastructure

However, there is another side to this issue. Some of what is advocated for the health care system has already been adopted in other industries. It is remarkable, for example, that you can take your ATM card to thousands of places, put it into a machine, get out money, and have the correct amount taken from the correct account at your bank. At the same time, there is no similar insurance card you can take to thousands of emergency rooms or doctor's offices that tells what your insurance covers and doesn't cover, whether you need authorization for treatment (and if so, how to obtain it), and what providers should know about your health history, recent laboratory tests, or current medications. If information is instantly available in banking, it can be instantly available in health care—what we lack is the infrastructure.[25,26,27,28]

Why is the infrastructure present in banking and not in healthcare? In banking, all of the data are numbers, which simplifies data transmission. When you use an ATM, you do the work of the teller, so there is less need for people at the bank to service your account, allowing banks to save money on teller salaries. Initially, many banks added a service charge (and most still do for transactions on another bank's account), which means that by using the ATM you are directly increasing the bank's income. In banking, therefore, the data processing demands are less stringent and there is an immediate monetary return on investment.

In health care, the business case for information transparency is not there. To have insurance and patient information readily available at multiple locations requires a significant infrastructure. There must be compatible systems at all locations where information is either generated or utilized. There must be ways to get the information into the system when and where it is generated and retrieve it later in a reasonably usable form when and where it is needed.

Medical record-keeping has never been uniformly usable by anyone other than the generating entity. Medical records have ranged from chaotic to cryptic, and from overly brief to ridiculously voluminous. Generally, like the prescriptions that no one but a pharmacist can read, they have been handwritten and illegible. Unlike banking, where almost all transactions are numerical (ten symbols), most health care transactions are verbal. I have seen physician office records kept on 3x5 cards—sometimes with the billing data on the same cards and with many years of data on a single card. Recently, computerized medical record systems have made it easy to enter excessive narratives that no one would ever want to read.

Ideally, the information should be compact, organized, and comprehensive. The person accessing the information should be able to receive all relevant information in a short transmission time (compact). She should be able to find the key elements rapidly and accurately (organized). She should be confident she has received all available information (comprehensive).

This affects quality of care. Clearly, in an emergency, you will receive better medical care from someone who knows your past history than from someone who does not. This is especially true if you are brought to the emergency room unconscious from an automobile accident or incoherent from a stroke. The issue is far from trivial when you are taking medications the doctor should know about before giving you other medications that might conflict.

This is also an issue about the utilization of resources. Every year, my insurance company pays for a second set of prenatal laboratory tests on a number of women whose first set was on file at a hospital different from the one at which the baby was delivered. It is not uncommon for tests to be repeated in the ER or by a specialist merely because the treating physician does not have access to tests done in the recent past. It is not clear how much money is wasted in this manner, but it is not a trivial amount.

What infrastructure do we need? I would propose the following expectations as a minimum, and will amplify where needed:

- Electronic order entry for all hospital orders, with artificial intelligence review and instant feedback on orders that are "out of bounds"

- Electronic transmission of prescriptions to pharmacies

- Complete hospital medical records in electronic format

- All office records in electronic format

- Standards for all of the above (electronic records should be transportable from one system to another, whether for temporary use or because the patient has moved or shifted care to a new group of physicians)

Electronic order entry for all hospital orders, with artificial intelligence review and instant feedback on orders that are "out of bounds." Electronic order entry can do several important things. The first, and perhaps most important, is that it makes the physician's orders legible to everyone. The pharmacist gets the right medication at the right dose. The nurse understands the frequency of treatments.

Second, it flags information the physician needs if there is a problem with the medication and/or the dose prescribed.[29] For instance, if the medical record says the patient is allergic to penicillin and the physician prescribes penicillin, it should require the physician to override the caution not to prescribe a medication the patient is allergic to. Or if the physician inadvertently writes a dose that is ten times the usual dose for a particular medication, it will immediately ask the physician to correct it before proceeding. In addition, if the physician prescribes medications that should not be administered together, the system can alert the physician to the conflict. In all of these examples, the system alerts the physician to the conflict before the order is officially registered so he or she can change it to something acceptable (or override the warning if that is appropriate). No one has to find the physician to request clarification, and the "outmoded" order never appears on the chart.

Third, the system can take in the diagnoses provided by the physician and suggest where there are care pathways that would apply to the care of this patient—and even offer the standard order set for review.[30] As I shall discuss below, a major obstacle to following care pathways is not having them at hand when care decisions are made. This takes care of that objection, at least in some circumstances.

Electronic transmission of prescriptions to pharmacies. As with electronic hospital order entry, this is another path to more accurate communication.[31] Like hospital order entry, it also has the virtue of allowing an electronic algorithm to check for medication interaction and contraindicated medications as well as inaccurate dosing, so that the order transmitted to the pharmacist is not only legible, but also accurate. Finally, transmission of prescriptions electronically precludes the patient from changing prescriptions on the way to the pharmacy. While this is not a problem with most medications, patients do sometimes change the number of doses prescribed on narcotic prescriptions, and this is a way to control that.

Complete hospital medical record in electronic format. One of the problems with hospital records is that they create huge hunks of paper with very little important information on them. Much of the information recorded may be of vital importance from the perspective of the next shift, but of no importance three days later, much less at the time of discharge. Much of this information, entered in tabular form, could easily be summarized in ways that would make the overall flow of care in the hospital much more obvious. Laboratory values are entered on separate lab slips in paper charts on separate days. In an electronic chart the values are entered into a database that can display the results of key lab studies on a daily basis, so trends are easier to see.

Advantages accrue to the attending physician in being able to follow several numerical trends more easily. Advantages accrue to the consultant, who can summarize the care given to date more readily and discern patterns in care and response. Advantages accrue to the patient, whose care becomes more apt and is better based in the actualities of the patient's medical status.

On top of all of this, it becomes possible to organize care around care pathways, and record the care in relationship to the care pathway. Checking for adherence to the pathway becomes easier. Obstructions to pathway care become obvious more rapidly. Deviations from the pathway for cause are more easily recognized and reported or commented on. It must be perfectly acceptable to deviate from the pathway when the deviation is planned, is done for cause, and is documented from the planning all the way through the execution. Finally, the only way hospital records can become portable is if they are electronic.

All office records in electronic format. Currently, electronic medical records are in use predominantly in large medical groups, where the advantages of improved communication outweigh the disadvantages of increased cost. This is not to say that electronic medical record-keeping is not done in some number of small group or solo physician offices, but such systems are not always designed to make data easily available to others. Ideally, the office medical record should have several important characteristics:

- Information developed at other locations should be easily and rapidly incorporated into the record.

- The record system should have built-in alert values for lab studies to flag out-of-bounds laboratory reports for physicians.

- The record should be easily transmitted to and accepted by other electronic medical record systems.

- The system should make needed information readily available to the physician at the time of each office visit.

- The system should be connected to sources of information to allow the physician to access information vital to the management of any patient.

These are not lightly announced characteristics. Office medical records should incorporate information generated outside of the office—such as x-ray reports, laboratory reports, summaries of hospital records, and reports or letters from consultants. These records should become rapidly and reliably available to the physician at the point of care—when the physician next sees the patient. In addition, if those results indicate some abnormality worthy of the physician's immediate attention, the record system should issue an alert to the physician. Communication is also important. The record should be in a format that can be sent to other systems, and the system should be able to receive records from other sources.

Information availability is also important. The best use of the electronic medical record is, as noted above, at the point of care. When the physician sits down with the patient, information needed about that patient should be available to the doctor. The doctor should also have scientific information from respected sources available from the Internet, and the system should offer care pathways to the physician while with the patient. Such information will help the physician comply with the pathway—or deviate from it knowingly for reasons to be documented in the record.[32]

Standards for all of the above. Electronic records should be transportable from one system to another. It doesn't matter whether the patient has arrived at an emergency room or the patient is traveling three states from home. Whether for temporary use or a permanent change of physician, the medical record should be able to follow the patient from physician to physician. As noted above, communications between systems is important, just as it is among banks in allowing patrons to use one bank's ATM to withdraw money from an account at another bank. There is now movement at the federal level to push these needed standards.[33,34]

Practice Parameters

Practice guidelines come in a number of varieties. Some have to do with the general way in which healthcare is delivered—such as the implementation of rapid response teams in a hospital, which have been shown to decrease hospital deaths. Some guidelines have to do with general process parameters—such as admission criteria for pneumonia,[35,36] and criteria having to do with the timing of care for pneumonia when admission is appropriate, when rapid care is important in reducing complications and deaths. Some have to do with specifying details of care that should be fulfilled, such as which medications should be prescribed to patients with heart attacks.[37]

Practice parameters have had problems in the past. Some have been slanted by a distinct bias on the part of the authoring group. Some have been more about opinion than science. Recently, parameters have tended to be more scientifically based and unbiased, but there are still too many of them coming from too many organizations, and they are not available enough at the point of the interaction between the physician and the patient. This latter problem should improve with the implementation of the electronic interface and the integration of the parameter into that interface. The diversity of guidelines is beginning to merge as authoring organizations collaborate more in the production of those guidelines.[38]

Practice guidelines may relate to hospital practices. These guidelines are designed to reduce complications or untoward events; by doing so, they are often lifesaving. Recently, Don Berwick, MD, president of the Institute for Healthcare Improvement, announced a new hospital program that will save 100,000 lives that might otherwise have been lost due to avoidable complications.[39] This program includes six practice changes to be adopted in hospitals. It does not require adoption at all hospitals in the country for success. In fact, it will save one life per year for every two hospital beds affected by it. The power of such structural changes to increase the safety of hospital care at the same time they decrease the cost of care is a powerful testimony to their importance. These guidelines increase the safety of patients who seek care. They decrease complications and death rates. (These are generally not the deaths referred to in the IOM report "To Err is Human.") These guidelines also increase the effectiveness of the underlying treatment being provided in the hospital.[40,41]

Practice guidelines may also affect office management of outpatients. These guidelines outline scientifically supported best practices. Because patients seen in office practices are less sick than those hospitalized, such guidelines are more likely to be designed to save costs (management of low back pain) or to prevent long-term consequences (management of diabetes mellitus) than to save lives.[42,43] This does not make them necessarily less important in the long run, but it does make them less urgent in the short run. These guidelines are much less important to the safety of healthcare practices, but they are very important to the overall effectiveness of the care provided.

In Summary

I believe we need a system that is safe and provides effective care for patients. I believe we can improve both safety and effectiveness by doing several things:

1. Change the tort system. Tort law should not apply to medical injuries. Instead, we need a patient compensation system that truly compensates injured patients and provides clear incentives for quality improvement efforts to reduce errors.

2. Establish infrastructure expectations and standards for all healthcare providers, regardless of the role they play. The initial steps in this process have already begun, having to do with specifying how data sets should be transmitted and received.

3. Practice guidelines should be implemented for safety and effectiveness. While there will always be exceptions to any such standard, general compliance should not be a matter at the general option of the provider, but should be expected as a matter of routine unless there are good reasons to do otherwise.[44,45]

4. Build provider compensation systems that recognize high performance in the above areas and reward it.[46,47]

The health care delivery system is replete with sincere, quality people who want to do a better job. Improvements in quality and safety are within reach, but getting there will take removing barriers (such as the tort system) and changing some physician thought patterns.[48]

Chapter 21

Uniform Availability

"Don't judge each day by the harvest you reap, but by the seeds you plant."

—*Robert Louis Stevenson*

By "uniform availability," I mean that available care is close to the patient both geographically and temporally, no matter where the patient happens to be or when the need for medical care occurs. Obviously, some exercise of good judgment is called for—it is unlikely that a routine annual physical examination will ever be as available at 2:00 a.m. as it is at 2:00 p.m. Similarly, if a person is in one of the vast unpopulated areas on our map, it is not reasonable to insist on immediately available care. On the other hand, within some reasonable boundaries, care should be readily available to all who find themselves in urgent need, and to all who are in any area with reasonable population.[1] We should begin by being more definite about the availability of care.

In terms of time of day, wherever care is available, it should be available 24/7 (24 hours a day, seven days a week). Providing care 24/7 is not a light undertaking. There have been times and places where a single physician undertook 24/7 care for a community, but it is an inhuman undertaking with an inhumane effect on the physician and often results in less than satisfactory care for the community. If three physicians agree to conduct a normal office practice 48 hours a week and to alternate call for the remainder of the week, we can end up with each working about 40 hours in the office and taking call for another 40 hours each week. I do not wish to dispute over the advisability, wisdom, or acceptability of such an arrangement. I know it has been done, since I have done it myself; I believe it is at the upper limit of the workload we should expect of a physician.

There are 168 hours in a week. If the three physicians share an office that they keep open 48 hours a week (five days and two evenings a week, or five days, one evening and Saturday morning), that leaves 120 hours when the office is closed. Shared three ways, that is 40 hours of call each. Three primary care physicians should be able to provide 24/7 coverage for about 6,000 people—an average of 2,000 patients each. I will provide one vision of how that could happen.

In addition to the physicians, the community will need a facility—which could be anything from the physicians' office to an urgent care office or hospital clinic—to function as a first-aid station where the physicians can examine patients. What matters is that the facility is recognized to provide 24-hour care, with ancillary staff on duty 24 hours a day, and with at least some rudimentary capability for laboratory and imaging studies. When the first-aid station is near a hospital, it may rely on the hospital to provide some ancillary services. When the first-aid station is remote from the hospital, it must provide services that might not ordinarily be found in a physician's office—the ability to do some necessary laboratory studies, imaging facilities, a minor surgery area, supplies to enable starting an IV, stopping bleeding, some acute stabilization care, a rudimentary pharmacy.

This facility, which I will refer to as a "first-aid station," becomes much more like a small, free-standing emergency room, except that ambulances never bring patients here. They only take them away. The less the capability of the local facility, the more important reliable transportation to a more capable facility becomes. It is not necessary that a local facility in a remote town be able to treat everything; what is necessary is that the facility and staff are available to evaluate any ill person and make prompt arrangements for care that cannot be rendered locally.

As we get to larger or less isolated towns, it becomes more and more tempting to utilize the services of the emergency room to provide all after-hours care—it is clearly less work for the physicians not to have to be truly available 24/7, and the emergency room is an easy focal point. The problem with this approach is that it continues to result in the ER availability problem we have today.[2]

As more and more people who do not have emergency conditions crowd into emergency rooms, several things happen. First, the ER must staff up for a larger volume; the staff's experience with true emergencies is diluted by caring for a large number of people with minor illnesses who do not really need emergency room care. This tends to decrease the efficiency and expertise of the ER staff. In addition, the increased volume creates a care backlog in the ER. There are times when true emergencies must wait because all of the places available for patient care are filled, many with patients whose problems are not emergencies. Further, patients with non-emergency problems must generally wait for the emergencies to be taken care of first (out of the order of their arrival), making the wait very long for patients with non-emergency problems.

For a variety of reasons, it is vastly preferable for most patients to see their own doctor, or one of their doctor's partners, when they require care after hours. It may be possible for this to happen in the ER or in a facility adjacent to the ER. Or it may happen in the physicians' office, or in a more local first-aid station. As I will discuss later, the continuity of care allowed by seeing the personal physician is an advantage that probably outweighs the risk that the patient will need to be transferred to another facility because the illness proves to be more severe than can be handled in the local facility. This is not to deny the importance of transporting people with conditions that are clearly an emergency to an emergency room—but the care they receive there will be prompter and more expert if the ER staff are not also having to deal with a lot of minor problems that merely couldn't be handled during the day or arose in the evening or over the weekend.[3]

This is not to say we need a first-aid station for every 6,000 people. Given the 24/7 nature of the first-aid station, it may be more desirable to consolidate a number of practices to a single first-aid station when geographic proximity permits. For example, in a community of 60,000 people, there might be 30-35 primary care physicians, all of whom could use the same evening and night clinic. The total volume of use would ensure that there would be enough work to justify 24/7 staffing, but it might only require one receptionist and one nurse between 2:00 a.m. and 6:00 a.m., making the consolidated facility easier and more economical to operate than ten smaller ones.

The first-aid station is not the emergency room. In a community with a hospital, it certainly could be located near the emergency room, but it should be a separate entity administratively and functionally. It needs to be staffed for a different set of needs. For example, the physicians should be community physicians, not dedicated ER staff. More than anything, it should have a separate patient flow so that the volume of ambulatory patients to the first-aid station never interferes with the proper functioning of the ER. The intrusive nature of ER care should also never impinge on the function of the first-aid station.

Why go into so much detail about the delivery of ambulatory medical care? It is precisely our expectation for the minimal distribution of ambulatory services that will drive the issue of distribution of physicians and facilities. If it takes 6,000 people to support a single ambulatory care delivery unit (ACDU), then the smallest community to which we should expect to deliver such a unit is a community of 6,000 people. (An ACDU is three generalist physicians sharing a practice covering 24/7, with a first-aid station for after-hours care.)

What do we do with smaller communities? In some areas, smaller communities will be close enough to share one or two

ACDUs. When communities are too remote to combine resources and are too small to justify a single ACDU, some other arrangement must be made. In some instances, this will entail "broken" ACDUs in which there are too few physicians, or the first-aid station is in the next town, making some care available, but not 24/7. Below a certain size, communities simply cannot support any full-time care, and all residents will have to travel for health care services.

However, some combination of communities will often work. I practiced for many years in a rural area. There were four towns, none with as many as 6,000 residents. Three of the towns were about ten miles from the fourth, in three different directions. Including the people in the unincorporated areas surrounding the four towns, there were about 19,000 people in the area. This is clearly enough for three ACDUs. (We had about ten primary care physicians in the area, and a small hospital.) After hours and on weekends and holidays, people often had to travel to the community with the hospital for care—but it was never more than a fifteen-mile drive.

We managed to combine four small towns and their surroundings into a single service area that could be well serviced by several ACDUs. We had an ER, but what we lacked was a first-aid station. When the ER was not staffed by dedicated emergency physicians, it functioned pretty well as a "small time" emergency room and also as a first-aid station. As the traffic through the area increased and the number of tourists increased, though, the emergency room function became too onerous for the local physicians to handle, so a full-time physician staff was employed. Then it became too easy for physicians to "sign out" to the ER physicians. Patients lost contact with their personal physicians, and the quality of care for routine ambulatory problems decreased because of the care discontinuity. Soon, patients with less serious medical conditions began to be regarded as obstacles to the care of the "real emergencies." This is a problem common in many communities, and it results in care being less available. Taking after-hours non-emergency care out of the ER would improve the quality of care as well as its availability.

What do we need to do to have a system in which every community of at least 6,000 has an ACDU, and people are able to receive medical care when they need it? Let us look at the obstacles:

- Getting physicians to live in communities as small as 6,000
- Rewarding physicians for committing to the time burden imposed by 24/7 availability
- Developing and financing first-aid stations
- Having enough primary care physicians available to fill all the positions in such a system

Let us consider these obstacles one by one:

Getting Physicians to Live in Communities as Small as 6,000

How are you going to keep them "down on the farm" after they have seen Paris? This conundrum in song is, as the author of the song knew, not just a rhetorical question; it is part of the quandary of modern life.

Physicians in training spend four years in college or university, generally in a town or city of some size. Then they spend four years in medical school, certainly at least in a metropolitan area of several hundred thousand, if not in a large urban center. Then they spend three to seven additional years in "residency" training for the specialty of practice. Residency training may take place in smaller cities, but most residencies are in cities of nearly the same size as those of the medical schools. At a minimum, residency training virtually always happens in towns with at least ten times the population of the town of 6,000 we are trying to staff with three primary care physicians.

An aphorism of thirty years ago probably still applies: no physician will practice in a town smaller than the one in which his wife (or her husband) grew up. Most physicians do not meet their spouses in small towns—they meet them in the cities, at the colleges, universities, and medical schools. The odds of a future physician marrying a "small town girl" or "small town boy" are small.

There has been a countervailing movement of the population in the last thirty years. There are actually people leaving the cities and seeking "the country life." This applies to some physicians as well. This movement is likely to make it easier to recruit physicians to smaller communities. However, many rural areas remain underserved even after many years of this movement. It is not clear that physicians are moving back to the rural environment as quickly as non-physicians are.

One of the drawbacks for physicians in a small community is isolation. A group of three physicians in a small town may see a lot of one another, but not have much interaction with physicians outside of their local enclave. The sense of isolation is an issue that must be confronted. Similarly, access to the world of culture available in the city is impaired for those living far from the nearest city. Isolation is not just distance and size dependent, it becomes time and money dependent—it costs time and money to get to the nearest city for sophisticated recreation.

There is work being done to understand these barriers. To get doctors to the towns that need them will require more than understanding the issues. It will require finding ways to deal with them in a concerted way, and to do so in a positive way that encourages persistence in the small town, not just a two-year stint of mandatory duty followed by a relieved "escape" back to suburbia or a big city. The solution will be partially monetary. It may also be partially setting the right expectations. In a small town that will support only one ACDU, it may be appropriate to staff with four physicians, to reduce the call burden somewhat and to allow the physicians additional time to be away from the community.

Rewarding Physicians for Committing to the Time Burden

There is a significant burden imposed by 24/7 availability—and the reward should be proportionate to how that availability is

231

shared. A physician who takes call one in three nights deserves more compensation than one who takes call one in six nights. In the fee-for-service compensation paradigm, there may or may not be some extra compensation for after-hours visits, but if there are few or no such visits, there is little or no compensation. However, the burden of availability is there in any case.

In the capitation compensation paradigm, there is no compensation for after-hours visits or after-hours availability. The time burden is dependent on the size of the group being capitated; the capitation payment is likely to be the same regardless of the size of the group. If we really expect physicians to be available in small groups to care for their own patients after hours, there must be compensation for that duty that goes beyond the satisfaction derived from doing it. Whatever we do in building a compensation scheme, we need to build it in such a way that it recognizes frequency of "call" or total hours of availability and compensates accordingly.

Developing and Financing First-Aid Stations

As I have outlined it here, the "first aid station" is a new concept for civilian medicine. A first-aid station need not be substantially more complex than most primary care physicians' offices. The problem with using the physician's office is that it is designed, constructed, and staffed for daytime use only. The "first-aid station" represents a new concept in care delivery because it will operate during the hours physician offices are not open, but it is not the ER.

First, we must confront the issue of what capability the first-aid station would have. In all probability, we need to think of the first-aid station in two contexts—adjacent to or part of a hospital, and remote from a hospital. If the first-aid station is adjacent to or part of a hospital, then laboratory and imaging facilities can be made available through the hospital, as can the possibility of observing a patient for a few hours. In these cases, the first-aid station need only be close enough to the hospital to permit inter-operability and most of the issues are resolved.

When the first-aid station is remote from the hospital, it must incorporate services not ordinarily found in a physician's office, as I have already mentioned. This would include enhanced laboratory studies, imaging facilities, a minor surgery area, supplies and facility for acute stabilization care, and some basic pharmacy services. This first-aid station becomes much more like a small, free-standing emergency room, except that ambulances never bring patients here. They only take them away.

The physical plant must be laid out to provide for the possibility of 24-hour service. It must be staffed for 24-hour service. And it must have capacity to reflect the population and area served. In all likelihood, such facilities must be constructed and supported through some process different from the physicians' ownership. This is not to say that the physician might not see patients in the facility during "normal operating hours." If a physician becomes a full-time tenant of a first-aid station, that physician should be paying rent and salaries for staff, just as that physician would in some other office somewhere else in town. Whether these facilities are operated by hospitals (and charges rendered to the system for the use of the facility), or by the government, or by someone else—I don't know. The means of providing financial payment to the facility is also not entirely clear to me.

Medical record availability is key. If the physicians are seeing patients in a first-aid station that is not where they normally practice, medical records need to be electronically available—and any transaction the physician could do in his/her own office should be possible from the first-aid station. It will cost money to build and upgrade facilities to meet this requirement. There is a good deal more design work to be done. But in the face of the total bill for medical services, the cost will be relatively small.

Having Enough Primary Care Physicians

Currently there are not enough primary care physicians to fill all the positions in the system I have described.[4] In the current sys-

233

tem, we have a shortage of primary care physicians, which is not likely to improve in the short run without some stimulation.[5,6]

Why don't physicians choose careers in primary care medicine? Primary care is not highly esteemed within the medical community, and is not well paid (refer back to Chapter 18). If we value what primary care physicians do enough to want more of them, we also must elevate their stature to recognize the value of what they do. A moderate culture shift will be needed in many medical schools to recognize and esteem the value brought by primary care physicians.[7] There have been medical schools founded in the desire to train more primary care physicians, and even these medical schools have suffered a lack of esteem in the eyes of other medical schools designed to produce physician researchers and super-specialists.

However hard it is to change the social pecking order in healthcare, it should be much easier to change the financial pecking order. Admittedly, reducing the incomes of some of the more highly paid specialties may be both difficult and painful—but at some point we need to stop providing ultimate value to the physician who is able to provide the ultimate intervention to a vanishingly small number of patients, and transfer some of that value back to the physicians who take care of most of the problems of most of the people most of the time.

Physicians graduate from medical school after eight years of undergraduate and graduate education, often $100,000 or more in debt for the costs of their education. At age 26 or 27, as newly minted MDs, they face an additional three to seven years of residency training at relatively low wages. Sometime after age 30, they finish training and step into the business world, heavily in debt, needing to buy and furnish an office and a home, and still have money left over to live on. The financial expectations of different specialties will have a significant bearing on how decisions are made about which specialty to pursue.

Primary care physicians are at the bottom of the earning scale. I would not contend they should be at the top, but they should at least be paid in the same range as other specialties. After two decades of work to create equivalency between them, we still have not gotten rid of the pricing distinction between "cognitive" and "procedural" services. Procedural services, provided almost exclusively by sub-specialists, are still paid at a higher rate per hour than cognitive services (see the discussion in Chapter 18).

Telemedicine

Telemedicine is a new undertaking that combines new electronic communication techniques to increase the availability of care in remote locations. A physician in an urban medical center can treat patients in the remotest rural area if there is the communication capability available to permit the right information to flow. This would require high-speed, high-volume telephone lines and the computers, monitors, and cameras that allow videoconferencing. The ability to transmit images from paper or transparency may be important, depending upon the use to which the system is put. There clearly needs to be an operator at the remote end who is capable of supplementing the visual and auditory communication with tactile input when needed by the consulting physician.

Telemedicine is a way to link the first-aid station to the nearest emergency room (when it is farther away than across a parking lot) or with specialists in a full-service community. Telemedicine is currently being used to extend the consultative resources of tertiary medical centers to provide availability in rural communities.[8]

Telemedicine may also be used as a way to deliver the "presence" of a physician to a patient when the patient is remote from the physician. I have a friend who foresees a system wherein the remote telemedicine terminal travels with nurses to the patient. The nurses tend to the patient at a hands-on level; the physician provides guidance and input through the remote connection. Not only might this be the way to deliver services to remote areas, it might also be an alternate way to deliver services to those people in any area who may have difficulty getting to a physician's office, or who might not wish to travel, but would prefer for medical services to come to them. Regardless of exactly how they are used overall, first-aid stations should include telemedicine links to a tertiary medical center and/or emergency room in all instances where it is not co-located with such a center.

In Summary

Geographic distribution of healthcare resources so that medical services are available where and when they are needed is a challenge. I have offered one vision for what such a system could look like. There are certainly other visions that could fill this need. It will require some rethinking of how the smallest units of the care delivery system are organized, operated, and distributed. Staffing will require some significant reconsiderations of how physicians are paid, and will require adjusting the relationship between specialty and primary care compensation.

In the past, we have left to the marketplace and the individual physicians the job of organizing and distributing care. This approach has not worked in the past and it seems unlikely to work in the future.[9,10] Significant system-level planning needs to be applied to creating a delivery system designed to ensure that care is there, where and when it is needed. Whatever plan is chosen, it will have to reflect high-level, system-based thinking if it is to succeed.

Chapter 22

Comprehensive Coverage:
Finding the Best Scientific Methods
for Treating and Preventing Disease

"Science is an integral part of culture. It's not this foreign thing, done by an arcane priesthood. It's one of the glories of human intellectual tradition."

—*Stephen Jay Gould*

Why would we ever choose not to cover a medical intervention that is safe, effective, and inexpensive? Comprehensive coverage means that diagnosis and treatment paid under the plan should not be limited by last year's view of how medical coverage should be structured. It should not be limited by last year's science. To a major extent, we must take the authority for decisions about what will or will not be covered out of the hands of politicians and put that authority into the hands of some group of experts charged with making coverage decisions.

In much this way, we have taken the job of licensing new medications out of the hands of legislatures and have vested that authority solely in the Food and Drug Administration. The intent of the FDA is that decisions are made by a panel of experts after a significant amount of study and understanding of the nature of the proposed new drug—including scientific information about how effective and how potentially dangerous it is. We would not be happy if new medications could not be introduced in the market without an act of Congress—or worse, if dangerous medications would remain on the market because it would take an act of Congress to get them removed. We understand that Congress is slow, is swayed by political pressure, and has no inherent expertise in pharmacology. We want the medications we use to be safe and effective. We count on the FDA, not Congress, to keep them that way.[1]

The current problem with the FDA is that it does not seem to be immune enough to pressure from the executive and legislative branches of the government. It has had problems garnering an adequate budget. Some medications have been approved, or not approved, seemingly in response to political or financial pressures from outside the agency. One recent article actually looked at the actions of the Advisory Committee in assessing financial conflicts of interest.[2] One recent medication seems to have had a very delayed release because it did not match the political concerns of the sitting U.S. President.

The only agency that seems to be more independent of federal manipulation is the Federal Reserve Board. Convened to watch over the currency and to set interest rates, the Federal Reserve Board members are nominated by the President, approved by Congress, and remain in place for terms that overlap political terms and help to insulate the Federal Reserve Board from political "packing." We need the FDA to have the same level of independence as the Federal Reserve Board.

In a similar way, we need to be certain the techniques of prevention, diagnosis, and treatment to which we are subjected are safe and effective. If new evidence shows that a treatment we considered ineffective is in fact effective, we want it to become available. Similarly, if an old standby treatment we always thought was effective turns out to be dangerous or not very effective, we want to know right away and expect action to be taken. We need a coverage organization, like the FDA (with the independence of the Federal Reserve Board), to make decisions about what should be covered.[3] Those decisions should not be bound by restrictive legislation that either demands or prohibits any particular treatment.[4-7]

For convenience, let us call this organization the Health Coverage Administration. The HCA would be tasked with painting the broad strokes of what would be covered (e.g., will we cover prescription medications, chiropractic, acupuncture?). The HCA would also be tasked with interpreting the desires of the electorate about the extent of coverage—one of the limiting factors discussed under controlling the cost of care.[8] Some of this would flow from the allocation we are willing to make to support the program financially. (Congress has a voice here.)

Answering the "What Works?" Question

The HCA would evaluate surgical and medical procedures, diagnostic protocols, the use of MRI, CT, and PET scanners, and laboratory tests. Some would be worth doing and produce value; some would not. The HCA would also monitor the literature on Disease Management, Case Management, and Utilization Management programs to determine which ones accomplish the goals of improving health and/or controlling expenses. They would then authorize the ones that work to be part of the basic health plan.

The FDA is quite capable of telling a pharmaceutical house that it needs to do more study on a drug before it can be licensed. The HCA should be able to do the same with any new device or procedure. Since the HCA will be overseeing the care of the entire population, it is in an excellent position to design and execute studies to determine what works and what doesn't work.[9]

The U.S. Population as a Testing Ground

This may sound coldly scientific—using the entire population of the United States as an experimental testing ground. However, individual physicians are currently performing such experiments by doing whatever makes sense to them at the moment, but no one is watching. We are all guinea pigs to the random whims of the health-care system, but no one is tallying the results to understand whether we are doing better or worse than we were before.

An example of how this would work has been modeled for us, in reverse, by the treatment of breast cancer with high-dose chemotherapy and bone marrow transplant. This treatment was introduced as a possible pathway to longer survival of breast cancer patients. There was initial interest based on a small study indicating that it might be helpful. Larger, longer-term studies were soon developed to help us figure out whether it really was helpful. In the meantime, the publicity stirred by the effort resulted in women demanding to be treated with the new regimen. Ten years later, we finally had enough patients enrolled in the studies to determine that the new treatment was of no extra value compared to the older regimens. In the meantime, thousands of women underwent what was essentially an experimental treatment, but no one was watching to see if it made any difference to those women. We could have reached the correct conclusion much sooner if all the women treated had been enrolled in a protocol to capture the results of their treatment.

How Is This Done?

How do we learn about what works and what doesn't work? To some extent, it is a trial-and-error effort, and certainly if each physician had to find a way to treat each new symptom, it would be very much a matter of trial and error. One way we systematically discover what works is with carefully designed studies that compare outcomes between a "control" group and a "test" group. There are several requirements to make the comparison most meaningful. First, the two groups must be as close to identical as possible. To accomplish this, the grouping technique is often "randomized" so that no one—neither the patient nor the physician—gets to choose who goes into the control group and who goes into the test group.

The next step is to make every attempt to hold everything the same except the intervention being tested. One way to do this is to "blind" both the subjects and the evaluators to the assignment of the subjects. If the subject does not know if he is receiving the active medication or not, then the subject's expectations cannot interfere in the result; if the evaluator also does not know, then the evaluator's hopes for (or against) the test cannot interfere in the evaluator's assessment of the subject. When both subject and evaluator are unaware of the assignment of the subject, the test structure is said to be "double blinded."

If we wish to know how effective medication "x" is for patients with the common cold, we could now derive an experiment. (We will need to define what we mean by a "cold" to ensure that all patients fulfill the diagnostic criteria.) Patients who have a cold will be randomly assigned to either the test group or the control group. Someone not directly involved in the patient's care will draw a ball from a container with 50 red and 50 white balls in it. If the ball is white, the patient gets "x"; if the ball is red, the patient gets an inert pill that looks the same as "x". Regardless of test/control assignment, all patients will be given a standard set of instructions about how to take care of a cold, and all will be given a follow-up appointment in one week. At one week, the patients are quizzed about how they are doing, and the results are recorded on a standard questionnaire—all patients are asked the same questions in the same order.

We have now done a randomized, double-blinded study of "x." What did we find out? If the responses to the questionnaire were significantly better in the test group, we may presume that "x" had a beneficial effect. If not, we assume that "x" is not effective in the treatment of the common cold.

The problem is that the doctors who say "no two people are alike" are correct. We will not get a uniform set of results. It would be nice to have results that were like flipping a coin: the coin either comes up heads or it comes up tails. Instead, we will have a spectrum of results. If the one-week questionnaire scores 0-10, we will

241

have some people scoring 10 and others scoring 0; it would not be a surprise to find some of each in both the test group and the control group. How do we decide?

The key is statistical analysis. How well does our model do at predicting the right process? One of the lessons has to do with sample size. The larger the number of people who can be enrolled in a study, the faster we can have a conclusion, and the more reliable that conclusion will be. One of the advantages the HCA may have is the ability to recruit very large numbers of patients into these studies.[10] One of the problems in the breast cancer studies noted earlier is that the free availability of the treatment without being in a controlled study meant that women who thought they had been randomized to "usual care" could change from being an experimental subject to being a recipient of the care they sought. This reduced the number of participants dramatically, making it much harder to get a meaningful result.

Long Studies versus Short Studies

The power of some studies is in how long the study lasts; the power of others is in how many people can be enrolled in the study. Both kinds can be enhanced by the availability of a central patient registry and central data repository such as the HCA.

Long-duration studies, like the Framingham study, follow people for decades to discern differences in longevity and health consequences that may be affected by any number of factors. Long-term studies may also be needed for the study of long-duration diseases —breast cancer and diabetes are two good examples—and their treatments. Because the HCA would have the data-warehousing facilities, it could be in the position to follow people for long periods of time to ascertain long-term health outcomes—and not lose people to follow-up just because they moved.

Short-term studies achieve their power from the sheer number of people who can be enrolled. If we are studying a treatment for the common cold, the larger the number of people we can enroll in the trial, the more quickly we will know the outcome.[11] Since colds are brief in duration, measurement of outcomes happens soon after the intervention. On the other hand, the question of whether the difference between six days of illness and seven days of illness is significant can only be resolved by the weight of numbers of people studied. Because the HCA is in a position to oversee the health care of a huge population, such studies can achieve discriminatory power very rapidly.[12]

What Don't We Know?

What do we need to study? What issues in the diagnosis and treatment of diseases are not yet settled? Do we really need the power of a central data repository to accumulate data and oversee large-scale trials to determine what works and what doesn't work?

The answer here is distressingly clear. It would appear that about 80% of what physicians do daily has no basis in science as we are discussing it. That doesn't mean it is wrong, but only that it has generally not been studied. Given the size of the budget and the relative ease of data collection, it should be possible to study a lot of medical practices to see if what we are doing really does what we think it does. While we are at it, we might as well test most of "alternative and complementary medicine"—that hazy realm that includes chiropractic and acupuncture[13], herbal medications, naturepathy, and homeopathy. Many of these therapies will require large-scale studies to see if they work. If they do, we should adopt them for general use and coverage by our program. If they do not, they should not be covered. Anything found to be detrimental should not only be discarded, but also well publicized so the general use of it stops.

More than that, we also need to understand a lot about payment mechanisms.[14] In the chapters on affordability, I indicated that no one really understood exactly what the real-life implications of some of the payment structures were. The HCA and a national program will not only need to implement some of the payment structures I discussed, but the system also will be in a good position to study the payment structures. How do we discover which payment strategies tend to reduce waste? Which payment structures discourage inappropriate use without being a barrier to necessary access to care?

Big Brother, the Researcher

Does all of this sound very much like something out of a George Orwell novel? It should. What are the guarantees that the kind of centralized information repository I am contemplating will not be used for some less-than-desirable purpose in controlling, intimidating, or defrauding the American people? Clearly, the risk is there.

However, I believe the risk can be minimized through several expedients. As I see the research arm of the HCA, it would be predominantly a data repository and a dispenser of grants. The research would primarily be done by non-HCA researchers, working under investigational protocols developed and approved by academic or professional institutions and subject to Investigational Review Board (IRB) approval and oversight. (The IRB acts like an ethics committee for research protocols.) The only research to be done by HCA employees would be related to the statistical evaluation of the accumulated data.

One role of the statistical research would be to detect variations in care that are worthy of more definitive research. Any research having to do with establishing treatment groups, altering treatment patterns, or potentially changing patterns of care would have to be done by independent researchers. HCA would, by virtue of its position as source of funds for such research, have some influence on the direction the research might go.

In Summary

In the effort to ensure that medical coverage keeps pace with medical science, I am proposing a federal agency called the Health Coverage Agency that would have the following duties:

- Using public input, determine a ranking for effective healthcare services for cost-effectiveness and appropriateness.

- Using the fiscal input of Congress, determine how far down the list of effective healthcare services the basic plan should cover.[15]

- Publish widely the coverage provided by the basic plan.

- Using the medical scientific literature, evaluate the validity of various purported healthcare services to determine which should be listed on the ranking of effective healthcare services.[16]

- Serve as the data warehouse for all information gathered regarding care and payment for care provided to people covered by the government-sponsored basic medical coverage plan.

- Perform statistical evaluation of care provided, based on the data in the data warehouse.

- Using funds allocated by Congress for this purpose, sponsor and fund research designed to test hypotheses about the most effective healthcare services.

This structure is designed to promote knowledge over speculation regarding the way diseases should be treated, and to ensure that coverage extends to cost-effective treatments and diagnostic techniques, but not to treatments and diagnostic techniques that have been shown not to be effective. Because the basic program sets the benefits for both government-sponsored coverage and private insurance, this will have the effect of bringing all coverage into line with what is scientifically appropriate.

Chapter 23

Personal Care

"We make a living by what we get; we make a life by what we give."

—*Winston Churchill*

One of the recurrent criticisms of the "modern" healthcare system in our country is that it is impersonal. No one seems to care. I am not sure exactly what the distractions are—whether it is making money or being angry with insurance companies—but healthcare professionals seem to have become distracted from the central goal of taking care of real people who have real problems.

The happiest doctors I have met in the last decade have been those whose focus has been on their patients. They have wanted, more than anything, to be helpful, kind, and supportive. They have not only succeeded in that, but they have also been financially successful.

The happiest patients I have met have been those who have been convinced that someone in the healthcare system really cared about them and how they were doing. Sometimes it is not especially important who that someone is. Amazingly, it may be a nurse at the medical plan! Or it may be the pharmacist. Or it could be the primary care physician.

The personal relationship is supportive to the patient during times of stress. (And when is illness not stressful?) The personal relationship offers the patient assurance that the provider is paying the special attention the patient needs. It offers an assurance that the particular wishes of the patient will be understood, remembered, and followed in case of an emergency. It offers the patient some assurance that his or her personal concerns will be addressed in a positive way during the course of an illness. And it offers those who are worried about their health status the assurance that they have a friend and ally who will help them get a reliable evaluation and appropriate treatment.

I believe the emphasis on making money has driven much of the personal-ness out of the medical relationship. In earlier times, when medical practice was simpler and money seemed to be less important, it was possible for the physician to spend more time with the patient and less time with the administrative duties surrounding the patient visit. Personal relationships developed easily in this less time-pressured practice pattern.

Now, medical practice is more complex, and there is more pressure to earn more money. The physician must have more employees:

- to submit bills to insurance companies

- to find "lost" medical records

- to run the electronic systems

- to answer the telephone

- to schedule appointments

- to transcribe dictated office notes

- to file all of the various bits and pieces in the medical record

- to move patients into and out of examination rooms

- to take weights and blood pressures, draw blood, and run other tests

- to assist in and "witness" examinations

- to manage all the other employees

In the meantime, the physician is working more quickly in an effort to see more patients (to raise more revenue to pay for all those employees and to take more money home).

The time spent with each patient diminishes as the amount of record-keeping increases. Record-keeping tasks increase with the intervention of third-party payers, who want a coherent account of the visit. Record-keeping tasks increase in response to the threat of being sued for malpractice. In the 1950s, many primary care doctors kept medical records on index cards, a word or several words providing the entire record of each visit. Now, a page of typewritten record per visit is not unusual. The time for creating this record is time not spent with the patient.

Computers are both a blessing and a curse. To the extent that they work and are able to relieve some of the record-keeping and function-tracking burden, they are a blessing. The curse is that every activity must somehow be adapted to the computer. Many physicians are frustrated by this, and it is not always clear whether the computer is helping or hindering.

To restore the personal touch to the system will require unraveling some of the complexity. It will require helping primary care physicians feel less pressed to see too many patients a day. It will require that the system help the physician get the job done efficiently. It will require helping the physician to bring the transaction time back into the examining room with the patient.

One of the strongholds of personal care is primary care medicine. Primary care medicine is represented by the "old fashioned" general practitioner whose modern successors are family physicians, general internists, general pediatricians, and some obstetrician-gynecologists. These are all well-trained physicians whose interest in people drives them to provide preventive services and screenings. They are trained to care for most of what goes wrong with people, and to recognize and refer the rest. At their best, they not only care for us, they are also our best guide to the system, helping us to get to the right people for the right tests and care. At their very best, they are our friends and our advocates.

This is time consuming. It is not easy to keep up with "all of medicine" as a primary care physician must do. And the primary care physician must be available to patients after hours as well as during office hours. Days can get long even without reading medical journals.

The work is rewarding to those who do it well, though—and to their patients. People who have had a personal physician for a friend know how wonderful it is. Unfortunately, there are not enough primary care physicians to go around. Many areas in the country—in fact, the majority of the counties in the country—do not have enough primary care physicians. And we are not training enough to keep up with the rate at which they are retiring. We are falling behind in training personal physicians to practice personal medicine. Why?

For a number of reasons, not the least of which is that primary care physicians are underpaid relative to other physicians (see Chapter 18). For another, the stature of the primary care physician is low in the hierarchy of the medical profession. Third, the specialists who congregate to form university medical centers are not primary care physicians. Often, they do not understand or honor the role of the primary care physician. The subspecialist is interested in training more physicians in his or her own narrow subject, not in training primary care physicians. Not only is this orientation not helpful in the current context, it is ultimately self-defeating.

What are the possible solutions?

In discussing the geographic distribution of care in Chapter 21, I talked about some of the solutions for training more primary care physicians. There are other alternatives. I offer these with the caveat that any change in the primary care infrastructure of the system will necessitate a change in the concept, structure, and distribution frequency of the Ambulatory Care Delivery Unit as conceived in Chapter 21.

Nurse practitioners and physician assistants are individuals who have been trained to provide some services within the spectrum of physician practice. They have not been to medical school, so in some ways may be less well prepared. They may have left other occupations to seek second careers in caring—generally a positive thing for forming caring relationships. Nurse practitioners frequently have practiced nursing for a number of years before undertaking training to be a nurse practitioner. (In some areas, the term is "advanced practice nurse" rather than nurse practitioner.) In many rural communities, these "mid-level providers" are providing some or all of the primary care services available in that community.

Another possibility is to increase training requirements for chiropractors so they could truly function as primary care providers —not just for illnesses falling within the proper scope of chiropractic, but for a broad array of other diseases as well. This has generally happened with osteopaths, who are now generally as well trained and as skilled in "allopathic" medicine as MDs are.

The need to expand the availability of primary care providers is paramount when we begin talking about preserving and expanding personal care. Personal care happens within the context of an extended and stable relationship. Such a relationship evolves most easily with a primary care provider, especially when the patient is healthy. Primary care providers are generally capable of handling most illnesses of any patient. (Estimates for family physicians run on the high side of 90%.) This means the patient should be seeing the same physician over and over again—which encourages a personal relationship.

For otherwise healthy people, the occasional visit because of an illness may not fall into normal office hours. The more primary care providers sharing call, the less chance that the patient will see the same one each time. Thus, while decreased frequency of call is a benefit to the providers, increased frequency of call is a benefit to the patients in establishing continuity of care and personal relationships. As I indicated in Chapter 21, frequency of call is something we need to compensate physicians for. More frequent call means that call is shared by fewer physicians. Fewer physicians means a smaller number of patients will be served by each physician while on call. More physicians will be needed "on call" to care for everyone. The personal-ness of the care improves, but the cost per patient goes up.

One of the issues with the use of non-physician providers to provide primary care has been that those non-physician providers do not substitute for physicians in the call system. If the non-physician provider who is available to patients tonight requires a physician to be backup, then two people must be on call—both the non-physician and the physician who is the backup. If we are going to increase the supply of primary care providers by using more non-physicians, we must design the system so that whatever backup resources are needed do not require extra nights of call from the local primary care physicians. One solution might be a central backup service (or telemedicine service) to provide backup to an entire region of non-physician providers.

To create a system with this much emphasis on primary care involves creating a system that would ultimately have more primary care providers who are better paid (compared to the medical profession in general). It would appear that this would mean spending a lot more money on physician services. Or it may be about the same amount, but more for primary care physicians and less for specialists. We don't really know. But we do know two things about cost and quality. We know that the overall cost of care is less in areas of the country where there are more primary care physicians. We know that the death rate in counties appears to go down as the number of primary care physicians increases (and up as the number of specialists increases).[1]

So, in adding to the number and compensation of primary care physicians, we may actually be reducing the overall cost of care. There are three issues to be considered in this, all of which may help make this a cost-effective maneuver:

1. Paying primary care physicians better in comparison to the medical profession in general does not necessarily mean that primary care physicians should receive a lot more money. This goal could be achieved by reducing the compensation of the more highly paid specialists.

2. When people see primary care physicians, they may receive less unnecessary care. The specialists, after all, are the ones who make the profit from the surgical procedures and special tests they perform. A patient who sees a primary care physician is more likely to receive appropriate care without receiving "extra" tests and treatments because the primary care physician has no economic motivation to promote them.

3. The primary care physician who is truly providing personal care to the patient will involve the patient in the decision-making process. There is ample evidence that well-informed patients more often choose not to undergo marginal treatment. Between improved public education about health care and the personal relationship with a primary care physician advocate, people are more likely to receive less high-tech care and to be more satisfied.[2-5]

The goal of restoring the personal-ness to the system is a lofty one. It requires creating an encouraging system and hoping people respond. We may not be able to accomplish the goal despite our best efforts. The fallback goal is not to destroy what personal caring still exists. Whatever we do, we must not design a system that systematically drives personal-ness out of health care. As a society, we have been creating an environment that drives personal contact out of the medical encounter. We should stop doing that.

It seems to me the two most prominent forces discouraging personal care are the decreasing availability of primary care physicians and the bureaucracy of the delivery system. I think I have discussed primary care at sufficient length. We are certainly discouraging primary care right now.

Bureaucracy raises obstacles that must be overcome. Bureaucratic systems, whether they are large group practices or a single-payer system, want all providers to look the same. While I think much medical decision-making can be standardized by reliance on scientific evidence, when we talk about personal relationships, we are talking about style issues. Style issues should not be standardized. In this process, we must allow for individual expression and individual commitment to the practice. We must allow the individual physician and his/her support staff to be identifiable in some special way that they choose.

There clearly are many different patient-friendly approaches to managing medical practices and hospitals, whether large or small. Despite the distaste many physicians feel for "customer service" efforts, they must be supported to the extent they help the patient feel and have a personal identification with the physician. There is no better measure for this than patient satisfaction—and the measurement of patient satisfaction should be built into the compensation system.

Large organizations need ways to measure how individual physicians are performing. While the volume of work done is certainly an important measure, we must resist the temptation to believe it is a sufficient measure. Pressure to increase the volume of work—whether it is measured in patient visits, dollars billed, or Relative Value Units (see Chapter 18)—will only have two effects: it will increase the number of marginal or unnecessary things done (to support the volume measurement) and it will decrease the time the physician is willing to spend with any individual patient. It is very important to measure such things as resource utilization, patient satisfaction, and outcomes to be sure the job is being done well.

I continue to believe that a personal relationship between the care provider and the patient is important to both, and particularly crucial to the patient in receiving the best care. My bias is that such relationships are most likely to occur in the primary care arena. I have now added another reason to encourage primary care practice.

I also believe we should be sure physician compensation encourages the aspects of service that are important.

Chapter 24

Professional Providers

"The problem of power is how to achieve its responsible use rather than its irresponsible and indulgent use—of how to get men of power to live for the public rather than off the public."
—Robert F. Kennedy

In Chapter 11, I outlined some of the essential features of a profession, and why professionalism in our healthcare providers is so important. A profession is an occupational group of whom expectations are different from the rest of our society. The profession is characterized by offering a service not easily mastered or understood, so the most obvious way to judge quality may be by the judgment of the profession itself. For this reason, the profession establishes its own educational course and standards for entry and continued participation. And the profession establishes and enforces its own ethical standards.

No matter how much information we derive about the qualities of individual health care providers and how well we disseminate this information, the average layman is ill equipped to understand or judge the quality of care they provide. For this reason, our expectation of professionalism from health care providers is the quality that allows us to trust the person who is about to minister to our ills.[1] It is not only that the individual subscribes to a code of ethics

—although this is important. We also trust the individual because he and his colleagues have an interest in seeing that all practitioners adhere to that code.

The history of American medicine in the 19th and early 20th centuries is a history filled with unscrupulous practitioners, poor educational standards, and a battle for dominance among groups with diverse diagnosis and treatment philosophies. In the wake of World War I, the profession yielded the control of professional entry to state licensing agencies. These agencies are still responsible for licensing and disciplining of physicians.

In the meantime, the litigiousness of our society has placed a pall on the self-policing activities of the professional associations. With the state taking some of the disciplinary authority from the profession, and with lawsuits for libel and slander, defamation of character, economic damage, and restraint of trade threatened by many professionals facing censure, the professional societies have devolved into social clubs and lobbying organizations. Barred from unionizing because they are largely self-employed, physicians have resorted to their medical societies to exert political influence to improve the economic position of the profession. At this, they have been quite successful.

These medical organizations have occasionally provided surprisingly good and unselfish advice. Early in the 20th century, the profession opposed health insurance on the grounds it would introduce a third party into the physician-patient relationship—and they were right. In opposing Medicare (repeatedly over several decades), the profession indicated that it would cost much more than anyone expected. It did. Professional opposition came in spite of the economic boon that both programs have been for the provider community.

But the role of the professional organization in setting, supervising, and enforcing ethical standards has disappeared.[2] I believe this role is actually one of the keys to the professionalism of the practitioners. Being ethical in one's dealings with patients and their payers should be as much the exemplar of the health care professional as intellectual honesty is to the scientist. Any scientist caught deliberately falsifying experimental results to suit his theory will be banished in shame and disrepute. This is exactly what should happen to any physician caught in an unethical transaction.

We should expect the profession to set the standards and enforce them. We should expect that the mere appearance of impropriety would be enough to justify an investigation. And if the physician is brought before his peers, he would be required to justify his acts—quite the opposite of the Anglo-Saxon jurisprudence rule of "innocent until proven guilty." If a physician's behavior gives the appearance (to his colleagues) of impropriety, an investigation should result. Misbehavior deserves a warning and counseling; if the behavior persists, the physician should be ejected from the profession. Significant ethical misconduct might merit expulsion without a warning or a second chance.[3,4]

What are the standards? I discussed the three central ones earlier: beneficence, non-maleficence, and self-effacement. Do good. Do no harm. Serve others (not oneself). There are other ethical standards, and there are details. The code of ethics of the American Medical Association is considerably longer than this, but it centers on these three principles.

When a physician owns a share of the hospital to which he sends patients and receives payment from that hospital based on the hospital's profitability—is that an ethical problem? If the physician owns stock in the company that makes a very expensive medication or manufactures a piece of hardware he can use frequently in his practice—is this an ethical problem? If a physician lies to an insurance company about what disease a patient has or the reasons for a surgical procedure in order to secure coverage for a procedure desired by the patient—is that an ethical problem?[5]

These things clearly raise ethical issues. They are the kinds of activities that gently but persistently undermine our confidence in the healing professions.[6] It is not my task here to unravel health care professional ethics. I merely point to some ethical issues.

What is the current reaction to these issues?[7] The licensing agencies do not pay attention to them if they are not illegal.[8] If the pattern of abuse becomes so bad as to be subject to prosecution, the physician will lose his or her license. The AMA may or may not approve, but it has no power to bring any sanction to bear on the individual physician.

If we want the professional organizations to have teeth, then we have to give them teeth. If membership in an ethical organization were a requirement for licensure, then ejection from that organization would be a serious issue. If the ethical organization were to be held economically responsible for damages caused by the unethical behavior of its members, then there is a reason for it to act. Such an ethical organization must be structured in a way that it cannot possibly become a lobbying organization. It should not be able to change the laws by which it is created and run through the brute force of lobbying and campaign contributions. If the laws are to be changed, it should be by negotiation and the force of moral and ethical weight.

I think the healing professions have wandered a long distance from their traditions of ethical behavior. This is not to say that professionals have done so. I think the vast majority of physicians and nurses hold themselves to strict standards of ethical behavior. The problem is that this is an individual activity and responsibility, not one relegated to the profession as a profession. So long as we tolerate unethical behavior, we allow the base of trust on which the profession is built to erode. It does not matter whether we tolerate that behavior with a wink and a nod or with a wince and a groan. So long as the profession is constrained from effective action by a lack of power to do anything effective, the base of trust erodes. But society will not grant that power without bestowing responsibility to go with it.

Regardless of what else we do to reform healthcare, I think restoring professional stature and trust[9] and professional power and responsibility to the healing professions is important. Will the healing professions embrace such a bargain? I do not know. For the existing professional organizations, it offers a choice—end their current labor union-like activities to become the universal ethical organization, or risk a declining role when members fail to rejoin because they have switched to a different ethical organization. Outside of the context of a major reorganization of the delivery system, I don't think this change would develop enough steam to get moving. Would such a bargain allow disparate professions to come together into the same ethical organization (physicians, nurses, chiropractors, acupuncturists, etc)? I don't know, but I would hope so. Do I think it is a good idea? Yes.

Part Three:

Gap Analysis

Chapter 25

Gap Analysis

"Destiny is not a matter of chance, it is a matter of choice; it is not a thing to be waited for, it is a thing to be achieved."
—*William Jennings Bryan*

During the first chapters of this book, I laid out a method of inquiry and set some goals for the health care system. I did so by asking a few questions: "What do I think the health care system should do? What should it produce as a set of outcomes?" I answered with seven characteristics I thought would be appropriate:

- Universal financial access
- Affordability
- Safety
- Geographic availability
- Comprehensive coverage
- Personal care
- Professional behavior of providers

In the subsequent chapters, I have been discussing how we could construct a health care system that would manifest these characteristics or provide these results. I believe that everything I have described is within the realm of what we can accomplish. I have provided some references that indicate I am not the only one who believes the things I have written.

I promised at the beginning I would also describe the gap between where we are today and where I think we should go. In reality, I have been discussing that gap all along. In the early chapters, I discussed the seven goals in terms of the gap between where we are and where we ought to be. In the implementation sections, I have talked about current reality in the process of discussing how to construct a different reality. Much of the gap analysis work is already done. Therefore, I will only summarize here and consolidate the discussion without going back over territory already well covered.

Universal Financial Access

How are we doing? The fact that there are 45 million uninsured in our country says that we are not doing very well, at least for 45 million Americans.

Medicaid programs around the country generally pay well below what commercial payers and Medicare pay. (Medicaid is a federally subsidized state program, so eligibility, levels of coverage, and prices to providers vary from state to state.) Physicians who wish to do so can refuse to see Medicaid patients. This improves the finances of the physician's practice, but causes financially-related access problems for many Medicaid recipients.

The Medicare program physician fee schedule is tied to an arcane formula that has recently been calling for fee reductions. Since Medicare already pays less than commercial insurance in most communities, physicians may decide not to see Medicare patients as well as Medicaid patients. Every time Medicare threatens to reduce physician fees, lobbyists for the medical profession raise the specter of physicians refusing to participate in the program. To the extent this physician exodus from Medicare takes place, Medicare patients may also start to have access problems.

Commercial insurance is generally asked to pay top dollar to make up for what the government programs and the uninsured do not pay. (Remember the emergency room we ran in Chapter 14?) As commercial rates rise, so do commercial premiums. As premiums rise, more people opt out of the system. We should expect the number of uninsured to rise.

In summary, financial access to care is uneven, varying from the sublime to the ridiculous. Even the best programs are in jeopardy. We have a major gulf to cross, but I suspect the crossing of this gulf will be relatively easy, and it can be done in a heartbeat by the action of an importuned Congress. I believe that we, as a nation, will solve this problem. I am worried about the effects of our solution on the other characteristics I have described.

Affordability

We continue to spend almost twice as much per capita on health care as the second highest spending nation in the world. As a nation, we rank below 30th in life expectancy. There are lots of possible explanations for this excess of spending in comparison to results, and a lot of research has been done to elucidate the issue.

First, we pay physicians more in absolute dollars and more in comparison to the average pay in our society than any other country in the world. We certainly wish to honor and respect our physicians, but I am not sure we physicians are worth what we are being paid.

Second, we pay hospitals very well for inefficient, unsafe, redundant, and unnecessary care. We need to help hospitals attain greater efficiency and safety—and lower costs.

Third, we waste resources on interventions, both diagnostic and therapeutic, that do not produce better health outcomes. Trends indicate that as the number of specialists per capita increases in a population, the cost goes up and the quality goes down. This is hardly an accolade for the delivery system. We must find ways to drive waste from the system.

Fourth, as a nation, we still tend to believe that "more is better." We believe this of the healthcare system in spite of its high ranking as a cause of death in our country. Public education must encompass not only healthy behaviors, but also an understanding of healthcare that helps us get over our lust for unnecessary care.

Fifth, it seems clear to me that merely adding 45 million uninsured to the list of those covered will not necessarily bankrupt the system, provided we take steps to be sure payment equity is maintained, and that the providers do not turn this addition into a financial windfall.

We are in the midst of a number of experiments designed to improve affordability, but the results are not known yet. We are also in the midst of a coverage-affordability meltdown. One reason there are 45 million uninsured is the high cost of coverage.

Ultimately, who pays for medical care? We do, as the individual members of this society. We pay in reduced wages so our employers can purchase medical coverage. We pay in the premiums we pay out of our paychecks or out of our pockets. We pay in the form of taxes to county, state and federal governments. We pay in the increased cost of the goods we buy. (For example, the price of a General Motors car includes more dollars for medical coverage than for steel.) The way we pay is haphazard, disorganized, and inefficient—and it is creating a new financial elite in the United States: physicians and healthcare executives.

The solution is to get the system organized. I have suggested a number of ways to do that. I firmly believe that a system providing universal coverage will cut the cost to employers who continue to provide medical coverage—but there is much more work than that to be done. We must help to restrain the lust of our public for healthcare interventions and the avarice of our healthcare providers. This is a more difficult problem than financial access; we have a significant distance to travel, and there are no shortcuts.

Safety

Whether health care is the third, fourth, sixth, ninth, or tenth most common cause of death in the United States is not the issue. Health care ought not to be on the list at all.

The Culture of Blame: One of the lessons from industrial quality assurance programs has been that a culture of blame will not result in quality improvement. Quality improvement begins when one lets go of "fixing blame" and begins "fixing systems." The professional ethos of individual responsibility is an obstacle to making this transition. To the extent that the ethos of blaming individuals is supported by the tort system, the tort system itself stands as an obstacle to quality improvement.

Part of the process of establishing a culture of quality improvement will entail ending the application of tort law to medical events and applying an alternative compensation system that does not entail seeking a scapegoat. Not only will plaintiff attorneys likely oppose this change, but so will malpractice insurance companies and defense attorneys (whose roles will also go away). And so will many physicians and nurses who are so imbued with the culture of individual culpability that they will see this change as being a move AWAY from quality rather than toward it.[1] The gulf seems immense, but there are a number of quality initiatives under way right now that will help to demonstrate the value of "fixing systems" and may help to change some of the imbedded opposition to this change.

The horror of "cookbook" medicine: Another lesson from industrial quality assurance is that standardization is good. In healthcare, standardization appears to be an undermining of professional prerogatives and is seen as being anti-quality. The similarities in the disease from one person to another are what make a particular disease recognizable as a disease rather than a miscellaneous assortment of symptoms and signs. It is precisely this thread of commonality within the disease that can drive a standardized approach to dealing with that disease.

The argument of the skilled clinician is that every patient is a unique individual. No disease presents in exactly the same way every time. Therefore, the clinician requires a certain flexibility to deal with different individuals in different ways. Standards are seen as precluding that flexibility.

There is a third interpretation, to which I subscribe, that believes both in the need for standardization as a means to reach quality goals and in the need for variation from the standard to meet the needs of individual patients. This interpretation specifies that the pathway (the standard) is necessary to ensure that all of the baseline things are done every time they are indicated. The variation for individual differences should be superimposed on the standard process, as a reaction to a non-standard aspect of the patient or the clinical presentation.

The reality is that many excellent cooks are excellent cooks precisely because they use a standard recipe. It may be one they wrote themselves, but to achieve consistent results, they follow the same steps over and over again. Should they want to produce a slightly different result, they do not discard the cookbook. They use it to create a recipe variation that accomplishes the goal. Stated another way, it is impossible to know when you are leaving the pathway for a particular and defined reason if you do not have an established pathway to which to refer. If there is no established pathway, there is nothing to vary from. Without a standard, the pathway of care of any process risks degenerating to a random walk —which will produce random results.

This third interpretation demands pathways and standards. It demands expectations and measurement of expectations. It defines quality as adherence to the standards in a measurable way, but it allows reasoned variation from the pathway when the provider clearly knows where the pathway is and has chosen to depart from it for a particular reason.

There is still considerable opposition even to this interpretation of the world of standards, but there is gradually increasing acceptance that meeting minimum standards helps to improve the quality of care. What providers have not yet seen is that setting and meeting maximum standards is also a quality and safety issue. This is especially true in a world where medical interventions are among the top ten causes of death. We avoid smoking because it contributes to a leading cause of death. Should we not also avoid health care because it does the same?

Geographic Availability

I have offered one pathway to equitable geographic availability. The weakness of the present system is that it is built without a particular design for availability, and with only weak incentives to fulfilling the needs of underserved areas. Over the last two decades, geographic distribution of physicians has improved, but the preponderance of underserved areas has increased. Primary care availability is decreasing as we fail to train enough new primary care physicians to replace those who are retiring.

Solving the geographic availability problem will require creating a vision for what geographic availability would look like, followed by a game plan to achieve the goal. If we proceed without a design, we have few specifics to work on at the local level and no way to measure progress except by counting the underserved counties. With a particular vision of what the solution looks like and how to reach it, we can proceed to solve the problem of availability on a community-by-community basis. In the meantime, we can take that vision, multiply by the number of underserved communities, and have an idea what we need in the way of personnel, equipment, and construction over the entire nation. This will allow us to set funding, training, and construction budgets and goals, and give us ways to measure progress.

I am not particularly concerned about what vision is chosen, so long as we choose one. There is serious conversation among the primary care physician specialties. What we are lacking is any motion toward a social consensus. We have a long way to go.

Comprehensive Coverage

The ideas I bring to the comprehensive coverage discussion also have significant impact in the arenas of cost and quality of care. I believe we deserve to be treated in proven, helpful ways, and unscrupulous providers should not be able to use methods that are lucrative but ineffective.[2] My proposal is for a new government agency to evaluate healthcare techniques and regulate payment to fund only those with enough evidence to suggest they are appropriate. This is one way to achieve the goal.

Establishing the data warehouse I referred to is not an extraordinarily difficult task. Currently, Medicare data is being accumulated and can be accessed by researchers—but not until about two years after the date of service. The warehouse needs to be larger. Inter-communicability is important. The warehouse should be able to receive and incorporate data from a number of different systems. Ideally (but not a necessary part of my vision), the same warehouse would be used by commercial carriers. This kind of data-processing ability currently exists in the commercial market.

Establishing the "Health Coverage Administration" would require an act of Congress, the signature of a friendly and understanding president, and both funds and personal efforts by many people to get it going. Over the long run, some structure like this will be required to support any federal healthcare program. There is evidence that the Center for Medicare and Medicaid Services is moving in this direction already.

The gulf seems wide. From the conceptual standpoint, it is narrowing. Careful design work will be required to bring it to fruition.

Personal Care

Those of us who have found personal physicians with whom we can have a personal relationship are fortunate. Too many of us cannot do that. One of the obstacles to forming such a relationship is good health. If you never see a doctor, it is hard to have a personal relationship with one. On the other hand, anyone who sees the same physician once or twice a year over several years is in a position to begin forming a positive relationship.

Developing this relationship involves two issues: the patient being able to see the same doctor at most visits, and the doctor having the time and attention available to spend on the relationship. In many ways, we are much closer than one might think. In some ways, we are far apart.

One of the major barriers is economic expectations that push income-producing activities at the expense of relationship-producing activities. There are a number of motivators behind this push. One is the disparity in income between the doctors with whom one might form a personal relationship. On one hand are the primary care physicians and specialists who care for people over time, and on the other are the physicians who just do procedures and only relate to patients for a short time. Why do we think the latter should be paid two or three times as much as the former? The fact that we are all participating in an avaricious society does not help.

I have suggested that changes should be made in physician training and compensation. I have also suggested that we might wish to turn to non-physician providers to increase the manpower sufficiently to allow providers to take more time per patient. Changing physician training is the easy hurdle of this group. Changing incomes is difficult at best and nearly impossible if the higher paid specialties are asked to take a cut in pay. Within the context of a variegated system in which different payers pay different amounts, it is possible for physicians to choose which programs to serve in order to maximize their income; in a system where fee schedules can be set by a national fee-setting body, the pick-and-choose option goes away. There will still be resistance.

Training more primary care physicians takes time—but a change in compensation would shorten that time considerably. Training more physicians who enter medical education without the expectation of becoming rich during a career of medical practice will take longer.

There are obstacles large and small. But the rewards are so great that it would be a mistake not to include a goal like this in our expectations and to incorporate steps to implement it into the overall plan. In addition, most of these steps will work to help contain overall cost and improve the geographic distribution of services.

Professional Behavior of Providers

A profession is a class of people within a society who are accorded special status by virtue of their membership in the profession. We accord them trust and esteem based on their status as members of the profession. We may not (often do not) accord them high personal incomes, but we do offer them compensation in the form of an esteem that is ennobling.

The health care professions have largely lost that cachet in the United States. Instead, they have reaped financial well-being and an abiding sense of distrust from much of the lay public. I think it is still possible to reverse this trend. It would require granting the caring professions not only the authority to set and enforce ethical standards, but also the responsibility and accountability for doing the job well.

I think we are some distance from being able to accomplish this, for a variety of reasons discussed in the last chapter. If it is incorporated into an overall system change, I think it could be done. If it is well done, it could be perceived as a benefit restored to the caring professions—a restoration of something they have lost. Seen in that light, it may actually make some of the other changes work more easily.

On the other hand, approaching this issue separately from the others is likely to be seen as an imposition on the caring professions. As such, it might be counter-productive and would likely produce unanticipated results in other parts of the system.

How far are we from being able to produce the changes suggested? I think we are not far from it. The bulk of the individuals in the caring professions strive mightily to be ethical in both appearance and act. This support of the underlying ethical nature of the caring professions will be embraced by many.

In Summary

Where does that leave us? With seven goals, each with a complex pathway filled with obstacles, dangers, and opportunities. Each with unforeseen twists and turnings in the pathway. Many with surprising consequences.

We need to begin the voyage, even if we cannot anticipate all of the adventures we shall have. If we do not start, we can never arrive. The ocean is wide. The gap is large. But there is a way across —if we will but plan and act.

Chapter 26

Concluding Words

"Every new opinion, at its starting point, is precisely a minority of one."
—Thomas Carlyle

After all of the foregoing discussion, the reader might well wonder which of the many tasks I have set for our society is the one we should start with. After all, I have outlined changes in the healthcare system that are somewhere between a great upheaval and a revolution.[1] Surely, there must be some key point at which we can begin—some simple things we can do to help now while we get ready to do the rest.

Herein lies grave danger. The danger comes in two forms:

- The danger that we will do some little things and succeed and stop.

- The danger that we will do some little things and fail and stop.

How Success Can Lead to Failure

Let us say that we start in to improve a single aspect of the system in a not-too-threatening way. To our gratification, there is some improvement in the parameters we are measuring. We think "Roger Howe wasn't so smart after all—it didn't take so much of a

277

change and look at all the improvement we have gained." We then rest on our laurels, believing that we have actually fixed something.

Remember that healthcare is a complex system. It conforms in every way to system theory/complexity theory. There is nothing in complexity that says we cannot fix one aspect of the problem. The difficulty is that we cannot do it in isolation. Whatever we do will somehow, sooner or later, produce unexpected consequences in some other part of the system.

We have been doing this over and over again for at least six decades, and very intensely for the last forty years. What have we wrought? We started insurance policies because it was a way of getting and keeping employees (and for the minor added reason that it improved employees' access to health care). The government thought it was such a good idea we got a tax break on our health insurance policies. Doctor visits only cost a couple of bucks, so we insured hospital care. The result is an escalating hospital industry that is still out of control and is the number three or six or nine killer of people in the country.

We thought the poor elderly among us deserved access to health care and were not getting what they needed, so we made Medicare to help the elderly—Part A to take care of hospital costs and Part B to take care of outpatient costs. We now have a very expensive program with archaic provisions. We have had to get around the lack of preventive services by instituting Medicare HMO coverage and making special exceptions. We have had to pass legislation to provide some kind of coverage for medications.[2] Costs continue to spiral upward, and every time we seem to be able to get Medicare costs under control, private insurance suddenly gets more expensive.

If the threat to the system is significant enough, then some programs will be adopted and some changes will occur. And as soon as we are lulled into a sense of security that we have actually accomplished something, we will discover that things are worse than they ever were before.

Failure Can Lead to Failure

The other danger is to start with a small project—goodness knows we have had plenty of them—and find we are unable to bring it to fruition because of unanticipated, cascading opposition. And then we give up.

The reality is that there will be tremendous inertia against making all the changes that need to be made. Some of the changes will generate heated opposition, but we should not mind that as long as the conversation continues. "Okay. We understand you don't like our solution to Problem X. However, Problem X still needs to be solved, so please propose alternative solutions."

I have already signaled some areas where I think there will be intense opposition to change. Professional tort liability is one. There are others I have implied but not yet spoken of openly. For example, if we change the relationship between the incomes of primary care physicians and the incomes of super-specialists without changing the overall average income of physicians, some physicians will be earning less. No one should expect the more highly paid physicians to welcome this news, or accept it without a fight. There are many physicians who do not share my confidence that expanding primary care services is an appropriate pathway to improved quality at lower cost. They will oppose this vehemently.

If we embark on the "grand plan," then such opposition should help us know we are on the right pathway. If something we propose is easily and readily accepted by everyone and seems to be almost effortless to implement, it is probably because the system has already subverted what we are trying to do. Watch out.

Winning Through Advance Planning

But in the final analysis, the only way we can "win"—as a society, as patients, and as healthcare professionals—is to start at the basics and work toward a solution that cuts across all the issues, that builds the system we are hoping for.

To do this, one must start by answering the question, "What do we want the healthcare system to do?" Once we agree on a set of answers to that question, then we must ask and answer the next question: "What would a system have to look like to accomplish all of that?"

With the answers to these two questions, we have our sailing orders. Now we can see the entire task. And we can plot our progress toward it. We can use our goals to create measurements that will tell us when we are moving in the right direction. We will find that some of the things we do will work much better than expected —and something will fall apart behind us. We will find that some of the things we try to do will not work at all—and we will need to revise the strategy. But if we know what we want, we can know whether what we are doing is getting us any closer to where we want to be.

I have laid out for the reader my personal answers to the questions. I have discussed them at some length. I have brought in opinions and research from many areas to help the reader understand. But all of this is merely the warming up exercises.[3] The reality is that we must do this as a society.

I wish us well on that voyage.

Chapter Notes

Chapter 1

1. Kleinke, JD: Oxymorons—The Myth of a U.S. Health Care System: Jossey-Bass, San Francisco, CA, 2001.

2. Howe, Roger K: Where Have We Failed? A Systemic Analysis of U.S. Health Care: American College of Physician Executives, Tampa, FL, 2002.

3. Blendon, Robert J et al: Confronting Competing Demands to Improve Quality: A Five-Country Hospital Survey: Health Affairs, May/June 2004 (Vol. 23, No. 3):119-135. In a survey of hospital executives from the United Kingdom, Australia, Canada, New Zealand, and the United States, there was agreement about the importance of information technology in the process of improving quality. All expressed concerns about staffing shortages and emergency department waiting times and quality. However, the executives from the U.S. are the most negative about their country's health care system.

Chapter 2

1. Abramson, John: Overdo$ed America—The Broken Promise of American Medicine: Harper-Collins Publishers Inc., New York, NY, 2004. This is a wonderful and well-documented indictment of the pharmaceutical industry, and how the drive for profits has poisoned the entire healthcare system.

2. Bartlett, DL & Steele, JB: Critical Condition—How Health Care in America Became Big Business—and Bad Medicine: Doubleday, 2004. This is an amazingly accurate indictment of the current health care system, given that it comes from two outsiders. Not surprisingly, they fail to see some of what they should see and misinterpret some of what they do see, but overall, the book is a wonderfully readable, generally accurate account of what is wrong in health care today. Correcting the problem of health care has three major components: recognizing there is a problem, developing a solution, and gathering the political momentum to do something about implementing the solution. The authors do an excellent job of the first and a good job helping with the third. My job in my book is to do something about the second.

3. Goldman DP & McGlynn EA: U.S. Health Care—Facts About Cost, Access, and Quality: RAND Corporation, 2005. The authors point out, among other things, that about one third of several common surgeries are probably unnecessary, that one third of hospital admissions are probably unnecessary, and that Americans receive only about 50% of recommended care.

4. Herzlinger, RF & Parsa-Parsi, R: Consumer-Driven Health Care —Lessons from Switzerland: JAMA, September 8, 2004 (Vol. 292, No. 10):1213-1220. Switzerland spends less of GDP and fewer dollars per population and achieves longer life expectancy than the United States. In Switzerland, privately purchased, individual health insurance is mandated by law; there is an assistance program in place for those who cannot afford it.

5. Howe, Roger K: Where Have We Failed? A Systemic Analysis of U.S. Health Care: American College of Physician Executives, Tampa, FL, 2002.

6. Institute of Medicine: To Err is Human: Building a Safer Health System: Washington, D.C.: Institute of Medicine, 1999.

7. Institute of Medicine: Crossing the Quality Chasm: A New Health System for the 21st Century: National Academy Press, 2001.

8. Kleinke, JD: Oxymorons—The Myth of a U.S. Health Care System: Jossey-Bass, San Francisco, CA, 2001. Though now somewhat dated, this is an excellent rendering of some of the problems of the healthcare system.

9. Krugman, Paul: America's Failing Health: New York Times, August 27, 2004: page A23. When newspaper columnists begin to write editorials about health care reform, momentum must be building.

10. Lawrence, David: From Chaos to Care—the Promise of Team-Based Medicine: Perseus Publishing, Cambridge, MA, 2002. This is a warm and tender story of the breakdown in modern healthcare, and one of the approaches we must take if we are to fix it.

11. Blendon, Robert J et al: Confronting Competing Demands to Improve Quality: A Five-Country Hospital Survey: Health Affairs, May/June 2004 (Vol. 23, No. 3):119-135. In a survey of hospital executives from the United Kingdom, Australia, Canada, New Zealand and the United States, there was agreement about the importance of information technology in the process of improving quality. All expressed concerns about staffing shortages and emergency department waiting times and quality. However, the executives from the U.S. are the most negative about their country's health care system.

12. I should differentiate carefully at the outset among three terms that are often used almost interchangeably, but which, to me,

have different shades of meaning. These three terms are "medical care," "health care," and "healthcare."

- By "medical care," I mean services rendered in the diagnosis and treatment of disease or in the prevention of a specific disease. Medical care is predominantly rendered by physicians or under the supervision or orders of physicians. Medical care includes all of what happens in hospitals, as well as almost all of what happens in doctors' offices and clinics. It includes immunizations against specific diseases, and all of the examinations and tests that are done to diagnose, and all of the medications and surgery that are rendered to treat diseases.

- By "health care," I intend to encompass a much larger array of services, but still ones that are primarily oriented toward physical and mental well-being or health. Health care would include medical care, but would also include all of what is now called alternative or complementary medicine. It would include much of the general surveillance done by health departments, and it certainly includes all of the remedies and nostrums available in health food stores. In the broadest sense, health care includes all of the things that are done, bought, and sold for the purposes of enhancing health.

- By "healthcare," I intend to indicate a still larger array of undertakings. Healthcare, also "the healthcare system," is intended to indicate—in addition to the things done, purchased, or sold directly to improve health—the mechanisms for financing that care, or for doing or financing the research that establishes what correct care is. Thus, a health insurance company is not providing medical care or health care, but it is part of the healthcare system because it pays the cost of those services. Similarly, the Medicaid program in each state and the Center for Medicare and Medicaid Services at the federal government level are all part of healthcare. So, too, is the National Institutes of Health, and so are all of the medical schools, even the parts of them that do not render any direct patient care. Therefore, by "healthcare" I intend to denote the entire enterprise surrounding the development, financing, and provision of all goods and services related to the prevention, detection, or treatment of disease, or the maintenance or improvement of health.

13. Aaron, Henry J, et al: How Federalism Could Spur Bipartisan Action on the Uninsured: Health Affairs: Web Exclusive W4 (31 March 2004):168-178. The authors examine a somewhat different set of assumptions and come to the conclusion that the solution to the problem of the uninsured may come piecemeal, in portions of a solution tried and tested, and in experiments on a state-by-state basis. While this is a wonderful concept, and I wish it would work, the experience in Oregon is not reassuring. New experiments tend, over time, to migrate back to the mean —which is exactly what one would expect in trying to solve part of the problem in the context of a complex system-based problem.

14. Flower, Joe: Mapping the Future of Health Care: The Physician Executive: January-February 2005:60-62. Noting that "if you're not sure where you're going, that's where you'll end up," the author points to five goal statements from the Institute for Healthcare Improvement:

   1. Eliminate unnecessary deaths

   2. Eliminate unnecessary pain

   3. Eliminate helplessness

   4. Eliminate waiting

   5. Eliminate waste

Two things are important about this short article. One is the emphasis on having a goal in mind, and the other is that the five goals are entwined with the ones I have announced.

Chapter 3

1. Bush, George W.: Ensuring Access To Health Care—The Bush Plan: JAMA October 27, 2004 (Vol. 292, No. 16):2010-2011. Mr. Bush announces what he anticipates to be the results of his plan—more affordable health coverage, 11 million to 17.5 million more Americans insured, tort liability reform. His article places significant emphasis on HSA enactment.

2. Kerry, John: Ensuring Access to Health Care—The Kerry Plan: JAMA, October 27, 2004 (Vol. 292, No. 16):2007-2009. Mr. Kerry outlines a plan of expanded coverage, more affordable coverage, medical malpractice reform, a patient bill of rights, and emphasis on medical research.

3. World Health Organization: The World Health Report, 2005: available at http://www.who.int/whr/2005/whr2005_en.pdf. Here is a summary chart of some of the information contained therein (index. Pages 176-203)(the data year is 2002): (See WHO 2005 Report on Life Expectancy table on next page.)

4. Gabel, Jon, et al: Health Benefits in 2004: Four Years of Double Digit Premium Increases Take Their Toll on Coverage: Health Affairs, September/October 2004 (Vol. 23, No. 5):200-209. Since 2001, premiums have increased 59%, and employee contributions have grown by 57% for single coverage and 49% for family coverage. The percent of workers covered by their own employer's health plan has fallen from 65% to 61% during that time.

5. Mintz, Morton: Single-Payer: Good for Business: The Nation, November 15, 2004. While the author advocates a single-payer system, what he really does best is document how the current system is not working, and how a system of universal coverage would be preferable. He makes the case that the shrinking industrial base of the country is at least partially due to the high cost

of employees, of which the cost of their health insurance is a major component. It is a wonderful article.

6. Bodenheimer, Thomas: The Political Divide in Health Care: A Liberal Perspective: Health Affairs, November/December 2005 (Vol. 24, No. 6):1426-1435. The author examines and contrasts liberal and conservative thought and premises as regards health care. The liberal position includes both moral principles and utilitarian arguments attempting to balance the needs of the individual with the concerns of the entire population.

7. Gladwell, Malcolm: The Moral Hazard Myth: The New Yorker, August 29, 2005. The author presents a compelling case for "social insurance"—the insurance concept of spreading the cost of care as widely as possible to assure that everyone who needs care can receive it. This is part of the social contract—part of our interdependence. It is a sense of social contract understood in the other industrialized countries, but not in the United States. His advocacy is based, in part, on his understanding that the concept of "moral hazard" is a basically flawed one—though he tends to go to the extreme of discounting it completely, which is also an error as much as believing that moral hazard is the only explanation for increased utilization by the insured.

8. McWilliams, J Michael et al: Health Insurance Coverage and Mortality Among the Near-Elderly: Health Affairs, July/August 2004 (Vol. 23, No. 4):223-233. Not surprisingly, the mortality rate among near-elderly (age 55-64) people without insurance is significantly higher than among those with insurance. This is noted when mortality rates are adjusted for co-existing diseases. The difference is more pronounced among the poor and the ill (for example, those with high blood pressure or diabetes). Ethical justice concerns arise here.

9. Miller, Wilhelmine, et al: Covering the Uninsured: What is it Worth? Health Affairs: Web Exclusive W4 (31 March 2004): 157-167. The authors use data from the Institute on Medicine

Committee on Consequences of Uninsurance, and estimate the economic cost (in quality-adjusted life-years lost) of uninsurance at $65-130 billion per year. They also estimate the cost of coverage for the 40 million uninsured at $34-69 billion. This suggests an economic benefit to society in covering the uninsured.

10. Blewett, Lynn A, et al: Covering Kids: Variation in Health Insurance Coverage Trends by State, 1996-2002: Health Affairs, November/December 2004 (Vol. 23, No. 6):170-180. In the interval described, the rate of uninsurance in children changed. That change varied from an increase of 3.4% in Washington to a decrease of 9.5% in Arkansas. The actual rate of uninsurance in 2001-2002 varied from a high of 23.1% in Texas to a low of 5.5% in Rhode Island. The authors point to the dramatic variation from one geographic area to another.

11. Budetti, Peter P: Ten Years Beyond the Health Security Act Failure: JAMA, October 27, 2004 (Vol. 292, No. 16):2000-2006. Since President Clinton's proposal in 1993, the problems addressed by that proposal have continued and worsened. The problem of uninsurance is worse. The health care system deteriorates. The central goals of the HSA still form the components of a vision for future action: universal coverage, quality improvement, cost containment, subsidies for the economically vulnerable.

12. Robinson, James C: Consolidation and the Transformation of Competition in Health Insurance: Health Affairs, November/December 2004 (Vol. 23, No. 6):11-24. The health insurance industry is consolidating. Fewer and fewer companies are having larger and larger market shares. This is not what "managed competition" was supposed to do.

13. Gordon, S and Mills, A: Timely Care a Basic Right: Toronto Star, Friday, June 10, 2005. http://www.thestar.com/NASApp/cs/ContentServer?pagename=thestar/Layout/Article_Type1&c=Article&cid=1118353813412&call_pageid=968332188492&col=968793972154&t=TS_Home&DPL=IvsNDS%2f7ChAX

&tacodalogin=yes. A law in Quebec banned private health insurance; the Supreme Court (of Canada) invalidated that ban, indicating that the government cannot obstruct people from getting quality health care. The article discusses at some length the consequences of a two-tier system for the financing and delivery of health care. One of the concerns is that if many people leave the public system and take their money with them, the system will not be able to continue to deliver high-quality care to the remainder.

Chapter 5

1. See the listings at http://www.ahrq.gov/clinic/uspstfix.htm.

Chapter 7

1. Institute of Medicine: To Err is Human: Building a Safer Health System: Washington, D.C.: Institute of Medicine, 1999. The IOM published high and low estimates of the number of deaths: 44,000 to 98,000. These numbers are extrapolations from studies done in Colorado and Utah, which are pretty well documented. There has actually been some debate as to whether the number should be as low as 40,000 or maybe as high as 120,000. As I point out, it is not the actual precise number that is important. The order of magnitude speaks for itself. It is too many.

2. Deaths: Leading Causes for 2002: http://www.cdc.gov/nchs/ fastats/ lcod.htm

3. Arkansas Foundation for Medical Care: Community-Acquired Pneumonia Data: http://www.afmc.org/HTML/programs/ statisticaldata/medicare/hospital/cap.aspx?skin=print; April 29, 2005. The data, taken from Medicare part A claims in Arkansas, demonstrate the rates at which we see compliance with the same criteria discussed by Hahn, et al (NEJM:347;25:2039). The results are tabulated only for individual criteria—no attempt is made to assess the rate at which ALL criteria (or any subset of criteria) were met. Four criteria of interest were:

    • Initial antibiotic within four hours (actual rate 75.5%)

    • Correct antibiotic selected (actual rate 77.6%)

    • Blood culture done timely (actual rate 66%)

    • Blood culture before first antibiotic (actual rate 86.8%)

From these data, we may discern that at least 86.8% of patients received at least one of these four crucial treatment elements, but the number receiving all four may be as low as 5.9% or as high as 66%.

4. Arkansas Foundation for Medical Care: Heart Failure Data: http://www.afmc.org/HTML/progams/statisticaldata/medicare/hospital/chf.aspx?skin=print; April 29, 2005. The data, taken from Medicare part A claims in Arkansas, demonstrate the rates of adherence to four standards for the care of patients with congestive heart failure. All four standards have good science behind them. Alarmingly, only 8.4% of patients being discharged from the hospital received adequate discharge instructions!

5. Lee, Douglas S., et al: Risk-Treatment Mismatch in the Pharmacotherapy of Heart Failure: Journal of the American Medical Association, September 14, 2005 (Vol. 294; No. 10):1240-1247. "Patients with heart failure at greatest risk of death are least likely to receive ACE inhibitors, ACE inhibitors or ARBs, and beta-adrenoreceptor antagonists." The medications referred to are life-saving in congestive heart failure. The patients who need these medications the most are precisely the ones in whom it would be the most important to institute treatment with these life-saving agents. But these patients are the ones least consistently treated with these medications.

6. Chung, PJ and Schuster, MA: Access and Quality in Child Health Services: Voltage Drops: Health Affairs, September/October 2004 (Vol. 23, No. 5):77-87. "We find critical policy needs (such as expanded insurance opportunities, increased care coordination, and improved quality measurement) at all system levels. Comprehensive access to insurance and services does not guarantee that children will receive high-quality (safe and effective) care." I fully agree that access to insurance and services does not guarantee safety or effectiveness. These are two different problems requiring different approaches.

7. Variations Revisited: Health Affairs Web Exclusive Collection; October 7, 2004. This is a full edition (of 144 pages plus two articles from 13 Feb 2002 and 7 April 2004) of articles flowing from Jack Wennberg's work on small area variation. For anyone

interested in seeing some of the science behind the statement made about geographic variation that is not supported by geographic differences in demographics, this is a wealth of material. It starts with and develops some of the science about variations, then branches off into analysis and commentary. The viewpoints are telling. I will also be citing a number of the articles from this edition separately for particular points, but I found the volume to be an exciting read—I read it cover to cover and found article after article to be interesting and compelling.

8. Hussey, Peter S et al: How Does the Quality of Care Compare in Five Countries?: Health Affairs, May/June 2004 (Vol. 23, No. 3):89-102. The Commonwealth Fund International Working Group on Quality Indicators collected data on twenty-one indicators of quality related to care provided in Australia, Canada, New Zealand, England and the United States. No one country consistently scored high or low.

9. Rogowski, Jeannette A, et al: Variation in the Quality of Care for Very-Low-Birthweight Infants: Implications for Policy: Health Affairs, September/October 2004 (Vol. 23, No. 5):88-97. "The United States has one of the highest infant mortality rates among industrialized countries. This is particularly true among black American infants, whose mortality rates are 2.5 times those of white American infants. More than two-thirds of all deaths among Americans under age fifteen occur in the first year of life, and nearly half occur within twenty-eight days of birth." The authors find that improvements in neonatal care have improved the outlook dramatically, but that the quality of neonatal care is highly variable across hospitals. Either we must improve quality at the lagging hospitals, or we must move high-risk births to hospitals with the best outcomes. This is not a hospital system or a medical staff problem, it is a societal problem.

10. Halm, Ethan A., et al: Management of Community-Acquired Pneumonia: New England Journal of Medicine; Vol. 347, No.

25 (December 19, 2002):2039-2045. The authors review the assessment and treatment of community acquired pneumonia. They note that annually there are about 4 million cases in the United States with about 1 million hospitalizations. Hospital care of community acquired pneumonia costs more than 20 times as much as outpatient care—in excess of $9 billion a year. There are variations in the rate and length of hospitalization that are not explained by differences in the characteristics of the patients or the severity of their disease. This is a review article, gathering scientific material and recommendations made by various resources over a number of years to offer advice on the evaluation and treatment of this condition.

11. Damberg, Cheryl L, et al: The California Report on Coronary Artery Bypass Graft Surgery—1999 Hospital Data: available from Pacific Business Group on Health at www.pbgh.org. This is an extensive, detailed and revealing report on the quality of CABG surgery done in California in 1999. There are some problems: only 70% of the hospitals and 68% of the surgeries are represented; it took three and a half years to move from the end of the data year to publication. Case mix adjustment was used to adjust expected mortality rates in various hospitals. There were a few of the participating hospitals that did better than expected and a few that did worse; most performed as predicted. The performance of hospitals included in the report was, in aggregate, better than the performance of the hospitals not included. This is important work, but must be spread to include all hospitals; underperforming hospitals should either improve or stop doing the procedure.

Chapter 9

1. Aaron, Henry J: The Good, the Bad, and the Ugly: The Washington Spectator, January 15, 2004: 1-3. The author describes the Medicare Modernization Act as being confusing. He raises issues of process, issues of cost and funding, and issues of administration.

2. Fleming, Michael: Letter to Members of the American Academy of Family Practice: received in e-mail from Dr. Fleming (AAFP President) on January 29, 2004. Dr. Fleming wrote about the support of the AAFP for the Medicare Modernization Act. He noted six dramatic positive changes to be enacted by the law and several serious shortcomings that would need to be changed or overcome before the law went into effect.

3. Rubenstein, Sarah: Health Plans Embrace Alternatives: Wall Street Journal, September 22, 2004. The author notes the increasing prevalence in the use of and in insurance coverage for alternative (now called "complementary") healing techniques, such as acupuncture and chiropractic.

4. Ruggle, Mary: Mainstreaming Complementary Therapies: New Directions in Health Care; Health Affairs: Vol. 24, No. 4 (July/August 2005):980-990. The author tracks the emergence of complementary and alternative medicine (CAM) from denigrated obscurity to increasing recognition and respectability, and expresses optimism in the further integration of these treatments. She describes the establishment of the National Center for Complementary and Alternative Medicine in the National Institutes of Health, and its functioning.

Chapter 10

1. Information about this program was available on June 18, 2006,
    at this website: http://www.ihi.org/IHI/Programs/Campaign/
    Campaign.htm?TabId=1. In summary, the six items in the pro-
    gram are these:

    - Deploy rapid response teams at the first sign of patient de-
      cline

    - Deliver reliable, evidence-based care for acute myocardial in-
      farction to prevent deaths from heart attack

    - Prevent adverse drug events (ADEs) by implementing medi-
      cation reconciliation

    - Prevent central line infections by implementing a series of in-
      terdependent, scientifically grounded steps called the "Central
      Line Bundle"

    - Prevent surgical site infections by reliably delivering the cor-
      rect perioperative care

    - Prevent ventilator-associated pneumonia by implementing a
      series of interdependent, scientifically grounded steps called
      the "Ventilator Bundle"

    This program was announced in December 2004 as the "Save
    100,000 Lives" campaign, with the goal of saving 100,000 lives
    by June 30, 2006. The announcement on June 18, 2006, suggests
    that almost 125,000 lives have been saved. Not all hospitals are
    participating, so the potential is even higher. The amazing thing
    is that this campaign has proven that it can be done. Now the
    issue will be to demonstrate persistence. There is a tremendous
    tendency to backslide to old behaviors.

Chapter 11

1. Thom, David H, et al: Measuring Patients' Trust in Physicians when Assessing Quality of Care: Health Affairs, July/August 2004 (Vol. 23, No. 4):124-132. "A person who trusts a provider is more likely to seek care, to comply with treatment recommendations, and to return for follow-up care than a person who has little trust in a specific provider or the health care system." Thus do the authors start the examination. The effects of trust are discussed. Mechanisms for measuring trust are discussed. Methods of improving trust are discussed. The question is whether anyone will move forward with any of this.

Chapter 12

1. Gostin, Lawrence O, et al: The Future of the Public's Health: Vision, Values, and Strategies: Health Affairs, July/August 2004 (Vol. 23, No. 4):96-107. The authors support the Institute of Medicine (IOM) position in which the IOM in two documents (The Future of Public Health–1988 and The Future of the Public's Health in the Twenty-first Century–2002) has spelled out a vision of the goal of modern public health: "healthy people in healthy communities." The authors address a series of recommendations for change in the public health structure, including the following:

   • Establish a national Public Health Council.

   • Report annually to Congress the state of the nation's health.

   • Establish a funding mechanism to support state and local public health agencies.

   • Set conditions for providing support to state and local public health agencies based on progress toward and adherence to quality standards.

   • Provide health care coverage for every person residing in the United States.

   • Engage state and local governments in land-use planning to encourage healthier lifestyles and habitats.

   • Adopt more comprehensive strategies to reduce health disparities.

   Needless to say, this is a broad and sweeping vision for a change in the "public health" structure that essentially restructures health care.

Chapter 13

1. America's Health Insurance Plans: A Commitment to Improve Health Care Quality, Access, and Affordability: A statement from the Board of Directors of America's Health Insurance Plans, March 2004. http://www.ahip.org/ This organization of health insurance plans looks for a far-reaching set of changes based on private action in the context of a continuation of the current system organization. The changes suggested include advancing evidence-based medicine as the "gold standard" for healthcare—both with ways of measuring accomplishment and of encouraging adoption and use of evidence-based medicine. They advocate that all Americans should have access through public and private coverage and through support for the public health infrastructure. They note that about one third of the uninsured have incomes between 150% and 300% of the poverty level—people who are not eligible for government programs and cannot afford private insurance. Of these, about half are employed by small businesses that employ fewer than 100 employees. The authors note that ways must be found to encourage younger Americans to seek and maintain health insurance (to support the risk pool). They also advocate an improvement in affordability: "maximize cost savings that can be achieved through improvements in access and quality and, at the same time, take additional steps to make health care more affordable through regulatory and legal reforms." So, finally, there is recognition at the end of this ambitious plan that federal action will be required.

2. Howe, Roger K: Where Have We Failed? A Systemic Analysis of U.S. Health Care: American College of Physician Executives, Tampa, FL, 2002.

3. Fuchs, Victor R & Emanuel, Ezekiel J: Health Care Reform: Why? What? When?: Health Affairs, November/December 2005

(Vol. 24, No. 6):1399-1414. The authors consider individual mandates with subsidies, single-payer systems, and insurance vouchers as approaches to reforming the payment system. They tend to favor vouchers. They do not see the drive for health care reform having sufficient power to make changes short of a crisis.

4. Moran, Donald W: Whence and Whither Health Insurance? A Revisionist History: Health Affairs, November/December 2005 (Vol. 24, No. 6):1415-1425. The author looks at current trends and a cost comparison between Medicare and the VA system, and concludes that more direct provision of care systems and fewer insurance-like systems will be less expensive.

5. Cunningham, P and Hadley, J: Expanding Care Versus Expanding Coverage: How to Improve Access to Care: Health Affairs, July/August 2004 (Vol. 23, No. 4):234-244. Expanding publicly funded Community Health Centers does not expand availability of care nearly as much as providing medical coverage does.

6. Longman, Phillip: The Best Care Anywhere: Washington Monthly, Jan/Feb 2006.

Chapter 14

1. In early 2005, a report was issued indicating that the number is not 45 million but 35 million. The problem is that the new report counted only those individuals who were uninsured for the entire year. When you add all the people who are only uninsured for part of the year, it seems you get back to 45 million (reported by National Public Radio).

2. Miller, Wilhelmine, et al: Covering the Uninsured: What is it Worth? Health Affairs: Web Exclusive W4 (31 March 2004): 157-167. The authors used data from the Institute on Medicine Committee on Consequences of Uninsurance and estimated the economic cost (in quality adjusted life years lost) of uninsurance at $65-130 billion per year. They also estimated the cost of coverage for the 40 million uninsured at $34-69 billion. This suggests an economic benefit to society in covering the uninsured.

3. Paying a Premium—The Added Cost of Care for the Uninsured: Families USA Publication No. 05-101; Families USA Foundation; June 2005: http://www.familiesusa.org/. There is a very serious look here at the dollar impact on private health insurance premiums due to the care of the uninsured. The authors indicate that there will be "nearly 48 million Americans uninsured for the entire year in 2005." They believe that about two-thirds of the $43 billion in costs generated by the care of the uninsured is reflected in the cost of premiums paid by people with private health insurance. "Health insurance premiums for families who have insurance through their private employers, on average, are $922 higher in 2005 due to the cost of health care for the uninsured." This ranges to as high as $1,875 in New Mexico. Because of the increasing number of uninsured, this amount will increase by 2010 to $1,502 on average. The amount of "unreimbursed care" provided in 2005 is estimated to be $43 billion and will rise by 2010 to $60 billion. This article is well worth reading.

4. A set of six articles published in the Health Affairs Web Exclusive provide some insight, some contrasting of opinion, and some information about emergency department capacity and economics. Among the responses are a variety of different opinions about how to solve the problem of ER crowding. Only by implication do any of them recognize that increasing the supply of primary care physicians and people's access to those physicians would make a difference. The group of articles makes interesting reading:

- Melnick, Glenn A, et al: Emergency Department Capacity and Access in California, 1990-2001: An Economic Analysis: Health Affairs: Web Exclusive W4 (24 March 2004):136-142.

- Fields, W. Wesley: Emergency Care In California: Robust Capacity or Busted Access?: Health Affairs: Web Exclusive W4 (24 March 2004):143-145.

- Siegel, Bruce: The Emergency Department: Rethinking the Safety Net for the Safety Net: Health Affairs: Web Exclusive W4 (24 March 2004): 146-148.

- Kellermann, Arthur L: Emergency Care in California: No Emergency?: Health Affairs: Web Exclusive W4 (24 March 2004):149-151.

- Dauner, C. Duane: Emergency Capacity in California: A Look at More Recent Trends: Health Affairs: Web Exclusive W4 (24 March 2004): 152-154.

- Melnick, Glenn A, et al: Hospital Emergency Departments: The Authors Respond: Health Affairs: Web Exclusive W4 (24 March 2004):155-156.

5. America's Health Insurance Plans: A Commitment to Improve Health Care Quality, Access, and Affordability: A Statement from the Board of Directors of America's Health Insurance Plans, March 2004. This organization of health insurance plans looks for a far-reaching set of changes based on private action in

the context of a continuation of the current system organization. The changes suggested include advancing evidence-based medicine as the "gold standard" for healthcare—with both ways of measuring accomplishment and ways of encouraging adoption and use of evidence-based medicine. They advocate that all Americans should have access through public and private coverage and through support for the public health infrastructure. They note that about one third of the uninsured have incomes between 150% and 300% of the poverty level—people who are not eligible for government programs and cannot afford private insurance. Of these, about half are employed by small businesses that employ fewer than 100 employees. The authors note that ways must be found to encourage younger Americans to seek and maintain health insurance (to support the risk pool). They also advocate an improvement in affordability: "maximize cost savings that can be achieved through improvements in access and quality and, at the same time, take additional steps to make health care more affordable through regulatory and legal reforms." So, finally, there is recognition at the end of this ambitious plan that federal action will be required.

6. Buntin, Melinda B, et al: The Role of the Individual Health Insurance Market and Prospects for Change: Health Affairs, November/December 2004 (Vol. 23, No. 6):79-90. "The individual market is the only source of health insurance for the more than 20 percent of Americans not eligible for group or public health insurance, yet participation rates are low and shrinking." The authors note that the high cost of individual coverage is the dominant factor in determining the low participation levels, but there are other factors that are also barriers. Among other things, the uninsured "are … more willing to take risks." Which is to say that there are those who are uninsured because they see the probable cost associated with being uninsured as being lower than the cost of being insured.

7. Abelson, Julia, et al: Canadians Confront Health Care Reform: Health Affairs, May/June 2004 (Vol. 23, No. 3):186-193. Lest anyone consider that the Canadian system of healthcare delivery is set and static, here is a report about changes happening and changes being considered in how that system works. One of the more interesting bits of that discussion is about the degrees of allowance that are being considered for a two-tier system of physician and hospital services (one public, one private) and the recognition of the adverse economic effect that the private system has on the public system.

Chapter 15

1. Summary of National Health Expenditures 2002: Hospitals, Physician, Prescription Drugs, Home Health: CMS, national Health Expenditures 2002: Http://www.cms.hhs.gov/statistics/ nhe/. In 2002, hospital spending increased 9.5%; prescription drugs increased 15.3%; physician services increased 7.7%; home health expenditures increased 7.2%.

2. Center for Policy and Research, Americas' Health Insurance Plans: Center for Studying Health System Change Identifies Hospital Prices as a Key Cost Driver; Prescription Drug Spending Slowing: AHIP, 2004. http://www.ahip.org/ During the first half of 2004, hospital utilization grew at less than 1% per year but hospital pricing was up 8%, contributing to an overall increase in hospital spending of 8.6% annual rate. In the meantime, the growth in prescription spending was at an 8.8% annual rate, down from almost 20% in 1999. The decrease in pharmaceutical spending is partly accounted for by a change in plan design, with the insured patients paying a larger portion of the price of high-priced drugs, and partially by the conversion of a number of significant drugs from brand to generic.

3. Thorpe, Kenneth E: The Rise in Health Care Spending and What to Do About It: Health Affairs, November/December 2005 (Vol. 24, No. 6):1438-1445. The author is an advocate for prevention and believes that programs in the workplace focused on health promotion plus programs in the schools to increase physical activity and help prevent obesity are key to reducing the cost of health care. However, he includes: "A third reform would target the rise in high-cost, low-benefit medical technologies. The US health care system lacks the institutional capacity to discourage the adoption of such technologies."

4. Mello, M and Brennan, T: The Controversy Over High-Dose Chemotherapy with Autologous Bone Marrow Transplant for

Breast Cancer: Health Affairs, September/October 2001 (Vol. 20, No. 5):101-117. This is perhaps the first, best summary of the controversy and is well documented.

5. Johansson, Jan-Erik et al: Natural History of Early, Localized Prostate Cancer: JAMA, June 9, 2004 (Vol. 291, No. 22):2713-2719.

6. Prostate Cancer Screening—A Decision Guide: National Center for Chronic Disease Prevention and Health Promotion, CDC: found on the web at http://www.cdc.gov/cancer/prostate/decisionguide/ on September 1, 2005.

7. Prostate Cancer Screening: National Cancer Institute: found on the web at http://www.nci.nih.gov/cancertopics/pdq/screening/prostate/Patient/page3 and /page4 on September 1, 2005.

8. Lefevre, Michael L: Prostate Cancer Screening: More Harm than Good?: American Family Physician, Vol. 58, No. 2 (August 1998) found on the web at http://www.aafp.org/afp/980800ap/lefevre.html on September 1, 2005.

9. Kessler, Larry, et al: Clinical Use of Medical Devices in the "Bermuda Triangle": Health Affairs, January/February 2004 (Vol. 23, No. 1):200-207. This paper discusses the rapid pace of medical device development, and the three federal agencies that may have oversight: the Centers for Medicare and Medicaid Services (CMS), the Food and Drug Administration (FDA), and the National Institutes of Health (NIH). Each of the three may or may not evaluate any particular new technology—but each from a different perspective. Many new technologies are not addressed by any of the three.

10. Markel, Howard: Why America Needs a Strong FDA: JAMA, November 16, 2005 (Vol. 294, No. 19):2489-2491. Dr. Markel analyzes the history and current role of the FDA. Given the history of our country, in which eager entrepreneurs would adulterate and/or poison foodstuffs or medications in search of

greater profit, there is clearly a need for an agency to protect the public interest in pure food and pure and effective medication. It may not be perfect, but we could not do without it.

11. Mullins, C. Daniel, et al: Variability and Growth in Spending for Outpatient Specialty Pharmaceuticals; Health Affairs: Vol. 24, No. 4 (July/August 2005):1117-1127. The authors look at the cost trends of some of the higher cost medications, noting use patterns and the rapidly increasing potential cost of care caused by the use of these medications. Wonderful for those who really need them, they are excessively expensive if the patient will respond to a less expensive medication just as well.

12. Carpenter, Daniel P: The Political Economy of FDA Drug Review: Processing, Politics, and Lessons for Policy: Health Affairs, January/February 2004 (Vol. 23, No. 1):52-63. This is a wonderful, short and pointed assessment of the political and public pressures on the FDA.

13. Malenka, David J., et al: Postmarketing Surveillance of Medical Devices Using Medicare Claims: Health Affairs: Vol. 24, No. 4 (July/August 2005):928-937. The authors describe some steps to improve data collection and correlation to get better assessments of how new technologies are working in the clinical setting. They use the example case of drug-eluting stents in coronary artery disease as an example. For this technology, a significant number of recipients are Medicare enrollees, and data may be collected from the Medicare claims database; however, other procedures (for instance, those related to childbirth or the care of children) will have a very small prevalence among Medicare enrollees as the system currently works. Think how much better the analysis could be if all the medical claims on every American were equally available for such an analysis.

14. Kaufman M & Masters BA: After Criticism, FDA Will Strengthen Drug Safety Checks: Washington Post, November 6, 2004: A12. In the wake of criticism of the FDA for not being more

"out in front of the news" with Vioxx and the safety of antide-
pressants in children, the agency indicates it is taking steps to
become more aggressive about responding to reports of potentially harmful side effects of medications.

15. Mathews, AW & Hensley, S: FDA Stiffens Painkiller Warnings,
Pushes Pfizer to Suspend Bextra: Wall Street Journal, April 8,
2005: A1. This article was written as Vioxx was already off the
market, Bextra was being withdrawn, and Celebrex was still approved. The FDA was requiring more warning labels. Some of
what was public information on the subject was recounted in
this article.

16. Reinberg, Steven: COX-2 Inhibitors Not Safer for Stomach:
HealthDay, December 2, 2005 (http://www.healthday.com/
printer.cfm?id=529435). The final nail (or as close to the final as
needs be) is driven into the coffin of the COX-2 inhibitors
(Vioxx, Celebrex, Bextra). These drugs were introduced because
they would not cause the gastric distress and ulcers caused by
the standard non-steroidal anti-inflammatory drugs (NSAIDs,
such as aspirin, ibuprofen, Motrin, and others). They became
immensely popular, despite the fact that they were no more effective as pain relievers than aspirin or acetaminophen (Tylenol).
They have caused problems because of increased heart attack
rates in users. And now, it turns out, they are no more effective
at avoiding the stomach problems. And we spent literally billions
of dollars on these drugs!

17. Abramson, John: Overdosed America—The Broken Promise of
American Medicine: Harper-Collins Publishers Inc., New York,
NY; 2004. The author's story of his evaluation of the research
on the COX-2 inhibitors Vioxx and Celebrex is an eye-opener. I
portray this episode as a slip-up by an imperfect FDA. Dr. Abramson portrays it as prevarication and withholding of data by
pharmaceutical manufacturers. His story is worth reading.

18. The Zomax (zomepirac) issue is an interesting one. I have consulted the following studies to refresh my memory:

- Inman WHW & Rawson NSB: Zomepirac and Cardiovascular Deaths: Lancet 1983; 2:908.

- Budoff PW: Zomepirac Sodium in the Treatment of Primary Dysmenorrhea Syndrome: NEJM September 16, 1982; 307: 714-719.

- Levy DB & Vasilmanolakis EC: Anaphylactic Reaction Due to Zomepirac: Drug Intell Clin Pharm, 1984, Dec 18(12): 983-984.

- McQuay, HJ et al: Zomepirac, Dihydrocodeine and Placebo Compared in Postoperative Pain after Day-Case Surgery. The Relationship Between the Effects of Single and Multiple Doses: British Journal of Anaesthesia, Vol. 57, Issue 4:412-419.

- Lewis JR: Zomepirac Sodium: A New Nonaddicting Analgesic: JAMA Vol. 246, No. 4, 14 July 1981.

19. Barton, John H. & Emanuel, Ezekiel J: The Patents-Based Pharmaceutical Development Process: JAMA, October 26, 2005 (Vol. 294, No. 16):2075-2082. The authors note that the pharmaceutical companies are under significant criticism because of the concerns about the high cost of pharmaceuticals. While it is true that the high cost of new drugs does tend to support the business case for research and development, they note that more money is spent on marketing than on research. They also note that a major portion of the profitability of new drugs is developed in the USA marketplace. They suggest some reforms, but are not optimistic that the system can be fixed.

20. Cox, E et al: Generic Drug Usage Report: Express Scripts Research Study Findings, 2005. For additional information about the study e-mail Express Scripts at publicaffairs@express-scripts. com. Express Scripts is a major national pharmacy benefit man-

ager. The authors suggest that more aggressive use of generic prescriptions could have saved the healthcare system $20 billion in
2004. This amount, it is noted, is on the same order as the amount
written off by health care providers in the care of the uninsured.

21. Berndt, Ernst R: Unique Issues Raised by Drug Benefit Design:
Health Affairs; Vol. 23, No. 1 (January/February 2004):103-106.
The author tracks and discusses the various aspects of the pharmaceutical cost equation that make price difficult to control—
the need to support high research and development costs, intense
adverse selection determined by drug use, retail sector dominance in the delivery of pharmaceuticals, and the inherent incentive for sellers to engage in differential pricing for different buyers
within the same market. There are many forces at work that will
continue to work against the rationalization and stabilization of
pharmaceutical prices, and those forces must all be considered in
solving the problem.

22. Carter, Darrell: Generic Drug Use Varies Widely by State: Express Scripts, December 5, 2004. For additional information
about the study e-mail Express Scripts at publicaffairs@
express-scripts.com. Express Scripts, a large pharmacy benefits
management company, looked at the rate of use of generic medications by state. They found that generic medications were used
most frequently in Massachusetts (51.3% of the time), followed
by New Mexico (50.4%), and Oregon (50.2%). The lowest states
were New Jersey (39.5%), New York (40.8%), and Washington
DC (41.5%). There is nothing in these statistics that reflects on
the value or efficacy of the generic medications. In fact, the
FDA holds the generic medications to the same standard of efficacy and consistency as the brand name preparations. For every
1% increase in generic use rate, Express Scripts notes, the overall pharmacy cost decreases by 1%. In the face of a pharmacy
expense that is rising rapidly, this saving would be substantial.

23. Weisman, Jonathan: Drugmakers Win Exemption in House Budget-Cutting Bill: Washington Post, November 30, 2005. This article reports on a House bill designed to allow reductions in spending on Medicaid prescription drugs. Drug manufacturers (Eli Lilly is mentioned by name) joined with others to get a provision inserted into the bill that will prevent Medicaid programs from pushing generic drug substitution of drugs used for mental health treatment. While the Congressional Budget Office estimated the cost at $125 million over five years, Governor Arnold Schwarzenegger estimated that the provision would raise California Medicaid prescription costs by $50 million per year. Part of the problem here is that treatment decisions are being driven by the legislature.

24. Plotkin, Stanley A: Why Certain Vaccines Have Been Delayed or Not Developed At All: Health Affairs; Vol. 24, No. 3 (May/June 2005):631-634. One would think that vaccine development would be on the expedited track—encouraged and supported in every way. The author details reasons why vaccines are not developed—the obstacles we put in the way of the development and production of vaccines. While I have not discussed this, it is certainly another one of the many problems that need to be identified and fixed on the way to a healthy healthcare system.

25. Ignani, Karen: The 30% Solution: AHIP Coverage, May-June 2004:9. Two studies by RAND over the past two decades demonstrate that we are wasting about 30% of the money we spend on health care. If we are to make health care an economically viable process, if we are to be able to continue to afford health care for our population, we must come to grips with this level of waste and do something about it.

26. Berenson, Robert A.: Lumpers and Splitters: Different Approaches to Understanding Variations Research: Health Affairs—Web Exclusive on Variation (7 October 2004):98-103. While the general thesis of this paper is interesting enough, the author's

comments about the wastefulness he observed in his own practice is well and poignantly stated, and echoes the experiences of many physicians who are concerned about the cost of that waste of resources.

27. Ebell, Mark H: Antibiotic Prescribing for Cough and Symptoms of Respiratory Tract Infection—Do the Right Thing: JAMA, June 22/29, 2005 (Vol. 293, No. 24):3062-3064. This is an editorial comment on a study published in the same issue. The editorialist notes that cough is the most common presenting complaint for physician office visits, accounting for over 30 million visits a year, in 10 million of which the patient is otherwise healthy. Most of these patients receive prescriptions for antibiotics in spite of relatively scant evidence of a significant positive effect. The most significant effect of antibiotic treatment was to increase patient satisfaction with the visit. This hardly justifies the use of an important medication, opines the editorialist, who notes that, in "the current market-based health care system, it is tempting to confuse patient satisfaction with better outcomes and to confuse more care with better quality care." I could not agree more.

28. Little, Paul; et al: Information Leaflet and Antibiotic Prescribing Strategies for Acute Lower Respiratory Tract Infection: JAMA, June 22/29, 2005 (Vol. 293, No. 24):3029-3035. In this study of over 800 patients presenting with uncomplicated acute lower respiratory infection, patients were randomized to three groups: immediate antibiotics, delayed antibiotics if needed, no antibiotics. There was no difference in duration of illness among the groups.

29. Here is another example of an expensive technology used for decades without any evidence that it makes any difference. Three articles in a single issue of JAMA describe the current state of the science related to the use of pulmonary artery catheters in congestive heart failure or in critically ill patients. The pulmonary

artery catheter (also known as a Swan-Ganz catheter) was introduced over twenty years ago. Without going into technical details, this catheter provides information about heart function. The use of this technology has become routine enough that no ICU could currently be built without having the ability to monitor and display information generated by pulmonary artery catheters built into the hardware infrastructure of the ICU. And now, after much soul-searching and some very fine investigation, here are two articles and an editorial. The first article is a study of the use of pulmonary artery catheters in congestive heart failure, which shows no improvement in outcomes related to its use. The second is an analysis of the aggregated data from a number of studies of the use of the pulmonary artery catheter in critically ill patients, which also shows no benefit, but at least shows no increase in mortality associated with the use of this technique. The third article is an editorial, which, among other things, stresses that the gathering of the data does no good if there is not a way of reacting to the data—another way of saying that a test that does not influence clinical management is of no use.

- Stevenson, Lynne W., et al (The ESCAPE Trial): Evaluation Study of Congestive Heart Failure and Pulmonary Artery Catheterization Effectiveness: Journal of the American Medical Association (JAMA); October 5, 21005 (Vol. 294, No. 13): 1625-1633.

- Shah, Monica R., et al: Impact of the Pulmonary Artery Catheter in Critically Ill Patients: JAMA, October 5, 2005 (Vol. 294, No. 13):1664-1670.

- Hall, Jesse B: Searching for Evidence to Support Pulmonary Artery Catheter Use in Critically Ill Patients: JAMA, October 5, 2005 (Vol. 294, No. 13):1693-1694.

30. Variations Revisited: Health Affairs Web Exclusive Collection; October 7, 2004. This is a full edition (of 144 pages plus two ar-

ticles from 13 Feb 2002 and 7 April 2004) of articles flowing from Jack Wennberg's work on small area variation. For anyone interested in seeing some of the science behind statements made about geographic variation that is not supported by geographic differences in demographics, this is a wealth of material. It starts with and develops some of the science about variations, then branches off into analysis and commentary. The viewpoints are telling. I will also be citing a number of the articles from this edition separately for particular points, but I found the volume to be an exciting read—I read it cover to cover and found article after article to be interesting and compelling.

31. Neergaard, Lauran: Early Breast Cancer Growth Tough to Treat: Associated Press, March 22, 2004. http://www.ap.org/. Ductal carcinoma in situ (DCIS) of the breast represents an abnormality in which cells are found that look as though they have cancer potential. No one really understands exactly what the course of untreated DCIS is, or what the right treatment is, or how to differentiate between those who are likely to be long-term disease-free survivors and those who will develop breast cancer and die of it (2% of DCIS victims die of breast cancer within the next ten years). The author documents how treatment varies widely from one region of the country to another.

32. Weinstein, James N., et al: Trends and Geographic Variations in Major Surgery for Degenerative Diseases of the Hip, Knee and Spine: Health Affairs—Web Exclusive on Variation (7 October 2004):81-89. The authors trace the variations in the incidence of back surgery, knee replacement, and hip replacement in several neighbor communities in South Florida and use the incidence of surgery for hip fracture as the control case. Even between such geographically close communities as Fort Lauderdale and Miami, the incidence of these surgeries was remarkably different, and the best predictor of the variation found in 2000-2001 was the variation found in 1992-1993. Patterns of practice are remarkably persistent over time. Hip replacement in Fort Lauderdale

occurs almost 25% more often than the national average; in Miami it occurs only two-thirds as frequently as the national average. Without making any judgment about which pattern is correct, certainly BOTH cannot be correct. We should be moving toward a uniform standard, but we are not. (The difference between the two communities was greater in 2000-2001 than it was in 1992-1993). What will it take to move to "best practices?"

33. Vladeck, Bruce C.: Everything New is Old Again: Health Affairs —Web Exclusive on Variation (7 October 2004):108-111. "After thirty years of insightful research and debate, unexplained variations continue to persist throughout U.S. health care." This is a well-expressed voice of the frustration the researchers in variation must be feeling. In spite of documentation of variances in practice patterns, these geographic variations are extremely persistent. "The problem is that we still really don't know very much about why physicians do what they do, or how to get them to do different things."

34. Grove, Andrew S: Efficiency in the Health Care Industries: JAMA, Vol. 294, No. 4 (July 27, 2005):490-492. This is a fascinating article, and well worth the several minutes it takes to read. As the founder and head of Intel Corporation, Mr. Grove has the background to understand the drive to efficiency. He finds three problems in health care. First, the research cycle is long—the fact that we are dealing with human beings and human life-span means that it can take years to find out the results of a change in therapy. The second is the slow rate of adoption of new knowledge and technology; in the computer industry, there is no question of getting the latest information incorporated into today's product because if you don't, your competitor will. In medicine it takes almost two decades for new knowledge to be integrated. Third, he criticizes the operational efficiency of the healthcare industry—the rate of adoption of technologies that would increase the efficiency of operations is slow, and is slowed by the fact that the technology must be adopted by many people

at various levels of the system in order for there to be a system benefit. The lack of integration of the system is part of the cause of its inefficiency.

35. Wenger, Neil et al: Quality of Medical Care Provided to Vulnerable Community Dwelling Older Patients: Annals of Internal Medicine, November 4, 2003 (as summarized at http://www.rand.org/health/healthpubs/seniors.html on December 25, 2005). Older patients have particular susceptibilities that make assessment and treatment for age-related conditions particularly important. This RAND-sponsored study found that the most vulnerable third of senior citizens were getting indicated services only about 31% of the time. This same group was receiving recommended care for general medical conditions about 52% of the time. Among the geriatric conditions with the worst track record were dementia (35% of services received), falls and mobility disorders (34% of services received), urinary incontinence (29% of services received), and end-of-life planning and care (9% of recommended services received).

36. Naik, Gautam: Unlikely Way to Cut Hospital Costs: Comfort the Dying: The Wall Street Journal; Wednesday, March 10, 2004. The author details the efforts at Virginia Commonwealth University medical center to bring palliative care rather than intense medical interventions to patients who are clearly at the end of life. This approach seems to have wonderful patient acceptance and saves money that would otherwise be spent on increasing heroic, expensive, and futile interventions. Wonderful examples and discussions are provided.

Chapter 16

1. Nyman, John A: The Theory of Demand for Health Insurance; Stanford University Press, Stanford, California; 2003. Professor Nyman's book is a major underpinning of my discussion of "moral hazard." I am indebted to him for his thinking on this subject, and for the clarity in his writing that enabled me to understand the difference between what he was describing and what I had previously understood. At the end of his discussion, Professor Nyman still ends up with two categories of moral hazard: efficient moral hazard and inefficient moral hazard. The former is what people would be willing to pay for if they had the money; the latter is what people would be willing to have insurance pay for but would not be willing to pay for themselves, no matter how much money they had. My problem with this classification is the retention of the term "moral hazard" in relation to ANY service (or expense) that is justifiable in an environment where there are sufficient funds to cover the service. Appropriate medical care (which is different from efficient moral hazard, but the two have significant overlap) should not be discussed with terminology that is as emotionally loaded as "moral hazard" is. The other problem I have with his work is that it does not recognize the existence of medical interventions that uninformed consumers would pay for but that informed consumers would not pay for. This is, of course, a difficult area for an economist, but an "easy" one for physicians—but physicians do this classification in a very disorderly, descriptive way that defies the kind of classification or categorization that the economists are searching for. During the course of this chapter, you will watch my struggles with this set of differentiations.

2. Gladwell, Malcolm: The Moral Hazard Myth: The New Yorker, August 29, 2005. The author presents a compelling case for "social insurance"—the insurance concept of spreading the cost of care as widely as possible to assure that everyone who needs care

can receive it. This is part of the social contract—part of our interdependence. It is a sense of social contract understood in the other industrialized countries, but not in the United States. His advocacy is based, in part, on his understanding that the concept of "moral hazard" is a basically flawed one—though he tends to go to the extreme of discounting it completely, which is also an error as much as believing that moral hazard is the only explanation for increased utilization by the insured.

3. Reuters: Many middle-income Americans lack insurance: Reuters release Tuesday, April 25, 2006. http://www.reuters.com/. The study cites research by The Commonwealth Fund indicating that 40% of Americans making between $20,000 and $40,000 per year were uninsured for at least part of 2005. Interestingly, it also found that "people without health insurance were more likely to go without recommended cancer, cholesterol, and blood pressure screenings." This group not only scrimps on preventive care, they are more susceptible to an episode of illness precipitating a downward health/financial cycle which may also result in loss of employment, avoidance of "routine" health care, health care debt, and worsening health status.

Chapter 17

1. Agovino, Theresa: Study: Cost Trumps Choice in Health Care: Associated Press, March 24, 2005. http://www.ap.org/. The author is reporting on a study by the Center for Studying Health System Change. That study found that Americans with employer-sponsored health insurance are becoming more willing to accept limits on their choice of providers in order to save on medical expenses. There is an interesting cyclic effect going on here—when health care is inexpensive, people insist on choice; when health care becomes expensive, people will relinquish choice in favor of less expense. As consumers, we are price sensitive.

2. Wright, Bill J et al: The Impact of Increased Cost Sharing on Medicaid Enrollees: Health Affairs: Vol. 24, No. 4 (July/August 2005):1106-1116. The authors initiated a study of the impact of a 2003 change in Oregon Medicaid coverage that imposed a small monthly premium and co-payments. They demonstrate fairly convincingly that the least affluent enrollees dropped out of the program and did not seek or receive appropriate care.

3. Rosenthal, Meredith B: Doughnut-Hole Economics: Health Affairs, November/December 2004 (Vol. 23, No. 6):129-135. The author discusses the implications of a new approach to medical coverage—relatively better coverage for early dollars followed by no coverage as dollars expended increase, eventually followed by better coverage at much higher levels of personal expense. Even though a variety of high-deductible plans associated with tax-preferred savings accounts have been available for some time, their use has not been common and has been only by personal choice, up to now. In the wake of the Medicare Improvement Act of 2003 and at the cusp of 2005, we were just beginning to see this kind of coverage being purposely sponsored by the federal government in terms of pharmacy coverage for Medicare recipients and by employers.

4. Baskin, Brian: More Firms Say Health Accounts Offer Promise: Arkansas Democrat-Gazette, October 30, 2005. Page 1G. This article was apparently inspired by the adoption of a mandatory "high-de-ductible health plan" with a health savings account by a local large employer. The author notes that the employees have not been at all happy with this development. The author also notes that this combination plan is being adopted by about 15% of employees when it is offered, except at firms with more than 1,000 employees, where adoption rates are more like 3%.

5. Fuhrmans, Vanessa: Patients Give New Insurance Mixed Reviews: The Wall Street Journal, June 14, 2005. Early results from "consumer-directed" health plans show reductions in cost, but only 44% of enrollees were as satisfied as with their previous health plan, and 80% of enrollees said they needed more information about prices charged by doctors.

6. Sepucha, Karen R., et al: Policy Support for Patient-Centered Care: The Need for Measurable Improvements in Decision Quality: Health Affairs—Web Exclusive on Variations (October 7, 2004): 54-62. An excellent article looking at patient education and assessment of patient understanding of proposed treatment as a way of combating variation. The abstract summarizes well: "The phenomenon of practice variation draws attention to the need for better management of clinical decision-making as a means of ensuring quality. Different policies to address variations, including guidelines and measures of appropriateness, have had little demonstrable impact on variation itself or on the underlying quality problems. Variations in rates of interventions raise questions about the patient-centeredness of decisions that determine what care is provided to whom. Policies that support the development and routine use of measures of decision quality will provide opportunities to measurably improve the quality of decisions, thereby leading to more patient-centered and efficient health care."

7. Epstein, Richard A: It Did Happen Here: Fear and Loathing on the Vaccine Trail: Health Affairs; Vol. 24, No. 3 (May/June 2005):740-743. The author tracks the thimersol scare and its effects on immunization rates. While there was certainly publicity about thimersol, there was never any scientific evidence of untoward effects.

8. Werner, Rachel M, et al: The Unintended Consequences of Publicly Reporting Quality Information: JAMA, March 9, 2005 (Vol. 293, No. 10):1239-1244. The authors note that public reporting, while well intentioned, may have the effect of altering physician behavior in order to produce a "better report," even though the behavior change is not the one sought. For instance, avoiding certain classes of more difficult or less compliant patients would enhance one's rating. So would doing the measured test on those for whom it was inappropriate. The authors conclude that, while public disclosure may improve public trust, it may not improve quality.

9. O'Connor, Annette M., et al: Modifying Unwarranted Variations in Health Care: Shared Decision Making Using Patient Decision Aids: Health Affairs—Web Exclusive on Variations (7 October 2004):63-72. The authors add to the argument that informed patients make better decisions, and that those decisions frequently do not include some of the interventions proposed by physicians. "Patient decision aids are evidence-based tools designed to facilitate [shared decision making]. Numerous randomized trials indicate that patient decision aids improve decision quality and prevent overuse of options that informed patients do not value."

10. Newhouse, Joseph P: Consumer-Directed Health Plans and the RAND Health Insurance Experiment: Health Affairs, November/December 2004 (Vol. 23, No. 6):107-113. The author offers a brief and cogent summary of the RAND Health Insurance Experiment performed in the late 1970s, which is one of the very small number of studies done to look at benefit structure and

enrollee behavior on a prospective basis. Not surprisingly, the study showed a diminution in outpatient visits and overall costs as the patient bore a larger and larger proportion of the cost. The author speculates on how the interaction between higher deductibles and the principles of managed care will impact the consumption of health care services.

11. Doshi, Jalpa A, et al: The Impact of Drug Coverage on COX-2 Inhibitor Use in Medicare: Health Affairs—Web Exclusive, 18 February 2004:94-105. The authors demonstrate that among Medicare recipients, those with the most generous drug coverage, not those who best met the clinical criteria, were most likely to be taking the (more expensive) COX-2 inhibitor drugs. This is a pointed demonstration that it is neither the indications for treatment nor the need for the drug that drives medication compliance. It is the price to the patient.

12. Goldman DP et al: Pharmacy Benefits and the Use of Drugs by the Chronically Ill: JAMA, May 18, 2004 (Vol. 291, No. 19): 2344-2350 (as summarized on the RAND website at http://www.rand.org/health/healthpubs/on December 25, 2005). When patient co-payment doubled, the use of medications decreased, including a 32% reduction in the use of medications to control asthma, a 26% reduction in the use of medications to control high blood pressure, and a 25% reduction in the use of medications to control diabetes.

13. Kamal-Bahl, S & Briesacher, B: How Do Incentive-Based Formularies Influence Drug Selection and Spending for Hypertension?: Health Affairs, January/February 2004 (Vol. 23, No. 1): 227-236. Two observations flow from comparisons of drug use in differing pharmacy plans, especially comparing one-, two-, and three-tier plans, and from plans with lower co-payments to higher ones in the same category of plan:

- As tier differentials increase, there is a trend toward the use of lower cost drugs.

- As tiering and co-payments increase, the plan spends less and members spend more on treatment for hypertension.

- As absolute costs increase, there is a trend toward non-use of higher cost drugs.

- The decreasing use of higher cost drugs takes place regardless of the indications or the potential for the higher cost drug actually being the one indicated for the treatment of the patient.

14. Pauly, Mark V: Medicare Drug Coverage and Moral Hazard: Health Affairs, January/February 2004 (Vol. 23, No. 1):113-122. An early speculation about the result of the Medicare Improvement Act of 2003 and what the effect will be on drug availability to Medicare recipients. The author feels it is likely that the availability of drugs will not be greatly enhanced for most Medicare beneficiaries. He notes that the structure of the program puts a significant burden on the recipient to cover cost, which may well act as a significant barrier. The reference to "moral hazard" in his title and in his discussion are a reminder that all behavior on the part of insurance recipients that results in increased spending while insured compared to while uninsured is not bad.

15. Soumerai, Stephen B: Benefits and Risks of Increasing Restrictions on Access to Costly Drugs in Medicaid: Health Affairs, January/February 2004 (Vol. 23, No. 1): 135-146. The author starts with an acknowledgement that there are some studies that have shown dramatic reduction in the use of chronically essential drugs (such as insulin for diabetes) after a price increase to Medicaid recipients. Such studies have also shown a substantial increase in overall cost of care after the discontinuation of essential medication. The author looks at some carefully crafted programs which imposed significant barriers to use of medication, but with liberal granting of exceptions, and noted reduction in cost for medication without a consequent rise in cost of care. It

can certainly be done wrong; this is a hopeful indication that it can also be done right.

16. Tseng, Chien-Wen, et al: Cost-Lowering Strategies Used by Medicare Beneficiaries Who Exceed Drug Benefit Caps and Have a Gap in Drug Coverage: JAMA, August 25, 2004 (Vol. 292, No. 8): 952-960. The question is, what do people do when they have medical expenses they have difficulty in meeting? Do they make medically "wise" decisions? This study looked at Medicare recipients who were covered by a Medicare+Choice plan with a capped drug benefit. For the first part of the year, these members had coverage for their prescriptions, but toward the end of the year, that coverage was exhausted, and these people had to pay out of pocket for their medications. The authors found that "Medicare beneficiaries often decreased use of essential medications..."

17. Friedman, Mark: State Seeks Medicaid Waiver for Employee Groups: Arkansas Business, October 10, 2005. This article covers most of the basics of the plan and how it was assembled. The details of the plan were released somewhat later by the Arkansas Department of Health and Human Services on its web site in the form of a Request for Proposals. At this time, no vendor has been identified to administer the program, and there are a lot of details missing. However, what is clear is the intent to cover the "low end" of health care cost, and leave the "high end"—the expensive services—without coverage. While this will save some on costs, it is not clear what the magnitude of the cost saving will be. It is clear that this program will be better for enrollees than no insurance at all, but it is not clear what will happen when enrollees begin to top out. It will be interesting to see what happens when the first enrollee needs a coronary artery bypass operation or a kidney transplant.

18. Neuschler, Edward & Curtis, Richard: Massachusetts-Style Coverage Expansion: What Would It Cost in California?: Cali-

fornia HealthCare Foundation, April, 2006. http://www.chcf.
org/topics/healthinsurance/index.cfm?itemID=120742. This
article undertakes a detailed analysis of the intent of the Massachusetts law in an effort to create parallels and contrasts with
California.

19. Ibid.

Chapter 18

1. Robinson, James C.: Blended Payment Methods in Physician Organizations Under Managed Care: JAMA, October 6, 1999 (Vol. 282, No. 13);1258-1263. Already this is some time ago. The author found in a survey of IPAs (physician organizations) in the San Francisco Bay Area that there was a significant shift to mixed payment methodology.

2. Lowes, Robert: Exclusive Survey: Earnings: Primary Care Tries to Hang On: Medical Economics, September 17, 2004.

3. Starfield, Barbara, et al: The Effects of Specialist Supply on Populations' Health: Assessing the Evidence: Health Affairs Web Exclusive W5 (March 15, 2005):97-107. This fascinating study looks at the longevity (or death rates) on a county-by-county basis across most counties in the United States. It finds that death rates among the residents of counties are inversely proportional to the number of primary care physicians per 1,000 population and directly proportional to the number of specialists per 1,000 population. This strongly implies that more primary care physicians tend to reduce death rates, but that more specialists tend to increase death rates. There is now a significant volume of data on this subject, though adjusting out happenstance and coincidence is not easy to do. There are several commentaries that follow this article that are also worthy:

    - Goodman, David C: The Physician Workforce Crisis: Where is the Evidence?: Health Affairs Web Exclusive W5 (March 15, 2005):108-110.

    - Phillips, Robert L Jr, et al: Adding More Specialists is Not Likely to Improve Population Health: Is Anybody Listening?: Health Affairs Web Exclusive W5 (March 15, 2005):111-114.

- Salsberg, Edward: The Need for Real Evidence in Physician Workforce Decision Making: Health Affairs Web Exclusive W5 (March 15, 2005):115-118.

- Starfield, Barbara: Letter of Response to Edward Salsberg: Health Affairs Web Exclusive W5 (March 15, 2005):S7-S8.

4. Brennan, Troyen A, et al: The Role of Physician Specialty Board Certification Status in the Quality Movement: JAMA, September 1, 2004 (Vol. 292, No. 9):1038-1043. The authors make a good case for periodic assessment of competency among physicians, indicating that the only current way of doing this is through specialty maintenance of certification programs. "[A] Gallup poll demonstrates that certification and maintenance of certification are highly valued by the public. The majority of respondents thought it important for physicians to be re-evaluated on their qualifications every few years and that physicians should do more to demonstrate ongoing competence." In conclusion, the authors feel that board certification should be used as one of the criteria in quality assessment. On the other hand, one might point out that they are really supporting an ongoing program of competency assessment, which is something that has generally been strenuously resisted by the profession.

Chapter 19

1. Chernew, Michael E, et al: Barriers to Constraining Health Care Cost Growth: Health Affairs, November/December 2004 (Vol. 23, No. 6):122-128. The authors look at rising health-care-related spending and conclude that standard managed care constraints are not likely to slow the rising cost of health care significantly. The "forces pushing for innovation in health care are very strong." Policy focus needs to be directed toward value.

2. Groman, Rachel: The Use of Performance Measurements to Improve Physician Quality of Care: A Position Paper of the American College of Physicians: American College of Physicians; Approved by the Board of Regents on 19 April 2004 (available on the ACP website). The ACP makes several position statements, including the following: "The goal of physician performance measurement should be to foster continuous quality improvement of clinical care"; "Physician performance measures should be evidence-based, broadly accepted, and clinically relevant. These measures should assess and focus on those elements of clinical care over which the physicians have direct and instrumental control (as opposed to system constraints)." [It is interesting that here is a tacit admission that there may be system problems that require system-level solutions. This is interesting back-handed support for my comments about the tort liability system.]; "The College supports demonstration projects to evaluate the use of incentives."

3. Weinberg, Richard M, et al: Engaging Physicians in Cost Savings Initiatives: The Physician Executive, January-February, 2005:12-18. With the example being a new medication that is more expensive than its older counterpart, but which saves other resources and ends up being cost-effective (low molecular weight heparin versus unfractionated heparin), the authors study the resistance to change. They found resistance coming from five

areas: time management issues; physician autonomy issues; habits and accustomed styles of practice; knowledge deficits; data perception issues. The last related particularly to the use of administrative data to assess cost-effectiveness as distinguished from the clinical data in the more commonly used studies of efficacy.

4. Rosenthal, Meredith B., et al: Early Experience With Pay-for-Performance: JAMA, October 12, 2005 (Vol. 294, No. 14):1788-1793. The authors point to recent experience of one company (PacifiCare Health Systems) with a pay-for-performance program in California compared to control physicians in Oregon and Washington. The results of the program were positive, but not nearly as good as hoped. They observe that most of the reward went to the physicians and physician groups who had the highest performance level in the first place. I am not sure this is bad—though they imply that perhaps the money was "wasted" in that case. It would be interesting to see what would happen over a longer period of time. It is early yet. Engagement of the physicians is important, and may take quite some time.

5. Conklin, J & Weiss, A: Pay-for-Performance: Assembling the Building Blocks of a Sustainable Program: Thomson–Medstat; 2005. The authors review the recent history of pay-for-performance programs and the various ways these programs are being set up. They believe that pay-for-performance programs offer positive rewards for all parties: patients benefit from better care and better outcomes; physicians benefit from increased financial rewards; fiscal intermediaries benefit from improved profitability and better reputation; payers benefit from reduced costs.

6. Beck, Christine A., et al: Administrative Data Feedback for Effective Cardiac Treatment: JAMA, July 20, 2005 (Vol. 294, No. 3):309-317. One of the proposed ways of improving the quality of care is to provide quality feedback to providers. In this study, hospitals in Quebec were randomized between immediate feedback and delayed feedback on several criteria related to the care

of patients with heart attacks. The feedback was provided to the hospital CEO, the director of the cardiac unit, and the chief of professional services. There was essentially no effect that could be attributed to this intervention.

7. Dudley, R. Adams: Pay-for-Performance Research: JAMA, October 12, 2005 (Vol. 294, No. 14):1821-1823. The author discusses some of the steps we need to take to determine whether pay-for-performance programs make sense (are effective). The critique is an important one, as we are in danger of adopting a payment mechanism with no evidence that it works and unknown adverse side effects in the system.

8. Public Interest in the Use of Quality Metrics in Healthcare is Mixed—Unless it Allows Them to Reduce Their Health Insurance Costs: HarrisInteractive, May 24, 2005: http://www.harrisinteractive.com/news/allnewsbydate.asp?NewsID=931.
"A new survey shows that the US public is only modestly supportive of having health plans pay more to doctors if they have been shown to provide higher quality care to their patients. However, a sizeable majority is interested in this type of plan if it helps to lower their health insurance coverage costs." This article supplies the detail to support these two contentions, which begin the piece.

9. Villagra, Victor G, et al: Outcomes-Based Compensation: Pay-for-Performance Design Principles: American Healthways, 2005. Under the joint sponsorship of American Healthways (one of the nation's leading providers of disease management services) and Johns Hopkins, over 150 participants convened from November 11 to 14, 2004, in Rancho Mirage, CA, to work on creating a set of guidelines for pay-for-performance programs. The mere fact of the undertaking indicates how early we are in the process of developing and implementing pay-for-performance programs. The guidelines themselves are interesting and useful,

but the mere fact that so many people gave up so much time to work on them is the most important message.

10. Anderson, Gerard F., et al: Health Spending in the United States and the Rest of the Industrialized World: Health Affairs: Vol. 24, No. 4 (July/August 2005):903-914. The authors look carefully at issues affecting the cost of care difference between the United States and Canada, the United Kingdom, and Australia. They found that the "waiting list" phenomenon in especially the UK did not have a significant effect on overall cost, and that waiting lists for some services in the United States are as bad as they are elsewhere. The effect of malpractice litigation directly on the cost of care is minimal, the average cost per capita per year being $16 in the United States compared to $12 in the UK, $10 in Australia, and $4 in Canada. The authors conclude that the higher cost in the US is primarily related to the higher prices of services.

11. Holman, Halsted: Chronic Disease—The Need for a New Clinical Education: JAMA, September 1, 2004 (Vol. 292, No. 9): 1057-1059. The classic medical paradigm is that the patient becomes ill and goes to the doctor, who administers some care, and the patient becomes better. The author makes the point that the chronic disease paradigm requires that we recognize that the patient does not become ill, but IS ill; the doctor does not administer the "cure," but rather the doctor's job is to instruct the patient on self care to control the illness; the patient rarely "gets better," but more usually may become stable. The author's point is that medical education needs to shift to accommodate to this new concept of the role of the physician as a guide, a facilitator, and the leader of a care team that includes the patient.

12. MacStravic, Scott: Rethinking the Question "Does Disease Management Work?": HealthLeaders News, Oct 31, 2005. http://www.healthleaders.com/news/print.php?contentid=73187. The author looks at the research on disease management programs and finds the quality of the research not matching up to the rigor

we would require in "hard" clinical studies—and therefore the results are not nearly so reliable. There is much work still to be done to establish the effectiveness of particular disease management programs and particular disease management approaches.

13. Clarke, Janice et al: Evaluation of a Comprehensive Diabetes Disease Management Program: Progress in the Struggle for Sustained Behavior Change: Disease Management Vol. 5, No. 2 (2002):77-86. There are any number of issues that can be raised about how we should measure the effectiveness of disease management (DM) programs and whether this study has effectively overcome them. However, what the study did was important. It looked at the level of control patients were exerting over their diabetes—the level of adoption of lifestyle changes needed for diabetic control—and evaluated the correlations between more change, better control, and degree of contact with the DM program. What they found is that the more contact the patient had with DM program personnel, the more changes they were able to make and sustain. They also found improvement in all of the elements that are markers of exemplary care of diabetes in the participants in the program.

14. Villagra, VG & Ahmed, T: Effectiveness of a Disease Management Program for Patients with Diabetes: Health Affairs, July/August 2004 (Vol. 23, No. 4):255-266. A natural experiment is documented in which a multi-state company launched a diabetes mellitus disease management program at some sites and not at others. At the end of the first year, overall cost of care was lower at the disease management sites, and measures of quality were better.

15. Bayer, Ellen et al: CBO's Analysis of Potential Savings from Disease Management Programs in Medicare: America's Health Insurance Plans, 2004. The Congressional Budget Office released an analysis of the literature on disease management programs in 2004 and concluded that there was "insufficient evidence to in-

dicate that disease management programs could generally reduce overall health spending." The authors note that the CBO missed some recent studies that have greater power than earlier ones. They also note significant savings being documented by health plans pursuing disease management programs. One of the difficulties in this arena is performing studies that document the savings in a case-matched (or randomized), prospective study fashion.

16. Fireman, Bruce, et al: Can Disease Management Reduce Health Care Costs by Improving Quality?: Health Affairs, November/ December 2004 (Vol. 23, No. 6): 63-75. The authors report on disease management (DM) programs implemented at Kaiser-Permanente in Northern California for the management of coronary artery disease, heart failure, diabetes, and asthma. The programs were implemented gradually. Cost savings were not noted. Improvements in the quality of care were noted. The authors attribute the lack of savings to the increased use of underused treatments. The analysis is somewhat impaired by the fact that the measurement is happening in the Kaiser system—which had already achieved one of the lowest care costs in the country before these measured DM programs were commenced, and already had many aspects of DM programs in place, even though not formally organized as a DM program. There is an excellent commentary on this study:

   • Crosson, FJ & Madvig, P: Does Population Management of Chronic Disease Lead to Lower Costs of Care?: Health Affairs, November/ December 2004 (Vol. 23, No. 6):76-78.

17. Stone, Robert E: Outcomes-Driven Health Care Delivery: When Better Health Does Not Equal Higher Costs: Atlantic Information Services, Inc., 2002. The author points to the success of disease management programs in improving clinical outcomes, producing significant cost savings, and building bridges between the healthcare system's key constituencies. He notes that the next step in the process would seem to be a move from disease-

focused management to population-focused management. It is an interesting and informative look at the state of the art of disease management as of 2002.

18. Villagra, Victor G, et al: Effectiveness of a Disease Management Program for Patients with Diabetes: Health Affairs, July/August 2004 (Vol. 23, No. 4):255-266. The authors tracked the results of a disease management program implemented in some areas and not in others by a national health insurer. They found decreased overall costs of care with increased quality in the areas affected by the program compared to those not affected.

19. Kleinke, JD: Access Versus Excess: Value-Based Cost Sharing for Prescription Drugs: Health Affairs, January/February 2004 (Vol. 23, No. 1):34-47. Kleinke begins his article by noting the extraordinary successes of our current health care system, and how those successes act to reinforce disparities in the availability and access to care between the well-insured and uninsured. It is against this backdrop that he defends the pharmaceutical industry. He notes that there are alternative ways to evaluate whether or how a health plan should pay for a particular medication. One of those ways is by price, which he feels currently predominates and will put the pharmaceutical and health insurance industries on a collision path. He advocates for value-based decision making—using the value created by the drug's effect to balance against the cost. For a contrasting view, see Reinhardt [Chapter 22 reference 6].

20. Simpson, Lisa: Lost in Translation? Reflection on the Role of Research in Improving Health Care for Children: Health Affairs, September/October 2004 (Vol. 23, No. 5):125-130. As in many other areas in medicine, the author notes that increased funding for research leads to new knowledge, and to a growing chasm between the health care we have and the health care we could have. Putting new knowledge into practice is a major challenge.

21. Smith, PC & York, N: Quality Incentives: The Case of UK General Practitioners: Health Affairs, May/June 2004 (Vol. 23, No. 3):112-118. The UK is undertaking a major change in its contracting with general practitioners to include rewarding of high-quality care. The process is outlined. Early evaluation of the results will be important.

22. Berndt, Ernst R: Unique Issues Raised by Drug Benefit Design: Health Affairs; Vol. 23, No. 1 (January/February 2004):103-106. The author tracks and discusses the various aspects of the pharmaceutical cost equation that make price difficult to control—the need to support high research & development costs, intense adverse selection determined by drug use, retail sector dominance in the delivery of pharmaceuticals, and the inherent incentive for sellers to engage in differential pricing for different buyers within the same market. There are many forces at work that will continue to work against the rationalization and stabilization of pharmaceutical prices, and those forces must all be considered in solving the problem.

23. Newhouse, Joseph P: How Much Should Medicare Pay for Drugs?: Health Affairs; Vol. 23, No. 1 (January/February 2004):89-102. This was early after the passage of the 2003 Medicare Improvement Act to allow drug coverage. Already, the debate is on about how the federal government should control the cost of the program. This is one view about how the government might proceed.

24. Carney, Patricia A, et al: Educational Epidemiology—Applying Population-Based Design and Analytic Approaches to Study Medical Education: JAMA, September 1, 2004 (292:9):1044-1050. "[T]here is a paucity of rigorous and generalizable educational research to provide an evidence-guided foundation to support educational effectiveness." (See also: Holman, Halsted: Chronic Disease—The Need for a New Clinical Education; JAMA, September 1, 2004 [Vol. 292, No. 9]:1057-1059.) If the roles of physicians are changing and we need to change educa-

tional processes to accommodate those changes—yet we don't know what works and what doesn't work—how do we make the change?

Chapter 20

1. Leape, Lucian L & Berwick, Donald M: Five Years After To Err is Human—What Have We Learned? JAMA, May 18, 2005 (Vol. 293, No. 19):2384-2390. The authors note that the IOM report has "changed the conversation," but they also note that "although these efforts are affecting safety at the margin, their overall impact is hard to see in national statistics."

2. Eisenberg MJ, et al: Outcomes and Cost of Coronary Artery Bypass Graft Surgery in the United States and Canada: Archives of Internal Medicine: July 11, 2005: 165:1506-1513. The authors compared coronary artery bypass graft surgery in the United States and Canada for cost and quality. Hospital mortality rates were comparable. Hospital length of stay was slightly shorter in the United States. Overall cost was 75% higher in the United States.

3. National Committee on Quality Assurance: HEDIS 2006 Draft Measures Focus on Overuse: Monitoring, Follow-up Visits also Addressed: NCQA, February 22, 2005 (http://www.ncqa.org/communications/news/hedis2006 PubComment.htm printed on December 1, 2005). Even the NCQA and HEDIS are climbing on the "overuse is poor quality" bandwagon. Measures proposed would:

   - Measure for follow-up to monitor effectiveness and side effects in children being treated with drugs for ADHD.

   - Measure over-prescribing of sedative drugs to elderly patients —these prescriptions are highly associated with increased rate of accidents.

   - Measure follow-up to observe patients for possible problems associated with long-term use of certain medications.

   - Measure indicators of overuse of antibiotics.

4. Wennberg, John E, et al: Evaluating the Efficiency of California Providers in Caring for Patients with Chronic Illnesses: Health Affairs—Web Exclusive W5 (16 November 2005):526-543. Wennberg and his colleagues have done it again. Using previously established methodology, they have tied Medicare recipients to a dominant hospital for care within the last two years of life, and have then compared utilization patterns and cost against quality measurements, including customer survey data. What they found, not surprisingly, is tremendous variation in utilization use among hospitals caring for people at the end of life—even after making adjustments for severity of illness. (These were all people who were within two years of death, after all!) Such things as total dollars spent and number of days spent in the intensive care unit varied by as much as five-fold. What is surprising is the variation across regions, with no hospital in the Los Angeles region having statistics as low as the average in Sacramento—so it is not just a couple of "bad actors" spoiling the community numbers. It is a community of bad actors, some of whom are worse than others. Most surprising is the inverse relationship between cost and quality, in which the highest quality ratings were found in the lowest cost regions. The great American expectation that more is better, that "you pay more for better quality," is (at least in the present context) flat wrong.

There are five fascinating editorials accompanying this article. They are written, in order, by Max Baucus, Democratic Senator from Montana, who sits on the Senate Finance Committee; Thomas M. Priselac, of Cedars-Sinai Health System in Los Angeles (the fifth most expensive hospital in the area); Uwe E. Reinhardt, Professor of Economics at Princeton; Leonard Schaeffer and Dana McMurtry, both of WellPoint; and Barry Straube of the Centers for Medicare and Medicaid Services. The variety of responses based on the organizational biases of the writers is a very instructive study all by itself:

- Baucus, Max: Looking at the U.S. Health Care System in the Rear-View Mirror: Health Affairs—Web Exclusive W5 (16 November 2005):544-545

- Priselac, Thomas M: Getting the Most Benefit from the Variations Research: Next Steps: Health Affairs—Web Exclusive W5 (16 November 2005):546-548

- Reinhardt, Uwe E: Variations in California Hospital Regions: Another Wake-Up Call for Sleeping Policymakers: Health Affairs—Web Exclusive W5 (16 November 2005):549-551

- Schaeffer, Leonard D & McMurtry, Dana E: Variation in Medical Care: Time for Action: Health Affairs—Web Exclusive W5 (16 November 2005):552-554

- Straube, Barry: The CMS Quality Roadmap: Quality Plus Efficiency: Health Affairs—Web Exclusive W5 (16 November 2005):555-557

5. Marchione, Marilyn: False-Alarm Cancer Tests Called Costly, Troubling: Associated Press, as published in Contra Costa Times, December 21, 2004. http://www.ap.org/. The author very clearly and forcefully makes the case that doing more tests isn't necessarily helpful, and may increase both cost and anxiety.

6. Sage, William M: The Forgotten Third: Liability Insurance and the Medical Malpractice Crisis: Health Affairs, July/August 2004 (Vol. 23, No. 4):10-21. The author advocates consideration of liability insurance itself as one of the policy issues to be confronted in resolving the professional liability crisis. What his paper point out, however, is that there is an interplay among medical care, tort law, and the process of liability insurance; the malpractice crisis represents an interplay among all three—but I see the issues regarding tort liability and professional liability insurance as being distracters that take attention away from fixing the problems in health care that drive the process. I found it to be an excellent and thought-provoking article.

7. Thorpe, Kenneth E.: The Medical Malpractice "Crisis": Recent Trends and the Impact of State Tort Reforms; Health Affairs: Web Exclusive W4 (21 January 2004):20-30. The author takes a look at the change in premiums for professional liability insurance and the tort reforms enacted in that state. He finds significant reduction with limits on awards, but not with other changes. He then evaluates the changing professional liability climate in the light of the goals of the tort system "of deterrence and compensation." He quotes references indicating the low rate of lawsuits compared to the rate of negligent care and indicating the apparent stability in the rate at which negligent care is occurring. His final statement is to indicate that "it is also important to evaluate any such reforms [in the tort system] in the context of their ability to further the dual policy objectives of deterrence and compensation." If the rate of negligent care is not going down and the rate of applications for compensation is only one for every eight incidents of negligence, then the current system cannot be held to be doing a very good job of either deterrence or compensation. I have made this point repeatedly in print over the last four years; it is gratifying to see it made by others as well.

8. Howe, RK: Time to Discard the Entire Tort Liability System: The Leading Edge: 1:3 (Fall 2004): American College of Physician Executives.

9. Howe, Roger K: Where Have We Failed? A Systemic Analysis of U.S. Health Care: American College of Physician Executives, Tampa, FL, 2002.

10. Struve, Catherine T: Improving the Medical Malpractice Litigation Process: Health Affairs, July/August 2004 (Vol. 23, No. 4): 33-41. In this thoughtful article, the author looks at potential improvements in the malpractice litigation system that would address issues relating to the problems judges and juries have in determining liability and damages, as an alternative to moving the system to an administrative compensation system. The ex-

tent of revision required, to me, is merely another argument in favor of the change away from the "fault-based compensation system" we currently have.

11. MacLennan, Alastair, et al: Who Will Deliver Our Grandchildren?: Journal of the American Medical Association; October 5, 2005 (Vol. 294, No. 13):1688-1690. This rather pointed piece starts with "It has never been safer to have a baby and never more dangerous to be an obstetrician." It explores the myths and fallacies behind the lawsuits and settlements (median award $2,300,000) for cerebral palsy. And it concludes with a brief allusion to a no-fault system and the statement "Such a system could be far more efficient and fair than the current malpractice system."

12. Kessler, Daniel P, et al: Impact of Malpractice Reforms on the Supply of Physician Services: JAMA, June 1, 2005 (293:21):2618-2625. The authors used the AMA master file to look at physician populations in states over time before and after malpractice reform. The conclusion is "Tort reform increases physician supply. Further research is needed to determine whether reform-induced increases in physician supply benefited patients."

13. Austin, Marsha: Malpractice Insurance Rates Send Doctors Fleeing to Colorado: Denver Post, March 5, 2004. The article begins by noting that "the nation's rising malpractice insurance crisis is a talent boon for Colorado." The author then describes a migration of physicians to Colorado from states such as Illinois, Ohio, and New York, where malpractice premium rates were very high. "Nearly half of the 2,178 doctors who have moved to Colorado in the past year fled what the American Medical Association calls malpractice crisis states." The author describes the tort reform provisions in effect in Colorado.

14. Kachalia, A & Studdert, DM: Professional Liability Issues in Graduate Medical Education: JAMA, September 1, 2004 (292:9): 1051-1056. This is an interesting discussion of not only the lia-

bility issues affecting resident physicians, but also the set of legal issues confronting those who are involved in training resident physicians. "Professional liability considerations are prominent in the minds and practices of many physicians today. Liability concerns may affect not only how resident physicians practice, but also in which specialties and locations they choose to practice." They also note a change in the theories of wrongdoing evidenced by plaintiff attorneys: "The emphasis on systems approaches to patient safety can be expected to increase legal scrutiny of the administrative structures through which resident physicians deliver care." Is the threat of a lawsuit really the best way to drive process improvement?

15. Mello, Michelle M, et al: Caring for Patients in a Malpractice Crisis: Physician Satisfaction and Quality of Care: Health Affairs, July/August, 2004 (Vol. 23, No. 4):42-53. The authors surveyed physicians in Pennsylvania who were in high-risk specialties to find out what they thought and how they felt about the malpractice crisis there. They note that "opinion alone should not determine public policy, but physicians' perceptions matter for two reasons. First, perceptions influence behavior with respect to practice environment and clinical decision-making. Second, perceptions influence the physician-patient relationship and the interpersonal quality of care." After analyzing the surveys, they find that "the malpractice crisis in Pennsylvania is decreasing specialist physicians' satisfaction with medical practice in ways that may affect the quality of care." If the tort liability system is supposed to increase the quality of care, and the effect of the escalation in suits is to decrease the quality of care, then the system is moving retrograde instead of antegrade and deserves dramatic change; if the purpose of the tort liability system is not to increase the quality of care, then we should develop a system that does have this as a purpose.

16. Rice, Berkeley: Malpractice: Will a Jury Think Money Clouds Your Judgment?: Medical Economics, March 4, 2005. This is a

recounting of a judgment against a physician for negligence in which the presence of a compensation system that rewarded lower overall utilization was interpreted by the jury as being a reason why the physician might have withheld needed care from the patient. The lead line on the article reads: "Does it get more horrifying that this? You're sitting in a courtroom, accused not merely of medical incompetence, but of killing your patient in order to make a buck." Even if the presence of the compensation system was not a factor in the jury's decision, such a rendering of the event not only illustrates physicians' paranoia on the subject of lawsuits and jury decisions, it also highlights another reason for physicians not to collaborate with any cost-reduction efforts.

17. Studdert, David M, et al: Defensive Medicine among High-Risk Specialist Physicians in a Volatile Malpractice Environment: JAMA, June 1, 2005 (Vol. 293, No. 21):2609-2617. The authors surveyed for self-assessed behaviors among physicians in high-risk specialties in Pennsylvania in May 2003. They found a high prevalence of defensive medical practices, designed to avoid lawsuits, with consequences as regards the cost of care, access to care, and the quality of care.

18. Walshe, K & Shortell, SM: When Things Go Wrong: How Health Care Organizations Deal With Major Failures: Health Affairs, May/June 2004 (Vol. 23, No. 3):103-111. The authors looked at five countries (the United Kingdom, New Zealand, Australia, Canada, the United States) that have English common law as a shared legal heritage. They examine the detection, investigation, disclosure, and correction processes, and find them wanting. "Better systems are needed for reporting and investigating failures and for implementing the lessons learned. The culture of secrecy, professional protectionism, defensiveness... is central to such major failures." "[W]e believe that major failures in health care are... a product of the distinctive culture of the organizations, the health care professionals, and the health system...."

Ultimately, the most effective actions we take to prevent future major failures will be those that help to create a more open, transparent, equitable, and accountable health care culture."

19. Smith, Michael S: Owning Up: Tests that Were Not Done Were Reported as Normal: The Physician Executive, November/December 2004 (Vol. 30, No. 6):54-56. The author raises an example, then discusses a rational approach to error detection and prevention. But on the way, he acknowledges that one of the more common responses to errors is denial: Suppress the report, punish the reporter. We need to move away from the culture of denial and blaming.

20. Audet, Anne-Marie J, et al: Measure, Learn and Improve: Physicians' Involvement in Quality Improvement: Health Affairs; Vol. 24, No. 3 (May/June 2005):843-853. The authors undertook to assess the extent to which physicians engage in Quality Improvement activities. They found that most do not. "Physicians do not routinely use data for assessing their performance and are reluctant to share those data. They infrequently participate in redesign activities." And "Physicians in larger and salaried groups are more likely to be engaged in QI." Physician participation is essential if the quality of health care received by Americans is to improve.

21. Survey: 80 Percent of Doctors Witness Mistakes: Reuters, January 26, 2005: found on http://www.msnbc.msn.com/id/6872715/ on January 29, 2005. Forty-eight percent of nurses and 88% of physicians surveyed indicated that they felt they worked with colleagues who showed poor clinical judgment. Only 10% said anything about it.

22. Weissman, Joel et al: Error Reporting and Disclosure Systems: Views from Hospital Leaders: JAMA, March 16, 2005:1359-1366. Hospital CEOs, interviewed, felt that state-required reporting of medical errors would tend to drive down the number of incidents reported. CEOs felt that all forms of state reporting

encourage lawsuits, and most felt that state reporting had no effect or a negative effect on patient safety.

23. Arkansas Foundation for Medical Care: Surgical Infection Prevention Data: http://www.afmc.org/HTML/programs/statisticaldata/medicare/hospital/sip.aspx?skin=print: April 29, 2005. The data, taken from Medicare Part A claims in Arkansas, demonstrate the rates of adherence to three standards for surgical wound infection prevention. All three standards have good science behind them. In Arkansas, compliance to the three was 62.4%, 93.5%, and 30.9%. High quality wound infection prevention would encompass all three.

24. National Committee for Quality Assurance (NCQA): Diabetes Physician Recognition Program (DPRP) Frequently Asked Questions: http://www.ncqa.org/dprp/dprpfaq.htm; April 28, 2005. This is a quality assessment and recognition program run by the National Diabetes Quality Improvement Alliance (NDQIA). This is a significant effort to evaluate physician performance in the management of patients with diabetes mellitus. While recognition does not require that the physician pass every measure imposed, there is a point system that includes all of the measures and requires an aggregate score that passes the defined threshold.

25. Appleby, Julie: Case bets on business to heal health care system: USA Today, July 7, 2005. The story is about Steve Case, a cofounder of AOL, who is embarking on a health-care informatics company. He notes the poor penetration of information technology into health care and is quoted as saying: "It reminds me of 20 years ago when we were starting AOL." The author's conclusion is not sanguine about Case's chances of success.

26. Grove, Andrew S: Efficiency in the Health Care Industries: JAMA, Vol. 294, No. 4 (July 27, 2005):490-492. This is a fascinating article, and well worth the several minutes it takes to read. As the founder and head of Intel Corporation, Mr. Grove has the background to understand the drive to efficiency. He finds

three problems in health care. First, the research cycle is long—the fact that we are dealing with human beings and human life-span means that it can take years to find out the results of a change in therapy. The second is the slow rate of adoption of new knowledge and technology. (In the computer industry, there is no question of getting the latest information incorporated into today's product because if you don't, your competitor will.) In medicine it takes almost two decades for new knowledge to be integrated. Third, he criticizes the operational efficiency of the healthcare industry—the rate of adoption of technologies that would increase the efficiency of operations is slow, and is slowed by the fact that the technology must be adopted by many people at various levels of the system in order for there to be a system benefit. The lack of integration of the system is part of the cause of its inefficiency.

27. Health Affairs, September/October 2005 (24:5). This issue is titled "Health Information Technology" and has many articles worthy of careful study. How to achieve the potential rewards in the implementation of health information technology is one issue, and how to get the users to adopt the technology in the first place is another. The "business case" for the adoption of HIT by individual practitioners is absent—in fact, J. D. Kleinke argues that it is contrary to the self-interest of the provider to do so. The degree to which malice and/or consciously designed resistance is a factor can be debated, but the bottom line is that physicians are NOT adopting HIT at a rate that will reach appropriate public health goals in a reasonable time, and there is considerable resistance. Many authors speak with knowledge, experience, and passion about the reasons for the resistance and how it is to be overcome. Briefly, here are some of the highlights:

- Hillestad, Richard et al: Can Electronic Medical Record Systems Transform Health Care? Potential Health Benefits, Savings, and Costs: 1103-1117. Efficiency, considered from one perspective, is projected to be able to save $81 billion a year.

- Walker, James M: Electronic Medical Records and Health Care Transformation: 1118-1120. The current state of adoption of HIT precludes accurate estimates of savings.

- Himmelstein, DU & Woolhandler, S: Hope and Hype: Predicting the Impact of Electronic Medical Records: 1121-1123. An even more skeptical look at the hypothesized savings.

- Miller, Robert H, et al: The Value of Electronic Health Records in Solo or Small Group Practices: 1127-1137. The authors actually looked at the economic results flowing from physician adoption of EHR software by physicians and found uneven results. On the average, the practice saved enough to pay the $44,000 investment per physician back in 2.5 years. This is a very different assessment of the value to the small group or individual practice.

- Shortliffe, Edward H: Strategic Action in Health Information Technology: Why the Obvious Has Taken So Long: 1222-1233. Here is one of the pioneers writing on a subject he knows very well. Dr Shortliffe marks the lack of organized drive and the barriers, but notes that there is finally gathering momentum toward adoption.

- Taylor, Roger et al: Promoting Health Information Technology: Is There a Case For More Aggressive Government Action?: 1234-1245. The authors start by noting that the U.S. health care system is in trouble. The potential advantages of HIT adoption are noted. The market is noted for not working well toward adoption of HIT or of uniform standards. The authors clearly believe that federal governmental intervention will be required.

- Kleinke, JD: Dot-Gov: Market Failure and the Creation of a National Health Information Technology System: 1246-1262.

As noted above, Kleinke is not gentle with health care providers, insurance companies, or anyone else about the conflicted reward structure of the current system. So far as he is concerned, there has been a complete breakdown of the marketplace, and the federal government should step in, as it did with the transcontinental railroad or space exploration.

- Halverson, George C: Wiring Health Care: 1266-1268. "Trying to create an accountable system or a well-functioning health care marketplace without accurate, accessible, meaningful, and timely data is an exercise in futility. It simply cannot be done." In joining J. D. Kleinke in advocating for governmental involvement, the author also points to the Hill-Burton Act, which funded hospital construction, and the Rural Electrification Act, which turned poor rural areas into viable communities. The author argues for diversity, but for interoperability.

- Middleton, Blackford: Achieving U.S. Health Information Technology Adoption: The Need for a Third Hand: 1269-1272. The author concurs about the need for federal government involvement, but adds, "I would remind us all in passing... that the failed adoption of IT in health care is not the only problem that ails health care." He advocates for systemic reform. The author further notes that it may not be the failure to have HIT standards that causes the HIT market failure—it may in fact be the market failure that is causing the lack of HIT standards. In vigorous, active markets, buyers and sellers flock to standards because they offer greater value.

28. Study: Health Care Industry Behind in IT Adoption: CDC press release: found at http://www.ihealthbeat.org/index.cfm? Action= dispItem&itemID= 109635 on March 16, 2005. Electronic medical records are used in 31% of hospital emergency departments, 29% of hospital outpatient departments, and 17% of physician

offices. About 8% of physicians use computerized order entry systems.

29. Koppel, Ross, et al: Role of Computerized Physician Order Entry Systems in Facilitating Medication Errors: JAMA, March 9, 2005 (293:10):1197-1203. The authors studied a single computerized order entry system and found that there were aspects of the system that actually encouraged errors of particular kinds. Clearly, the work on computerized order entry systems is not complete. Additional consideration to user-friendliness and mitigation of potential error production is needed.

30. Poon, Eric G et al: Overcoming Barriers to Adopting and Implementing Computerized Physician Order Entry Systems in U.S. Hospitals: Health Affairs, July/August 2004 (23:4):184-190. This is an interesting discussion of the barriers the hospital faces in implementing a Computerized Physician Order Entry system.

31. Here is a set of articles about electronic prescribing which includes and expands on my concerns about getting the system right, having the right medical information built into the system, and having standards for communication of information from one system to another.

   • Bell, Douglas S., et al: Recommendations for Comparing Electronic Prescribing Systems: Results of an Expert Consensus Process: Health Affairs—Web Exclusive, W4 (25 May 2004):305-317.

   • Brailer, David J.: Translating Ideals for Health Information Technology into Practice: Health Affairs—Web Exclusive, W4 (25 May 2004):318-320.

   • Javitt, Jonathan C.: How to Succeed in Health Information Technology: Health Affairs—Web Exclusive, W4 (25 May 2004):321-324.

- Hammond, W. Ed: The Role of Standards in Electronic Prescribing: Health Affairs—Web Exclusive, W4 (25 May 2004): 325-327.

32. Garg, Amit X, et al: Effects of Computerized Clinical Decision Support Systems on Practitioner Performance and Patient Outcomes: JAMA, March 9, 2005 (vol. 293, No. 10):1223-1238. The authors looked for studies comparing performance with and without computerized clinical decision support systems (CDSS) to see what was available in the literature and what quality of research was being done. They found 100 studies; the number and quality has been improving. Results were scattered, but it was clear that those systems which automatically prompted users were more successful than those that required activation; those designed by the users were more successful than those not designed by the users. The potential for impact of CDSS is present, but we are in the early days.

33. Frist, Bill & Clinton, Hillary: How to Heal Health Care: Washington Post, August 25, 2004: A17. Writing together, this interesting combination of the Republican Senate Majority Leader and a Democratic Senator, in a presidential election year, join forces first to deliver an indictment of the healthcare system, then to propose solutions. Their joint solution is that patients must take charge of their own care and become active participants in the determinations about their care. To do this will require information—information about what care is appropriate, information about the quality of care delivered by providers, and information about the cost of that care and how cost varies from provider to provider. They recognize a substantial federal role in setting up such information systems.

34. Mullaney, Timothy J: This Man Wants to Heal Health Care: Business Week, October 31, 2005:75. This article is about David Brailer (the national coordinator for Health Information Technology in the Department of Health and Human Services) and

his campaign for electronic standardization in electronic systems for patient care.

35. Arkansas Foundation for Medical Care: Community-Acquired Pneumonia Data: http://www.afmc.org/HTML/programs/ statisticaldata/ medicare/hospital/cap.aspx?skin=print; April 29, 2005. The data, taken from Medicare Part A claims in Arkansas, demonstrate the rates at which we see compliance with the same criteria discussed by Hahn, et al (NEJM:347;25:2039). The results are tabulated only for individual criteria—no attempt is made to assess the rate at which all criteria (or any subset of criteria) were met. Four criteria were of interest:

- Initial antibiotic within four hours (actual rate 75.5%)

- Correct antibiotic selected (actual rate 77.6%)

- Blood culture done timely (actual rate 66%)

- Blood culture before first antibiotic (actual rate 86.8%)

From these data, we may discern that at least 86.8% of patients received at least one of these four crucial treatment elements, but the number receiving all four may be as low as 5.9% or as high as 66%.

36. Halm, Ethan A., et al: Management of Community-Acquired Pneumonia: New England Journal of Medicine: 347:25 (December 19, 2002):2039-2045. The authors review the assessment and treatment of community-acquired pneumonia. They note that annually there are about four million cases in the United States, with about one million hospitalizations. Hospital care of community-acquired pneumonia costs more than 20 times as much as outpatient care—in excess of $9 billion a year. There are variations in the rate and length of hospitalization that are not explained by differences in the characteristics of the patients or the severity of their disease. This is a review article, gathering scientific material and recommendations made by various re-

sources over a number of years to offer advice on the evaluation and treatment of this condition.

37. Arkansas Foundation for Medical Care: Acute Myocardial Infarction Data: http://www.afmc.org/HTML/programs/statisticaldata/medicare/hospital/ami.aspx?skin=print; April 29, 2005. The data, taken from Medicare Part A claims in Arkansas, demonstrate the rates of adherence to six standards for the care of patients presenting to the hospital with a heart attack. All six standards have good science behind them. Encouragingly, performance on five of the six improved during the intervention period.

38. CMS Provider Resource: Health Care Quality Leaders Join Forces —AQA and HQA Collaborate to Expedite National Quality Strategy: CMS Provider Resource email list serve, July 25, 2006. AQA is already an alliance of a number of provider and payer organizations concerned primarily with physician practice issues; HQA is the Hospital Quality Alliance and represents a somewhat different point of view. Both will be working closely with the Centers for Medicare & Medicaid Services (CMS) and the Agency for Healthcare Research and Quality (AHRQ). This alliance should be capable of producing optimized practice parameters.

39. McCue, Michael T: "I'm Losing My Patience": Managed Healthcare Executive, February 2005. Here are the six interventions outlined by the Institute for Healthcare Improvement (IHI):

- Create Rapid Response Teams to intercept unexpected deterioration in patient status;

- Improve care for acute myocardial infarction (heart attack) to the scientifically demonstrated standard;

- Improve ventilator care to prevent pneumonia;

- Improve central intravenous line care to prevent infection;

- Improve pre- and post-operative care to reduce surgical site infections;

- Prevent severe adverse drug events through the use of medication reconciliation procedures.

These six interventions are estimated to save nearly one life per two hospital beds per year. To be certain of saving 100,000 lives, Don Berwick, President of the IHI, is recruiting enough hospitals to bring the total number of beds committed to this intervention process to 400,000. See also the IHI website at www.ihi.org. Berwick figured he needed about 1,600 hospitals to reach this number; as of November 2005, 2,800 hospitals were participating.

40. Stobbe, Mike: Campaign against hospital mistakes says 122,000 lives saved: Associated Press (found at http://www. Signon sandiego.com/news/health/20060614-1457-hospitalsivers. html) on June 15, 2006. The challenge was to save 100,000 lives. The best estimate is that 122,000 were saved in the program. The next challenge will be to keep the improvements in place. This is like forming new habits or breaking old ones—there are no institutional supports to encourage these new activities except the enthusiasm of the people who implement them in the first place. As soon as any degree of complacency sets in, unless there continues to be an external stimulus, the efforts will tend to fade.

41. Ulrich, Roger et al: The Role of the Physical Environment in the Hospital of the 21st Century: A Once-in-a-Lifetime Opportunity: Report to the Center for Health Design, sponsored by the Robert Wood Johnson Foundation; Sept 2004. http://www.healthdesign. org/research/reports/physical_environ.php. The authors found "rigorous studies that link the physical environment to patient and staff outcomes in four areas:

- Reduce staff stress and fatigue, and increase effectiveness in delivering care

- Improve patient safety

- Reduce stress and improve outcomes

- Improve overall healthcare quality"

The upshot is that not only do you have to design quality into the processes; you actually have to design it into the physical plant.

42. Samore, Matthew H, et al: Clinical Decision Support and Appropriateness of Antimicrobial Prescribing: JAMA, November 9, 2005:(294:18):2305-2314. In a randomized, controlled trial, the authors demonstrate that a clinical decision support tool was able to reduce unnecessary antibiotic prescriptions for patients with upper respiratory illnesses.

43. Weber, JT: Appropriate Use of Antimicrobial Drugs: JAMA, November 9, 2005:(294:18):2354-2356. The author notes the publication of two important articles on antibiotic use in the current issue of JAMA. He comments that the appropriate use of antibiotics is becoming more important as the rate of development of new antibiotics slows. He points out the importance of studies to indicate how to reduce the antibiotic use trend, and notes that the trend must be reduced across all of the use patterns for antibiotics.

44. Mortensen, EM et al: Effects of Guideline-Concordant Antimicrobial Therapy on Mortality among Patients with Community-Acquired Pneumonia: American Journal of Medicine; Nov 15, 2004; 117:725-731 (as reported in Journal Watch, Vol. 25, No. 1, page 10). This study looked at 420 patients who were treated for community-acquired pneumonia, and adjusted for disease severity, concurrent other illness, time to administration of antibiotic, and admission status. What they found was 30-day mortality that was 5.7 times higher in patients who were not given the antibiotics recommended by a national guideline on the treatment of community-acquired pneumonia, but were given another antibiotic in-

stead. The moral of the story is that guidelines do work, and standard treatment is standard treatment because it works better than non-standard treatment in most cases. Why would doctors not want to follow standards that result in better outcomes for their patients?

45. NCQA: The State of Health Care Quality–2004: National Committee for Quality Assurance; 2004. This is a wonderful resource about a number of measures of quality performance, with some reservations. The first reservation is that it measures a single class of payer—the "HMO." Standard health insurance and variants thereof (such as PPO coverage) are not measured. The second reservation is that the measurements represent a compromise between importance and measurability—measurability being compromised primarily by the fact that the organizations being measured are generally not the ones performing the subjects of measurement. So, for instance, an HMO is measured on a standard relating to childhood immunization. No employee of the HMO ever administers a childhood immunization. The physicians who are contracted to the HMO administer such immunizations as they can and/or wish to administer. Many parents take their children to the public health immunization clinics, believing it to be less expensive. The public health clinics often not only do not but cannot bill the private insurer (the HMO). In the face of this, NCQA is probably measuring the wrong people—though on many of the right measures.

46. Kerr, Eve A, et al: Profiling the Quality of Care in Twelve Communities: Results from the CQI Study: Health Affairs, May/June 2004 (23:3):247-256. The authors note the long history of studies showing deficits in the application of identifiable standards of care. Fundamental redesign of the system is required. For improvements in quality, quality data should be available locally and in a timely manner to provide a measure of progress. To advance that process, RAND undertook a detailed examination of the quality of care in twelve metropolitan areas in the USA, based

on the analyses from the Community Quality Index (CQI) study of the Center for Studying Health System Change. They used a tool with 439 indicators across 30 conditions and preventive care. The indicators were developed by RAND and were independently validated. Overall scores, scores on preventive measures, and scores by chronic conditions varied among the cities, with no city being consistently best or worst, and none approaching either extreme in any score. Preventive scores ranged from 35% to 80%; disease-based scores ranged from just under 40% to 70%. The authors conclude that "although each community will need to grapple with how to improve quality of care locally, it is clear that considerable room exists for improvement in health care delivery at the community level."

47. Landro, Laura: The Informed Patient: The Wall Street Journal, May 6, 2004. The author describes a network of 4,500 physicians and 120 hospitals in Oklahoma initiating a program to reward both physicians and patients for following 117 evidence-based clinical guidelines. She notes that this is likely to be an improvement in an environment where patients receive recommended guidelines only about half of the time.

48. Paauw, Douglas S: Did We Learn Evidence-Based Medicine in Medical School? Some Common Medical Mythology: JABFP, March-April 1999 (Vol. 12, No. 2); 143-149. This is a well documented article that has taken several common medical myths and examined the lack of factual background to support them. In fact, there is plenty of evidence to refute them, but that evidence appears to be systematically ignored by the perpetuation of the false views expressed in the myths. We have to build systems that will repeatedly contradict misstatements and build on science; we must do what we can to overcome the human tendency of physicians to rely on what was once said by an acknowledged authority, or on the results of the most recent episode of care.

Chapter 21

1. Markel H & Golden J: Children's Public Health Policy in the United States: How the Past Can Inform the Future: Health Affairs, September/ October 2004 (23:5):147-152. Through a historical looking-glass, the authors mark the importance of three issues in treating children: focus on the environment that makes children sick; focus on the biggest problems, not necessarily the most interesting ones; provide services where the children are. This last is the distribution problem we are trying to approach in this chapter.

2. McCaig, Linda F et al: National Hospital Ambulatory Medical Care Survey: 2003 Emergency Department Summary: CDC Advance Data Number 358, May 26, 2005. In the period from 1993 to 2003, ED visits increased 26%. The population-based rate of ED use rose from 35.5 visits per 100 people per year to 39.9 visits per 100 people per year. Infants under 12 months of age had a visit rate of 97.5 visits per 100 babies per year. Utilization rates were highest for Medicaid enrollees (81.0 visits per 100) and lowest for patients with private insurance (21.5 visits per 100). Three percent of ED visits occurred within three days of a prior visit to the same ED. The most common diagnosis was acute upper respiratory infection. The mean waiting time was 46.5 minutes. These statistics clearly indicate a trend to higher use of the ED for problems that could be taken care of in another facility. The ED is the highest cost provider of these services.

3. A set of six articles published in the Health Affairs Web Exclusive provide some insight, some contrasting of opinion, and some information about emergency department capacity and economics. Among the responses are a variety of different opinions about how to solve the problem of ER crowding. Only by implication do any of them recognize that increasing the supply of primary

care physicians and people's access to those physicians would make a difference. The group of articles makes interesting reading:

- Melnick, Glenn A, et al: Emergency Department Capacity and Access in California, 1990-2001: An Economic Analysis: Health Affairs: Web Exclusive W4 (24 March 2004):136-142.

- Fields, W. Wesley: Emergency Care In California: Robust Capacity or Busted Access?: Health Affairs: Web Exclusive W4 (24 March 2004):143-145.

- Siegel, Bruce: The Emergency Department: Rethinking the Safety Net for the Safety Net: Health Affairs: Web Exclusive W4 (24 March 2004): 146-148.

- Kellermann, Arthur L: Emergency Care in California: No Emergency?: Health Affairs: Web Exclusive W4 (24 March 2004):149-151.

- Dauner, C. Duane: Emergency Capacity in California: A Look at More Recent Trends: Health Affairs: Web Exclusive W4 (24 March 2004): 152-154.

- Melnick, Glenn A, et al: Hospital Emergency Departments: The Authors Respond: Health Affairs: Web Exclusive W4 (24 March 2004):155-156.

4. Reschovsky, James D., et al: Access and Quality: Does Rural America Lag Behind?: Health Affairs: 24:4 (July/August 2005): 1128-1139. The authors chose to look at physician availability by comparing satisfaction scores and delay in receiving services between rural and urban communities. They found few differences, though they found that rural physicians worked longer hours and were more willing to care for patients on Medicaid and patients without insurance. This is extremely interesting work which needs more exploration of the process of determining how many physicians we really need.

5. Future of Family Medicine Project Leadership Committee: The Future of Family Medicine: Annals of Family Medicine, Vol. 2, Supplement 1 (March/ April 2004). This ambitious look at the future of family medicine (by which the authors mean a particular medical discipline akin to what was formerly called "general practice") covers a lot of ground. It includes a look at manpower needs for primary care (and finds primary care resources lacking in most American counties). It describes in detail a "new way" of delivering primary care services. It discusses the need for change and advocates, among other things, for universal coverage.

6. Sipkoff, Martin: Back to the Future: The Re-Emergence of the Primary Care Physician: Managed Care, 2005 June; 14(6) 24-6, 29-30. The importance of this article, and of the reference material it cites, is not precisely the path it advocates, but the recognition that a total reorganization of primary care medicine is needed. The reorganization proposed includes efforts to improve the effectiveness of PCPs, but also efforts to improve the accessibility of primary care physicians to assist their patients. This article reflects a considerable body of work done by the American Academy of Family Physicians in response to the current issues surrounding primary care practice. However, to succeed, this effort will need not only internal impetus from within primary care, but also considerable support from outside—the rest of the medical community and the payer community. The pathway proposed is similar in some ways to my proposals, but in most ways different both in the problems it seeks to confront and the solutions chosen, many of which might become portions of the solution as I outline it.

7. Starfield, Barbara, et al: The Effects of Specialist Supply on Populations' Health: Assessing the Evidence: Health Affairs Web Exclusive W5 (March 15, 2005):97-107. This fascinating study looks at the longevity (or death rates) on a county-by-county basis across most counties in the United States. It finds that death rates among the residents of counties are inversely propor-

tional to the number of primary care physicians per 1,000 population and directly proportional to the number of specialists per
1,000 population. This strongly implies that more primary care
physicians tend to reduce death rates, but that more specialists
tend to increase death rates. There is now a significant volume
of data on this subject, though adjusting out happenstance and
coincidence is not easy to do. There are several commentaries
that follow this article that are also worthy:

- Goodman, David C: The Physician Workforce Crisis: Where
  is the Evidence?: Health Affairs Web Exclusive W5 (March
  15, 2005):108-110.

- Phillips, Robert L Jr, et al: Adding More Specialists is Not
  Likely to Improve Population Health: Is Anybody Listening?:
  Health Affairs Web Exclusive W5 (March 15, 2005):111-114.

- Salsberg, Edward: The Need for Real Evidence in Physician
  Workforce Decision Making: Health Affairs Web Exclusive
  W5 (March 15, 2005):115-118.

- Starfield, Barbara: Letter of Response to Edward Salsberg:
  Health Affairs Web Exclusive W5 (March 15, 2005): Health
  Affairs Web Exclusive W5 (March 15, 2005):S7-S8.

8. Hill, L & Madara, JL: Role of the Urban Academic Medical Center in US Health Care: JAMA, November 2, 2005:(294: 17):
   2219-2220. The authors note the several conflicting roles of academic medical centers. Central to their role is the combination of
   teaching, research, and care for rare and complex problems not
   easily encompassed by the community physicians. More problematic is the need for a well-rounded patient population to support the teaching role. Substantially more difficult still is their role
   in the support of the surrounding community. Competition
   among roles and between the center and community physicians
   is a perennial problem. One of the pathways to resolution of this
   conundrum is through the control of process that can be exerted

by an astute payer. Does such an astute payer exist? Would a single-payer system help out?

9. Dimick, Justin B., et al: Regional Availability of High Volume Hospitals for Major Surgery: Health Affairs—Web Exclusive on Variations (7 October 2004):45-53. Some surgical procedures can be shown to be clearly safer if done at high-volume hospitals ("practice makes perfect"). In spite of the fact that this has been known for some time, many patients continue to have surgery in low-volume hospitals. What the authors found is that there are problems with surgical density—there are some regions where there are not enough procedures to support even a single high-volume hospital; there are other regions where several hospitals in competition each have inadequate volume, but adequate volume is present if it could be consolidated into one facility; in other regions, there are high-volume facilities and people still are operated on outside of those facilities. The marketplace does not seem to be capable of fixing this problem. A more consolidated system could go a long way toward optimizing the care received by Americans.

10. Goodman, David C.: Twenty-Year Trends in Regional Variations in the U.S. Physician Workforce: Health Affairs—Web Exclusive on Variation (7 October 2004):90-97. The author notes that in spite of continued growth in the physician workforce (aggregate supply per capita grew more than 50%), large variations (up to 300%) exist between different geographic areas. It is clear that most new physicians tend to locate to areas where there are already many physicians. This continued unequal distribution makes estimates of the appropriate supply difficult. The author notes that even in areas of very high supply, there may be underserved segments of the population.

Chapter 22

1. Gottlieb, Scott: Opening Pandora's Pillbox: Using Modern Information Tools to Improve Drug Safety; Health Affairs: 24:4 (July/August 2005):938-948. The author discusses pathways to improving the ability of the FDA to obtain, maintain, and process information to allow improved and more rapid assessment of the safety and effectiveness of medications in the post-approval period. Always, the approval process is based in studies of relatively small numbers of people followed for a relatively short period of time. Appropriate, carefully collected data could increase both the speed and the accuracy of evaluation during the period following the release of a new medication onto the market.

2. Lurie, Peter, et al: Financial Conflict of Interest Disclosure and Voting Patterns at Food and Drug Administration Drug Advisory Committee Meetings: JAMA, April 26, 2006 (295:16):1921-1928. The conclusion in the abstract begins with this statement: "Disclosures of conflicts of interest at drug advisory committee meetings are common, often of considerable monetary value, and rarely result in recusal of advisory committee members." It may be difficult to arrange that no one on the committee has conflicts of interest. It is certainly better to have such conflicts disclosed than for them to remain secret. On the other hand, the presence of such conflicts in committee members who remain present for the discussion and continue to have a vote in matters which are influenced by those conflicts represents a potential poisoning of the process.

3. Neumann, Peter J: Evidence-Based and Value-Based Formulary Guidelines: Health Affairs January/February 2004 (23:1):124-134. The author notes that hospital and health plan formulary decisions have, in the past, frequently lacked transparency. There is now a trend among formulary committees to request of

pharmaceutical manufacturers a standardized "dossier" of information, including scientific background, to enable the decision to be more standard and more rational. The effort is to have all pertinent information available for the formulary committee, and to have the decision whether to include the new drug on the formulary be based on objective data, not supposition. It may be that the decision is primarily an economic one where therapeutic alternatives are available. It may be that the decision is based on the evidence, or lack of it, of efficacy. In any case, if we can do this at the level of the hospital or local health plan, we can certainly do that on a national basis as well.

4. Foote, Susan B, et al: Resolving the Tug-of-War Between Medicare's National and Local Coverage: Health Affairs, July/August 2004 (23:4):109-123. The authors note that Medicare forms some national coverage policies, but leaves many issues up to local medical review policies for determination. There is considerable variation around the country based on the decisions by these local determinations. This variability raises questions about equity and about quality. The authors advocate for a national process for creating policies, especially those regarding new technologies and technology extensions.

5. Henry, David A et al: Drug Prices and Value for Money—The Australian Pharmaceutical Benefits Scheme: JAMA, November 23/30, 2005 (294:20):2630-2632. As a contrast to the NICE program in Great Britain (see next note), the authors describe the Australian approach. Though limited to pharmaceuticals, the charge is explicitly to include cost-effectiveness of pharmaceuticals. The work of the Pharmaceutical Benefits Advisory Committee has been as controversial as that of NICE. The resulting prices for drugs in Australia have been published on their website (http://wwwl.health.gov.au/pbs/index.htm). The Pharmaceutical Benefits Advisory Committee and NICE are programs doing what I describe, in English-speaking countries that share much of our national heritage.

6. Pearson SD & Rawlins MD: Quality, Innovation, and Value for Money—NICE and the British National Health Service: JAMA, November 23/30, 2005 (294:20):2618-2622. The National Institute for Health and Clinical Excellence (NICE) was established as part of the British National Health Service in 1999 to set standards for the adoption of new health care technologies and the management of specific conditions. In doing so, it was required explicitly to take into account both clinical effectiveness and cost-effectiveness. Its processes are largely open and make extensive use of panels of providers and members gathered to assist in the hearing process. The fact that NICE is under attack both for approving too many technologies and for approving too few indicates some degree of success. Prior to the institution of NICE, each local NHS office was able to make such decisions, and often what was covered by the NHS varied considerably from one postal code zone to another. From a national standpoint, this was even less tolerable than a central organization to make decisions. The NICE has, so far, been able to remain unpoliticized, which is important.

7. Reinhardt, Uwe E: An Information Infrastructure for the Pharmaceutical Market: Health Affairs; Vol. 23, No. 1 (January/ February 2004):107-112. As a response to the passage of the 2003 Medicare Improvement Act to allow drug coverage, Professor Reinhardt proposes an independent, publicly funded information infrastructure to study and disseminate results on pharmaceutical cost-effectiveness. The idea is clear—we should be willing to pay what a drug is worth, but not some exorbitant price promulgated by the pharmaceutical manufacturer solely bent on making a great profit.

8. Beal, Anne C: Policies to Reduce Racial and Ethnic Disparities in Child Health and Health Care: Health Affairs, September/ October 2004 (23:5):171-179. The set of policies proposes cuts across many parts of our society and requires the coordination of many efforts. The author suggests an oversight body based in

the U.S. Department of Health and Human Services to oversee the implementation.

9. Wennberg, John E., et al: Use of Medicare Claims Data to Monitor Provider-Specific Performance among Patients with Severe Chronic Illness: Health Affairs—Web Exclusive on Variations (7 October 2004):4-18. The authors used Medicare claims data to derive illness-adjusted, population-based information on the handling of severe chronic diseases. This permitted comparisons among a number of hospitals, ranging from academic medical centers to community hospitals, on practice patterns and consumption of resources. The information about variations is not surprising. The ease with which Medicare claims data was used to create the comparisons suggests that careful use of claims data will enable researchers to accomplish a great deal in understanding patterns of care.

10. CMS Public Affairs Office: CMS Launches Council to Improve Timely Access to New Medical Technologies: Centers for Medicare & Medicaid Services, Press Release, August 12, 2004. URL: http://www.cms.hhs.gov/apps/media/press/release.asp?Counter=1163&intNumPerPage=10&checkDate=&checkKey=&srchType=1&numDays=0&srchOpt=0&srchData=&srchOpt=0&srchData=&keywordType=All&chkNewsType=1%2C+2%2C+3%2C+4%2C+5&intPage=&showAll=1&pYear=1&year=2004&desc=false&cboOrder=date. Also in a telephone conference with Janet Anderson Brock, Project Coordinator, Center on Technology and Innovation, CMS: CMO Committee of the AHIP (America's Health Insurance Plans), November 2, 2004. The press release announced and Ms. Brock discussed the foundation of the Center on Technology and Innovation. The plan is to use the payment mechanism to drive research that will enable determinations about the effectiveness of new technology. CMS has already done something very like this with lung reduction surgery for emphysema. The trial was at a small number of institutions; patients were randomized to surgery or no

surgery, and participation in the trial was the only way Medicare patients had access to this surgery. This went on for five years, but has brought some indication about the overall effectiveness of this procedure.

11. Grove, Andrew S: Efficiency in the Health Care Industries: JAMA, Vol. 294, No. 4 (July 27, 2005):490-492. This is a fascinating article, and well worth the several minutes it takes to read. As the founder and head of Intel Corporation, Mr. Grove has the background to understand the drive to efficiency. He finds three problems in health care. First, the research cycle is long—the fact that we are dealing with human beings and human lifespan means that it can take years to find out the results of a change in therapy. The second is the slow rate of adoption of new knowledge and technology. In the computer industry, there is no question of getting the latest information incorporated into today's product because if you don't, your competitor will. In medicine, it takes almost two decades for new knowledge to be integrated. Third, he criticizes the operational efficiency of the healthcare industry. The rate of adoption of technologies that would increase the efficiency of operations is slow, and the technology must be adopted by many people at various levels of the system in order for there to be a system benefit. The lack of integration of the system is part of the cause of its inefficiency.

12. Califf, Robert M: Defining the Balance of Risk and Benefit in the Era of Genomics and Proteomics: Health Affairs, January/February 2004 (23:1):77-87. The individualization of care decisions will increase with the identification of genomic predispositions and physiologic propensities, combined with the increasing factor of patient choice. As this individualization increases, the ability to produce meaningful research results will require larger and larger trials. Not only does this require larger networks, it will require better coordination across regulatory and payment systems. It will also require an investment in the education of providers and patients to understand the results of that research.

This sounds like the job of the Health Coverage Administration to me.

13. Bakalar, Nicholas: Treatment: Remedy Is Fake but Relief Is Real: New York Times, May 17, 2005. The author reports on a study of acupuncture for migraine headaches done in Germany. The study showed that "sham" acupuncture (putting the needles in the "wrong" places) was as effective in this group as "real" acupuncture (putting the needles in the "right" places), and both were significantly more successful at relieving migraine than non-treatment. This kind of research will help to light the way to finding the best approaches to medical diagnosis and treatment.

14. Marquis SM, Rogowski JA & Escarce JJ: The Managed Care Backlash: Did Consumers Vote with Their Feet?: Inquiry, Vol. 41, Winter 2004/2005:376-390 (as summarized at http://www.rand.org/pubs/research_briefs/RB9121/index1.html on December 25, 2005). In comparing HMO enrollment from 1994 to 1998 to 2001, it is noteworthy that there was little drop in HMO enrollment despite the "HMO backlash." As the authors point out, this could either be because people were really more satisfied with their HMOs than had been thought, or because HMOs relaxed their cost containment restrictions to avoid losing market share. Or both.

15. Garber, Alan M.: Cost-Effectiveness and Evidence Evaluation as Criteria for Coverage Policy: Health Affairs—Web Exclusive, W4 (19 May 2004):284-296. The author looks at current research and evaluation techniques and finds "evidence of effectiveness" to be an inadequate tool for cost control, but finds that "cost-effectiveness" is not yet well enough developed, produces results in which the expression is different enough that they are not comparable, and is not entirely acceptable. However, he notes that "the current erosion of commercial health insurance and the growing burden of public health insurance programs may trans-

form it from an academic curiosity to an essential tool for health care decision making." This article is followed by two editorials:

- Ginsburg, Marjorie E.: Cost-Effectiveness: Will the Public Buy It or Balk?: Health Affairs—Web Exclusive, W4 (19 May 2004):297-299.
- Yeglan, Jill Mathews: Setting Priorities in Medical Care Through Benefit Design and Medical Management: Health Affairs—Web Exclusive, W4 (19 May 2004):300-304.

16. Health Affairs, January/February 2005 (24:1). This whole issue is crammed with articles about evidence-based medical care, opinions about how to implement scientific standards, and discussion of why it isn't already working better than it is. There is no single author or set of articles that stood out for me. What is important to the reader is that there is an accumulating body of knowledge not only about how health care should be delivered, but about the ways of moving from where we are to an appropriately science-based system. In my writing, I am dealing with the broad concepts. Much of what is in this issue of Health Affairs is the bits and pieces that will make up the detail blueprints to implement the system of the future.

Chapter 23

1. Starfield, Barbara, et al: The Effects of Specialist Supply on Populations' Health: Assessing the Evidence: Health Affairs Web Exclusive W5 (March 15, 2005):97-107. This fascinating study looks at the longevity (or death rates) on a county-by-county basis across most counties in the United States. It finds that death rates among the residents of counties are inversely proportional to the number of primary care physicians per 1,000 population and directly proportional to the number of specialists per 1,000 population. This strongly implies that more primary care physicians tend to reduce death rates, but that more specialists tend to increase death rates. There is now a significant volume of data on this subject, though adjusting out happenstance and coincidence is not easy to do. There are several commentaries that follow this article that are also worthy:

   - Goodman, David C: The Physician Workforce Crisis: Where is the Evidence?: Health Affairs Web Exclusive W5 (March 15, 2005):108-110.

   - Phillips, Robert L Jr, et al: Adding More Specialists is Not Likely to Improve Population Health: Is Anybody Listening?: Health Affairs Web Exclusive W5 (March 15, 2005):111-114.

   - Salsberg, Edward: The Need for Real Evidence in Physician Workforce Decision Making: Health Affairs Web Exclusive W5 (March 15, 2005): 115-118.

   - Starfield, Barbara: Letter of Response to Edward Salsberg: Health Affairs Web Exclusive W5 (March 15, 2005): Health Affairs Web Exclusive W5 (March 15, 2005):S7-S8.

2. Cunningham, Robert: Professionalism Reconsidered: Physician Payment in a Small-Practice Environment: Health Affairs, November/December 2004 (Vol. 23, No. 6):36-47. The author reviews a number of, so far, failed attempts to change

the locus of medical decision-making. As he clearly points out, it is not at all clear that patients will ever wrest decision-making authority from physicians. The challenge he issues is to acknowledge the preferred relationships that patients and physicians continue to have, and work on ways to improve quality within that relationship rather than to produce radical change in the relationship itself. A follow-up article comments and agrees, pointing out that the health plans, once thought to be the potential reorganizers of care, are probably not in a position to do that job. Allan Korn speaks with some authority as the Chief Medical Officer for the Blue Cross/Blue Shield Association. Here is his article:

- Korn, Allan: Professionalism Reconsidered: Physician Payment from a Health Plan Perspective: Health Affairs, November/December 2004 (Vol. 23, No. 6):48-50.

3. Forrest CB & Riley AW: Childhood Origins of Adult Health: A Basis for Life-Course Health Policy: Health Affairs, September/October 2004 (23:5):155-164. "Many common chronic and mental disorders have modifiable precursors that arise during childhood." Each person represents a continuity from childhood through adulthood. To the extent that we recognize and treat that continuity, we can intervene in childhood to produce outcomes in adulthood. This "requires health policies to foster positive long-term outcomes focused on the individual, family, and community." This is yet another argument for increasing primary care supply—to improve the continuity of care and the attention to the family and the community.

4. Kerr, Stacey Marie: Keeping the Fire Alive: JAMA, April 21, 2004 (291:15):1813-1814. No comment by me can elevate or detract from this carefully told, heart-rending story of a primary care physician, her patients, and her struggle with the health care reimbursement system. We have to do a better job of supporting physicians like Dr Kerr.

5. Starfield, Barbara: U.S. Child Health: What's Amiss, And What Should Be Done About It?: Health Affairs September/October 2004 (23:5):165-170. The health of children in our country is poorer in virtually every way than that of children in other countries. One of the advocated changes is recognition of the importance of primary health care in the health and sense of well-being of our children, and the advancement of that aspect of care. In general, the higher the ratio of primary care physicians to population, the better health outcomes can be expected. A plan that encourages primary care services and makes them more available is also a plan that improves health outcomes.

Chapter 24

1. Thom, David H, et al: Measuring Patients' Trust in Physicians When Assessing Quality of Care: Health Affairs, July/August 2004 (23:4):124-132. "A person who trusts a provider is more likely to seek care, to comply with treatment recommendations, and to return for follow-up care than a person who has little trust in a specific provider or the health care system." Thus do the authors start the examination. The effects of trust are discussed. Mechanisms for measuring trust are discussed. Methods of improving trust are discussed. The question is whether anyone will move forward with any of this.

2. Chimonas, Susan, et al: New Federal Guidelines for Physician-Pharmaceutical Industry Relations: The Politics of Policy Formation; Health Affairs: 24:4 (July/August 2005):949-960. The authors track and comment on proposed federal guidelines for pharmaceutical manufacturers giving gifts and favors to physicians as a way to influence physicians to prescribe medications manufactured by that company. The evolution of the standards in response to pressure from pharmaceutical manufacturers and the medical profession is an interesting commentary on the current status of professional ethics.

3. McCullough, Laurence B: Practicing Preventive Ethics—The Keys to Avoiding Ethical Conflicts in Health Care: The Physician Executive; March-April 2005:18-21. This article is the balance, the resolution, the "how to avoid that" response to Mr. Weber's immediately preceding article about the prevalence of unethical practices.

4. Weber, David O: Unethical Business Practices in U.S. Health Care Alarm Physician Leaders: The Physician Executive; March-April 2005:6-13. In the context of a survey of physician leaders about unethical practices, this article explored the alarming answer that these leaders, apparently regardless of what sector of

the health care system they work in, are concerned about the prevalence of unethical practices. It is a fascinating article with several editorial appendages of significant interest.

5. Robeznieks, Andis: Would You Fib for Your Patient?: American Medical News, June 13, 2005:13-14. Insurance fraud appears to be a common desire among patients and a disturbingly common option among physicians. Fifty-seven percent (57%) of physicians at least sometimes exaggerate the severity of a patient's condition to avoid discharge from the hospital. Fifty-two percent (52%) will at least sometimes change a patient's official diagnosis to help the patient secure coverage for a treatment or service. Twenty-nine percent (29%) are at least sometimes willing to report signs or symptoms that a patient did not have in order to help the patient secure coverage for a treatment or service. Is it any wonder that insurance companies do not trust doctors? How much additional cost has to be built into the system to combat fraud? In a real sense, the money spent to combat fraud is a waste, since it provides no medical care to anyone.

6. Vesely, Rebecca: Kaiser Halts Doctors' Freebies: Inside Bay Area, April 23, 2005. The author reports on a recent move by the Permanente Medical Group of Northern California to adopt strict conflict-of-interest rules. The new rules apparently forbid acceptance of any gift from a drug or device manufacturer representative unless that gift is particularly directed toward the care of a particular patient. A representative of the group is quoted making comments about the prevalence of gifts and the way that those gifts tend to undermine the duty of the physician to the patient.

7. American College of Physician Executives Ethical Behavior Survey Results, 2005: http://www.acpe.org/ethicalsurvey/May 8, 2005. Of 1,479 physician leaders who responded to the survey, 54.6% were "very concerned" about unethical business practices in U.S. health care. Very concerned or moderately concerned

about physicians being influenced by pharmaceutical companies: 76%. Physicians over-treating patients to boost their income: 78%. Physicians under-treating patients to boost their income: 51%. Is there a physician in your organization who is involved in unethical business practices?: 33.1% yes. Is there a health care organization in your community involved in unethical business practices?: 53.8% yes. First, this level of concern is a terrible indictment of the way we are currently doing business in health care. Second, it is interesting that the level of concern about over-treatment is much higher than the level of concern about under-treatment—which is certainly contrary to the public concern.

8. Medical Board of California, Annual Report 2004-2005. http://www.caldocinfo.ca.gov. The mission of the Medical Board of California is noted to be "to protect healthcare consumers through the proper licensing and regulation of physicians and surgeons and certain allied healthcare professions and through the vigorous, objective enforcement of the Medical Practice Act." During 2005, there were 120,027 licentiates under the aegis of this board. Of these, there were 365 (0.3%) monitored in diversion programs (drug and alcohol abuse) during 2005. There were 361 (0.3%) licentiates subject to administrative actions of one kind or another, from reprimand to license revocation. It is simply not credible that the level of misbehavior among licentiates of this board is this low. Our system is not detecting and/or not disciplining a significant amount of misbehavior.

9. Moore, David W: Nurses Top List in Honesty and Ethics Poll: Gallup Poll News Service, December 7, 2004. http://www.gallup.com/. Nurses top Gallup's annual survey on the honesty and ethical standards of various professions again for the fourth time since 1999. The only time they fell below first place was in 2001, when they were topped by firefighters. The nurse rating was 79%, down from 83% in 2003. Physicians were at 67%, lagging behind pharmacists, grade school teachers, and military officers.

Chapter 25

1. Inglehart, John: The Malpractice Morass: Symbol of Societal Conflict: Health Affairs, July/August 2004 (23:4):7-8. The author, in introducing a set of articles on professional liability reform, notes the political environment in Washington, D.C., that drives much of the conversation about professional liability. One political party advocates for the ability of people to "obtain just redress" of damages; the other wishes to limit the overall cost of the system. The Department of Health and Human Services estimates that the tort liability system costs the federal government $28 billion a year in direct and indirect spending. This is a significant problem, hung up in a political morass that prevents appropriate consideration of bona fide solutions.

2. Nahin, Richard L., et al: Racing Toward the Integration of Complementary and Alternative Medicine: A Marathon or a Sprint?: Health Affairs: 24:4 (July/August 2005):991-993. A short but apt discussion of the role of evidence-based evaluation in the integration of CAM into everyday medical practice.

Roger Howe

Chapter 26

1. Newhouse, Joseph P, et al: The Institute of Medicine Committee's Clarion Call for Universal Coverage; Health Affairs—Web Exclusive W4 (March 31, 2004):179-183. The authors praise the Institute of Medicine's report on uninsurance, but challenge the ability of our nation to make the radical changes called for. They believe that paying for insurance for all Americans will constitute a massive shift of resources from the rich to the poor, and they believe that an incremental approach is preferable to a revolutionary approach. Both of these argue against what I suggest will continue. I believe I have demonstrated that the shift of resources is already happening—in that the health care institutions providing care to the uninsured are being paid for that care in the form of "mark up" to the rest of the cost of care to reflect the "shrinkage" produced by non-payment from the uninsured. Universal coverage should decrease the direct cost of health care to those currently insured, but will increase the indirect cost of supporting the program—what the net effect will be depends upon the benefit design chosen. I have also discussed, and will discuss again in this chapter, the reasons why incremental approaches will not work. If our goal is a major change in the system, we must be prepared to implement that goal by making major changes in the system. If we try to make incremental changes toward a major goal, I fear we will be just as unsuccessful as we have been in the past.

2. In a nutshell, here is how the "Part D" pharmacy coverage program for Medicare recipients works:

   - There is a $250 annual deductible—so nothing is covered up to $250.

   - After the deductible is met, then Medicare covers 75% of the cost of the medication up to $2,250.

- After $2,250 is reached, there is no coverage until the member has spent a total of $3,600 of his/her own money on medications.

- Then, after the member reaches $3,600, Medicare pays for 95% of any other medication expense.

- The interval of zero coverage between $2,250 and $3,600 is called the "donut hole"—referring to the fact that there is a gap between the coverage at lower expense levels and the coverage at the higher level, which must be filled by the Medicare enrollee him/herself.

3. Collins, Sara R., et al: The Affordability Crisis in U.S. Health Care: Findings from the Commonwealth Fund Biennial Health Insurance Survey: Commonwealth Fund (www.cmwf.org), March 2004. This survey, leading up toward the 2004 presidential election, was particularly interested in the attitude of the American public toward healthcare issues as it related to that election. Fifty-seven percent (57%) of Americans indicated that candidates' views on health care reform would be a very important factor they would consider in choosing for whom to vote. This was more prominent among Democrats (69%) than among Republicans (45%) or Independents (56%). Sixty-two percent (62%) of Americans indicated they would be willing to give up the entire recent federal tax cut to help guarantee health insurance security for everyone—this included over half (54%) of those with household incomes in excess of $100,000 per year. Health insurance coverage was seen as unstable, and the instability was seen as decreasing financial security for families. Clearly, there is a rising political tide toward health care reform. For the moment, that seems to have been subsumed to concerns about national security and the war on terrorism.